BOYS' HANDBOOK

First published 1981 by
Octopus Books Limited
59 Grosvenor Street, London W1

© 1981 Octopus Books Limited
Reprinted 1981, 1982, 1983
ISBN 0 7064 1545 0

Printed in Czechoslovakia
50424/3

BOYS' HANDBOOK

CONTENTS

THE UNIVERSE

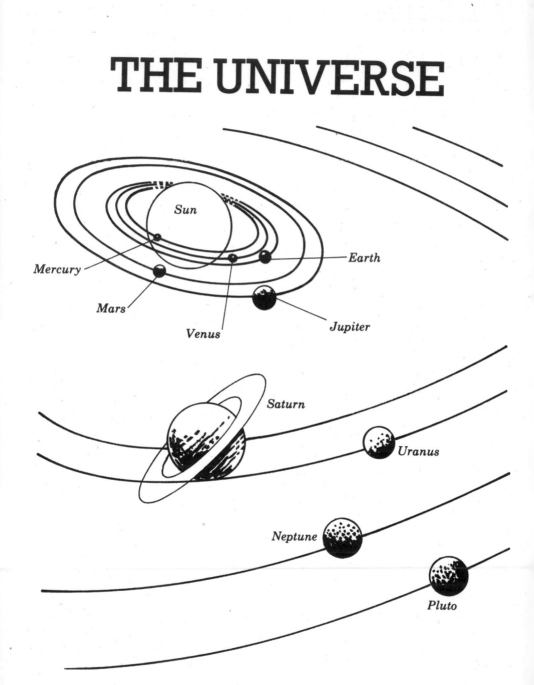

Sun

Mercury

Mars

Venus

Earth

Jupiter

Saturn

Uranus

Neptune

Pluto

The Scale of the Universe

If we imagine that our Sun is only 1 m (3.27 ft) in diameter, on that scale the planet Pluto, the most distant of the nine known planets, would be about 4.6 km (nearly 3 miles) away at its average distance. The nearest star would be about 26,000 km (16,000 miles) away.

Our Sun is just one of many millions of stars in the Milky Way, the name for our galaxy. The Milky Way is a spiral galaxy and almost all the stars we see at night lie in one of the spirals or 'arms'. Compared to the other stars, the Sun is unremarkable in either size or brightness. It lies about two-thirds of the way to one edge from the centre. On the scale we have adopted, the Milky Way would be about 1,300 million km (800 million miles) across. But even on that scale distances become quite impossible to visualize.

Outside our galaxy are hundreds of millions of other galaxies. One of the largest and nearest of these, visible to the naked eye in the northern hemisphere, is the great spiral galaxy in the constellation Andromeda. If the Milky Way were a mere 1,000 km (620 miles) across, it would be about 13,000 km (8,000 miles) away from us. The world's greatest telescopes have photographed galaxies more than 1,000 times farther away than this!

The mean distance between the Earth and the Sun, 150,000,000 km (93,000,000 miles), is known as an *astronomical unit*. But when we go beyond the solar system, kilometres and astronomical units are both inconveniently small for reckoning distances. The unit used is the *light-year*, the distance light travels in one year. Light travels at 2,997,925 km (186,282 miles) per second, so in a year it covers 9,470,000,000,000 km – nearly 6,000,000,000,000 miles.

Here are some facts and figures on the planets and the stars:

Number of stars in the Milky Way galaxy: 100,000 million (10^{11}) approx.
Distance across Milky Way galaxy: 100,000 light-years approx.
Distance of Sun from centre of Milky Way: 32,000 light-years approx.
Distance of Sun from most distant star in Milky Way: 75,000 light-years approx.
Distance to Magellanic Clouds (the two small galaxies which are nearest to ours): 160,000 light-years approx.
Distance to Great Spiral galaxy in Andromeda (limit of naked eye vision): 2,200,000 light-years
Distance of the most distant galaxies detectable by radio telescope: 17,500,000,000 light-years
Number of stars visible to the naked eye: 5,776
Number of galaxies in the detectable universe: 10^{11} to 10^{12} (100,000,000,000 to 1,000,000,000,000)

Total number of stars in detectable universe: 10^{22} to 10^{23}
(10,000,000,000,000,000,000,000 to 100,000,000,000,000,000,000,000)
Estimated age of the universe: between 17,500 million and 21,500 million years
Estimated age of the Sun: 4,600,000,000 years

THE TWENTY BRIGHTEST STARS

NAME	VISUAL MAGNITUDE	DISTANCE IN LIGHT-YEARS
Sirius	−1.43	8.6
Canopus	−0.72	98
Alpha Centauri	−0.27	4.3
Arcturus	−0.06	36
Vega	+0.04	26
Capella	+0.05	45
Rigel	+0.08	600
Procyon	+0.37	11.4
Betelgeuse	+0.41 (variable)	600
Archernar	+0.47	65
Beta Centauri	+0.63	300
Altair	+0.77	16.6
Aldebaran	+0.86 (variable)	52
Alpha Crucis	+0.87	390
Spica	+0.91 (variable)	274
Antares	+0.92 (variable)	420
Pollux	+1.16	37
Fomalhaut	+1.19	22.6
Beta Crucis	+1.24	490
Deneb	+1.26	1,400

The brightest stars

The stars in the night sky differ in apparent brightness, and these differences are measured on the scale of stellar magnitudes. Roughly speaking, the brightest stars in the sky are of the first magnitude. All the other stars visible to the naked eye on a clear night are divided into five lower magnitudes, the very faintest belonging to the sixth. The stars of each magnitude are 2.5 times as bright as those of the next lower magnitude. Negative magnitudes are brightest. A star that has a magnitude of −1 is ten times brighter than one of +1.5.

THE NEAREST STARS

STAR	DISTANCE IN LIGHT-YEARS	APPARENT MAGNITUDE
Proxima Centauri	4.28	+11.0
Alpha Centauri	4.38	−0.27
Barnard's Star	5.91	+9.5
Wolf 359	7.60	+13.3
Lalande 21185	8.13	+7.5
Sirius	8.65	−1.43

The Constellations

In ancient times the stars were divided into groups, each of which was named after a mythological character or common object. One of the great astronomers, Ptolemy (fl. AD 140), drew up a star catalogue containing 48 constellations. Since then the list has been extended because many star groups can only be seen from the southern hemisphere and therefore remained unknown to classical astronomers.

There are now 88 constellations recognized internationally; these are listed below in alphabetical order. N indicates the northernmost and S the southernmost star groups.

ALPHABETICAL LIST OF CONSTELLATIONS

NAME	MEANING	NAME	MEANING
Andromeda	Daughter of King Cepheus	Caelum	Chisel
		Camelopardalis	Giraffe
Antlia	Pump	Cancer	Crab
Apus (S)	Bird of Paradise	Canes Venatici	Hunting Dogs
Aquarius	Water Carrier	Canis Major	Greater Dog
Aquila	Eagle	Canis Minor	Lesser Dog
Ara (S)	Altar	Capricornus	Goat
Aries	Ram	Carina	Ship's Keel
Auriga	Charioteer	Cassiopeia (N)	Mother of Andromeda
Boötes	Herdsman		

Constellations of the northern hemisphere

NAME	MEANING	NAME	MEANING
Centaurus	Centaur	**Fornax**	Furnace
Cepheus (N)	King of Ethiopia	**Gemini**	Twins
Cetus	Whale	**Grus**	Crane
Chamaeleon (S)	Chameleon	**Hercules**	Hercules
Circinus (S)	Dividers	**Horologium**	Clock
Columba	Dove	**Hydra**	Water Serpent
Coma Berenices	Berenice's Hair	**Hydrus (S)**	Water Snake
Corona Australis	Southern Crown	**Indus (S)**	Indian
Corona Borealis	Northern Crown	**Lacerta**	Lizard
Corvus	Crow	**Leo**	Lion
Crater	Cup	**Leo Minor**	Lion Cub
Crux (S)	Southern Cross	**Lepus**	Hare
Cygnus	Swan	**Libra**	Scales
Delphinus	Dolphin	**Lupus**	Wolf
Dorado (S)	Swordfish	**Lynx**	Lynx
Draco (N)	Dragon	**Lyra**	Lyre
Equuleus	Foal	**Mensa (S)**	Table
Eridanus	River Eridanus	**Microscopium**	Microscope

Constellations of the southern hemisphere

NAME	MEANING	NAME	MEANING
Monoceros	Unicorn	**Scorpius**	Scorpion
Musca (S)	Fly	**Sculptor**	Sculptor
Norma	Rule	**Scutum**	Shield
Octans (S)	Octant	**Serpens**	Serpent
Ophiuchus	Serpent Holder	**Sextans**	Sextant
Orion	The Hunter	**Taurus**	Bull
Pavo (S)	Peacock	**Telescopium**	Telescope
Pegasus	Winged Horse	**Triangulum**	Triangle
Perseus	Son of Zeus	**Triangulum**	
Phoenix	Phoenix	**Australe (S)**	Southern Triangle
Pictor (S)	Easel	**Tucana (S)**	Toucan
Pisces	Fishes	**Ursa Major**	Greater Bear,
Piscis Austrinus	Southern Fish		Plough
Puppis	Ship's Poop	**Ursa Minor (N)**	Lesser Bear
Pyxis	Ship's Compass	**Vela**	Ship's Sail
Reticulum (S)	Net	**Virgo**	Virgin
Sagitta	Arrow	**Volans (S)**	Flying Fish
Sagittarius	Archer	**Vulpecula**	Little Fox

The Solar System

THE PLANETS (in order of distance from the Sun)

PLANET	EQUATORIAL DIAMETER KM	MILES	LENGTH OF YEAR (SIDEREAL PERIOD) IN EARTH YEARS OR DAYS	ROTATION PERIOD
Mercury	4,878	3,031	88 days	58 days
Venus	12,100	7,519	225 days	243 days
Earth	12,756	7,926	365 days	24 hours
Mars	6,793	4,221	687 days	24½ hours
Jupiter	142,880	88,780	12 years	10 hours
Saturn	120,000	74,600	29½ years	10 hours
Uranus	50,800	31,600	84 years	10¾ hours
Neptune	48,600	30,200	165 years	15¾ hours
Pluto	5,500	3,400	248½ years	6½ days

Our Sun
Mean distance from the Earth: 150,000,000 km (93,000,000 miles)
Time light takes to travel from Sun to Earth: 8⅓ minutes
Diameter: 139,000,000 km (865,000 miles)
Volume: more than one million times that of the Earth
Mass: more than 300,000 times that of the Earth
Mean density: about 1½ times that of water
Rotation period: equator, once every 25 days; poles, once every 34 days (the Sun does not rotate as a solid body)
Surface temperature: 6,000 °C
Temperature of interior: 20,000,000°C approx.
Power output: 3.8×10^{23} kilowatts

The natural satellites
Satellites are small planets orbiting larger ones. The Earth has only one satellite, the Moon, which is an exceptionally large one in proportion to the size of the Earth. Jupiter and Saturn have bigger moons than ours, but these are smaller in proportion to the size of their planets.

The Moon is 3,476 km (2,172 miles) in diameter and revolves around the Earth at a distance of 382,000 km (239,000 miles). It rotates on its axis in the same time that it revolves round the Earth; that is why we always see the same face of the Moon.

SURFACE TEMPERATURE °C	SURFACE GRAVITY COMPARED TO THAT OF THE EARTH	MEAN DISTANCE FROM SUN	
		KM	MILES
−180 to +420	0.38	58,000,000	36,000,000
+500	0.90	108,200,000	67,200,000
−88 to +58	1.00	149,600,000	93,000,000
−125 to +30	0.38	228,000,000	141,000,000
−25	2.64	778,000,000	484,000,000
−110	1.16	1,427,000,000	887,000,000
−160	0.94	2,870,000,000	1,780,000,000
−160	1.20	4,497,000,000	2,794,000,000
−220	0.24	5,900,000,000	3,658,000,000

SATELLITES OF THE PLANETS

Planet/ Satellite	Mean distance from planet		Diameter	
	1000s OF KM	1000s OF MILES	KM	MILES
MARS				
Phobos	9.3	5.8	23	14
Deimos	23.4	14.6	11	7
JUPITER				
Amalthea	181	113	200	124
Io	419	262	3,650	2,268
Europa	667	417	2,900	1,802
Ganymede	1,066	666	5,000	3,107
Callisto	1,872	1,170	4,500	2,796
Himalia	11,392	7,120	100	62
Leda	11,115	6,910	?	?
Lysithea	11,664	7,290	20	12

| Planet/ Satellite | Mean distance from planet | | Diameter | |
	1000s OF KM	1000s OF MILES	KM	MILES
Elara	11,680	7,300	30	19
Ananke	20,800	13,000	20	12
Carme	22,400	14,000	20	12
Pasiphae	23,360	14,600	20	12
Sinope	23,520	14,700	20	12

14th satellite (unnamed): details not fully established yet

SATURN

Janus	157	98	300	186
Mimas	181	113	500	310
Encelades	238	149	600	373
Tethys	293	183	1,040	646
Dione	376	235	820	510
Rhea	525	328	1,580	982
Titan	1,216	760	5,830	3,623
Hyperion	1,472	920	500	311
Iapetus	3,520	2,200	1,600	994
Phoebe	12,880	8,050	200	124

URANUS

Miranda	122	76	300	186
Ariel	190	119	800	498
Umbria	266	166	600	373
Titania	435	272	1,100	684
Oberon	582	364	1,000	621

NEPTUNE

Triton	352	220	3,700	2,300
Nereid	5,600	3,500	300	186

THE EARTH

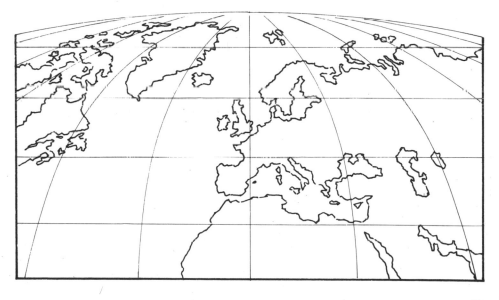

Features of the Earth

SOME FACTS ABOUT THE EARTH
Estimated age of the Earth: over 4,500 million years
Diameter of Earth at Equator: 12,757 km (7,927 miles)
Diameter of Earth at Poles: 12,714 km (7,900 miles)
Equatorial circumference: 64,496 km (24,902 miles)
Meridianal circumference: 64,387 km (24,860 miles)
Total surface area: 510,100,000 sq km (196,950,000 sq miles)
Land area: 148,950,000 sq km (57,510,000 sq miles)
Sea area: 361,150,000 sq km (139,440 sq miles)

PRINCIPAL OCEANS AND SEAS OF THE WORLD

NAME	AREA SQ KM	SQ MILES	AVERAGE DEPTH METRES	FEET	GREATEST DEPTH METRES	FEET
Pacific Ocean	160,000,000	63,986,000	4,280	14,040	11,033	36,198
Atlantic Ocean	81,663,000	31,530,000	3,926	12,880	9,188	30,143
Indian Ocean	73,427,000	28,350,000	3,962	13,000	7,000	22,968
Arctic Ocean	14,353,000	5,541,500	1,280	4,200	5,440	17,850
Mediterranean Sea	2,851,000	1,145,000	1,372	4,500	4,400	14,435
South China Sea	2,318,000	895,000	1,645	5,400	5,016	16,456
Bering Sea	2,274,000	878,000	507	1,665	4,091	13,422
Caribbean Sea	1,942,500	750,000	2,560	8,400	7,239	23,750
Gulf of Mexico	1,813,000	700,000	1,433	4,700	3,787	12,426
Sea of Okhotsk	1,507,000	582,000	914	3,000	3,847	12,621
East China Sea	1,243,000	480,000	186	610	3,200	10,500
Yellow Sea	1,243,000	480,000	49	160	106	348
Hudson Bay	1,222,500	472,000	134	440	457	1,500
Sea of Japan	1,049,000	405,000	1,474	4,835	3,109	10,200
North Sea	572,500	221,000	55	180	609	1,998
Red Sea	461,000	178,000	454	1,490	2,211	7,254
Black Sea	436,415	168,500	1,311	4,300	2,244	7,362
Baltic Sea	409,000	158,000	67	221	396	1,300

CONTINENTS OF THE WORLD

CONTINENT	AREA SQ KM	SQ MILES
Africa	30,259,000	11,683,000
Antarctica	16,000,000	6,178,000
Asia	43,250,000	16,699,000
Europe	10,360,000	4,000,000
America: North America	21,500,000	8,301,000
South America	17,793,000	6,870,000
Central America	2,750,000	1,062,000
Oceania (Australia, New Zealand and the Pacific islands – Polynesia, Melanesia and Micronesia)	8,935,000	3,450,000

THE WORLD'S GREATEST MOUNTAIN RANGES

RANGE	LENGTH KILO-METRES	MILES	HIGHEST MOUNTAIN	HEIGHT METRES	FEET
Himalaya-Karakoram-Hindu Kush-Pamir	3,800	2,400	Mount Everest	8,847	29,028
Andes	7,200	4,500	Aconcagua	6,960	22,834
Rocky Mountains	6,000	3,750	Mt Elbert	4,399	14,431
Trans-Antarctic Mountains	3,500	2,200	Mt Kirkpatrick	4,529	14,860
Great Dividing Range (E. Australia)	3,600	2,250	Kosciusko	2,228	7,310
Brazilian Atlantic Coast Range	3,000	1,900	Pico da Bandeira	2,890	9,482
West Sumatran-Javan Range	2,900	1,800	Kerintji	3,805	12,484
Tien Shan (S. Central Asia)	2,250	1,400	Pik Pobeda	7,439	24,406

The world's highest mountains
The Himalaya-Karakoram-Hindu Kush-Pamir Range of Asia includes the highest mountains of the world, with 104 peaks over 7,315 m (24,000 ft) above sea level. One of these, Mount Everest, in the Himalayas, reaches a height of 8,847 m (29,028 ft). The Andes Range, the second greatest, has 54 peaks over 6,096 m (20,000 ft).

OTHER NOTABLE MOUNTAIN PEAKS

	MOUNTAIN	HEIGHT METRES	FEET	LOCATION
Highest mountain in USSR	Communism Peak	7,495	24,590	Tadzhik
Highest mountain in USA	Mt McKinley	6,194	20,320	Alaska
Highest mountain in Canada	Mt Logan	6,050	19,850	Yukon
Highest active volcano	Cotopaxi	5,897	19,347	Ecuador
Highest mountain in Africa	Kilimanjaro	5,895	19,340	Tanzania
Highest mountain in western Europe	Mont Blanc	4,807	15,771	France/Italy

GREAT DESERTS OF THE WORLD

DESERT	APPROX. AREA SQ KM	SQ MILES	TERRITORIES
Sahara	16,835,000	6,500,000	Algeria, Chad, Libya, Mali, Mauritania, Niger, Sudan, Tunisia, Egypt, Morocco
Australian	1,550,000	600,000	Australia
Arabian	1,300,000	500,000	Saudi Arabia, Syria, Yemen
Gobi	1,040,000	400,000	Mongolia, Inner Mongolia
Kalahari	520,000	200,000	Botswana
Kara-Kum	350,000	135,000	Turkmen SSR
Taklamakan	320,000	125,000	Sinkiang (region of China)
Sonoran	310,000	120,000	Arizona, California, Mexico
Namib	310,000	120,000	Namibia
Thar	260,000	100,000	N.W. India, Pakistan
Somali	260,000	100,000	Somalia

THE WORLD'S LARGEST LAKES

LAKE	AREA SQ KM	SQ MILES	LOCATION
Caspian Sea (salt)	371,800	143,550	USSR and Iran
Superior	82,350	31,800	Canada and USA
Victoria	69,500	26,830	Kenya, Uganda and Tanzania
Aral Sea (salt)	65,500	25,300	USSR
Huron	59,600	23,010	Canada and USA
Michigan	58,000	22,400	USA
Tanganyika	32,900	12,700	Tanzania, Zaire and Zambia
Great Bear	31,800	12,275	Canada
Baykal	30,500	11,780	USSR
Malawi	29,600	11,430	Malawi, Mozambique and Tanzania
Great Slave	28,500	10,980	Canada
Erie	25,700	9,930	Canada and USA
Winnipeg	24,500	9,465	Canada
Ontario	19,500	7,520	Canada and USA
Ladoga (Ladozhskoye)	17,700	6,835	USSR
Balkhash	17,400	6,720	USSR
Chad	16,300	6,300	Chad, Cameroon, Niger and Nigeria
Onega	9,840	3,800	USSR
Eyre (salt)	9,585	3,700	Australia
Rudolf (salt)	9,065	3,500	Kenya
Titicaca	8,290	3,200	Peru-Bolivia
Athabasca	7,920	3,058	Canada
Nicaragua	7,770	3,000	Nicaragua
Reindeer	6,320	2,440	Canada
Torrens (salt)	6,215	2,400	Australia
Koko Nor (salt)	5,960	2,300	China
Issyk-Kul	5,895	2,276	USSR
Vänern	5,570	2,150	Sweden

THE WORLD'S LARGEST ISLANDS

ISLAND	AREA SQ KM	SQ MILES	LOCATION
Greenland	2,175,600	840,000	Arctic Ocean
New Guinea	831,390	321,000	W. Pacific
Borneo	738,150	285,000	Indian Ocean
Madagascar	590,002	227,800	Indian Ocean
Baffin Island	476,065	183,810	Arctic Ocean
Sumatra	473,607	182,860	Indian Ocean
Honshu	230,300	88,920	N.W. Pacific
Great Britain	218,041	84,186	N. Atlantic
Victoria Island	212,197	81,930	Arctic Ocean
Ellesmere Island	196,236	75,770	Arctic Ocean
Sulawesi (Celebes)	189,484	73,160	Indian Ocean
South Island, New Zealand	150,460	58,093	S.W. Pacific
Java	130,510	50,390	Indian Ocean
North Island, New Zealand	114,687	44,281	S.W. Pacific
Cuba	114,494	44,206	Caribbean Sea
Newfoundland	112,300	43,359	N. Atlantic
Luzon	104,688	40,420	W. Pacific
Iceland	102,846	39,709	N. Atlantic
Mindanao	94,628	36,536	W. Pacific
Hokkaido	88,775	34,276	N.W. Pacific
Ireland	82,460	31,839	N. Atlantic
Hispaniola	76,498	29,536	Caribbean Sea
Tasmania	67,897	26,215	S.W. Pacific
Sri Lanka	65,610	25,332	Indian Ocean

THE WORLD'S LONGEST RIVERS

RIVER	MAIN LOCATION	LENGTH KILO-METRES	MILES	OUTFLOW
Nile	Egypt	6,650	4,132	Mediterranean Sea
Amazon	Peru, Brazil	6,437	4,000	Atlantic Ocean
Mississippi-Missouri	USA	6,020	3,741	Gulf of Mexico
Yenisey	Siberia	5,540	3,442	Arctic Ocean
Yangtze	Tibet, China	5,494	3,434	East China Sea
Ob-Irtysh	W. Siberia	5,410	3,362	Gulf of Ob, Arctic Ocean
Zaire	Equatorial Africa	4,700	2,914	South Atlantic Ocean
Hwang-ho (Yellow River)	China	4,640	2,883	Gulf of Pohai
Lena	Siberia	4,400	2,734	Arctic Ocean
Mackenzie	Canada	4,241	2,635	Beaufort Sea
Niger	W. Africa	4,180	2,600	Gulf of Guinea
St Lawrence-Great Lakes	Canada	4,023	2,500	Gulf of St Lawrence
Rio de la Plata-Paraná	Brazil, Argentina, Uruguay	4,000	2,485	South Atlantic Ocean
Mekong	Tibet, China, Laos, Kampuchea, Vietnam	4,000	2,485	China Sea
Murray-Darling	Australia	3,780	2,350	Indian Ocean
Volga	USSR	3,690	2,293	Caspian Sea
Zambezi	S.E. Africa	3,540	2,200	Indian Ocean
Yukon	Canada, Alaska	3,200	1,988	Bering Strait
Madeira	Brazil	3,200	1,988	Amazon River
Rio Grande	USA, Mexico	3,040	1,885	Gulf of Mexico
Ganges-Brahmaputra	India	2,897	1,800	Bay of Bengal
São Francisco	E. Brazil	2,897	1,800	Atlantic Ocean
Salween	Tibet, Burma	2,880	1,790	Gulf of Martaban
Indus	Pakistan	2,880	1,790	Arabian Sea

Inside the Earth

If it were possible to drill a hole from the surface all the way to the Earth's centre (6,378 km, 3,986 miles), it would be found that the Earth is composed of a number of layers. Although the deepest hole ever drilled reached only 10 km (6.25 miles), scientists have obtained information about the interior of the Earth by studying seismic waves produced by earthquakes.

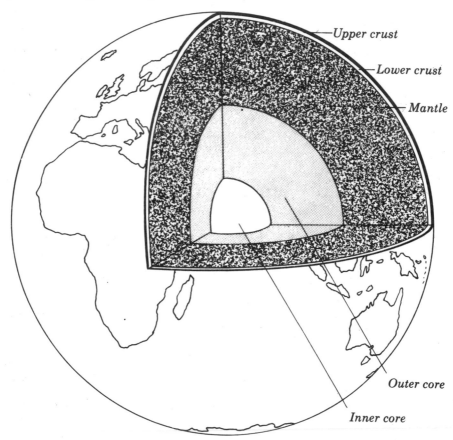

Structure of the Earth

STRUCTURE OF THE EARTH

DEPTH KM	MILES	LAYER	COMPOSITION	STATE
		Upper crust	Granite. Rich in silica and alumina.	Solid
17–25	10–15			
		Lower crust	Basalt. Rich in silica and magnesium. Temperature: 400–1,000°C	Solid
32–38	20–24			
		Mantle	Compressed iron and magnesium silicates. Temperature: 1,000–5,000°C	Probably solid to a depth of 725 km (450 miles)
2,900	1,800			
		Outer core	Mainly iron, probably with some nickel.	Fluid
5,000	3,100			
		Inner core	Mainly iron, probably with some nickel. Temperature: 4–10,000°C. Pressure: about 3.5 million atmospheres.	Solid
6,350	3,950			

Volcanoes

Volcanoes are openings in the Earth's crust through which magma (molten rock) reaches the surface, where it becomes lava or ash. Volcanoes are classified as active (including rumbling, steaming and erupting), dormant or extinct. It is estimated that there are about 535 active volcanoes on Earth, and 80 of these are submarine.

There are various types of volcanic eruption. Some are relatively quiet, although large amounts of lava may stream out. Others are quite violent, and some very violent – such as the eruption of Mt Pelée which destroyed the city of St Pierre in Martinique in 1902. An eruption can occur under the sea as well as on land, but if the depth is below 2,400 m (7,900 ft) there will be no sign of it on the surface of the water, and the lava simply spreads out over the ocean floor.

Many of the tallest mountains are volcanoes. Aconcagua, an

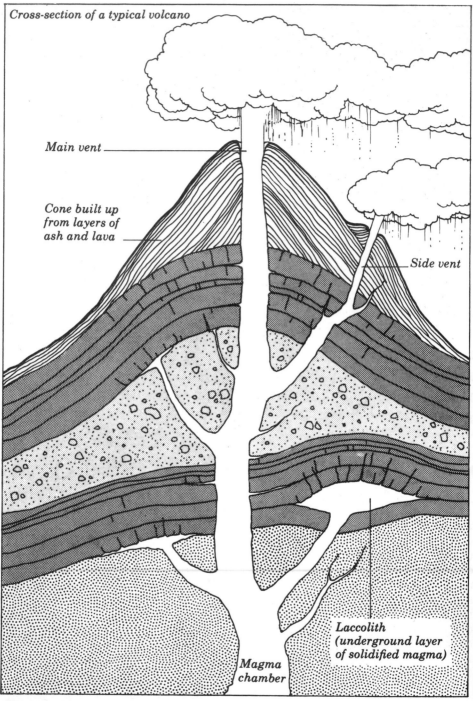

Cross-section of a typical volcano

Main vent

Cone built up
from layers of
ash and lava

Side vent

Laccolith
(underground layer
of solidified magma)

Magma
chamber

extinct volcano in Chile, is 6,960 m (22,834 ft) high. The summit of Mauna Loa in Hawaii is 4,200 m (13,780 ft) above the sea's surface. Measured from the sea floor, however, this active volcano reaches a height of 9,000 m (29,500 ft), rivalling Mt Everest.

New volcanoes have arisen in historic times, and have reached great heights in a short period.

Izalco in El Salvador has reached a height of 2,000 m (6,560 ft) in the 200 years since it first appeared. More recently, in 1943, Paracutin suddenly made its appearance in a quiet field in Mexico, building up a cone of cinders 150 m (490 ft) high in one week. In 1963, a new volcanic island, Surtsey, appeared near the coast of Iceland.

THE GREATEST VOLCANIC ERUPTIONS KNOWN

VOLCANO	COUNTRY	DATE OF ERUPTION	VOLUME OF LAVA, ASH, ETC. IN CUBIC KILOMETRES
Tambora	Indonesia	1815	150
Veidivatna	Iceland	before 870	43
Katmai	Alaska	1912	30
Krakatoa	Indonesia	1883	18
Laki	Iceland	1783	12
Eldgja	Iceland	930	9
Bezymianny	Kamchatka, USSR	1956	3
Bandaisan	Japan	1888	1

The Earth's Atmosphere

Air near the Earth's surface consists of a mixture of oxygen (21%), nitrogen (78%), carbon dioxide (0.03%), argon (0.93%) and minute quantities of the inert gases neon, helium, krypton, xenon and radon. There is also a variable quantity of water vapour. The atmosphere extends upwards for at least 1,600 km (1,000 miles) and can be divided into definite layers each

with its own characteristics. For example, the temperature of the atmosphere differs from one layer to another.

The *troposphere* extends up to a height of about 11 km (7 miles) and is the region where all weather phenomena take place. Temperature decreases with height to about $-56°C$. Above the troposphere is a 15 km (10 miles) thick layer known as the *stratosphere*. The temperature is usually −60°C.

About 30–50 km (20–30 miles) high there is an accumulation of ozone. This region is known as the *chemosphere*. Ozone absorbs some of the Sun's harmful rays. The temperature of the ozone belt is much higher than those around it.

The next layer, stretching up to about 250 km (155 miles) above the Earth is the *ionosphere*. In the ionosphere the air particles are electrically charged (ionized) by the Sun's ultra-violet radiation. There are four main layers within it: D, E, F_1 and F_2, and it is these layers which reflect radio waves back to the ground. The temperature is about −73°C in the D layer (height about 70 km, 45 miles) and increases rapidly with height to about 1,700°C in the upper ionosphere. The lower ionosphere is the region where most meteorites burn up when they meet increased air resistance. Auroras, thought to be caused by the deflection of charged particles from the Sun by the Earth's magnetic field, occur at heights between 65–1,000 km (40–600 miles).

Above the ionosphere is the *exosphere*. Here the air is so rarified that its density is only one million millionth of that at ground level. It consists mostly of hydrogen, helium and traces of oxygen and nitrogen.

Life on Earth

Life is believed to have originated some 3,000 million years ago. All the major groups of animals and plants subsequently developed from the first few relatively primitive forms. Ever-increasing numbers of species later evolved, but those that did not adapt to changing Earth conditions, or were not as successful as rival species, dwindled and became extinct.

Palaeontology (the study of fossils) traces the evolutionary paths of various animals and plants, some of which were the ancestors of present-day species. The development of modern life is rather difficult to trace, however, because the fossil record is incomplete.

Most fossils are found in sedimentary rocks formed long ago from mud, sand or clay, and even by microscopic sea organisms (limestone and chalk). The sediments were deposited in seas, lakes, deserts and river valleys, sometimes covering the remains of dead animals or plants and thereby preserving their forms.

In general, the older the fossil the deeper it lies in the beds or strata of any particular rock formation – a fact which allows events to be related in chronological order. The occurrence of a certain type of fossil which existed for a limited time only in beds of rock several miles apart proves that these rocks were formed at the same time. Some rocks can also be dated by the radioactive minerals they contain, enabling geologists to calibrate a

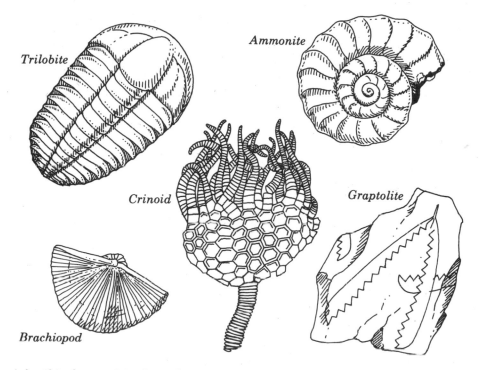

Trilobite

Ammonite

Crinoid

Graptolite

Brachiopod

A fossil is the remains of a prehistoric animal or plant, or some other evidence that it existed. Hard parts, such as bone, teeth or shells, have been found preserved with little alteration, but often the original material has been replaced by dissolved mineral matter, or it may *simply have disappeared and left a cast showing where it had been. Soft parts have rarely been preserved, but impressions made in soft mud which subsequently hardened into shale are occasionally found.*

time scale with considerable accuracy.

The record of life is mostly one of sea life, in particular that of shallow seas which swarmed with a large variety of animals. Marine sedimentary rocks containing these fossils tend to be less eroded than those deposited on land; they are thicker and display more complete sequences.

If you find a fossil, it will most likely be that of a sea animal – many areas that are now dry land were once under the sea. If you wish to see fossil land animals, such as dinosaurs, probably the best place to look is in a museum, because they are quite rare. The rarest fossils of all are those of man. Fragments of bone found in Africa indicate that humans, or near-humans, date back to nearly 1,750,000 years ago.

Coal and oil are known as *fossil fuels*, because they are the remains of ancient living organisms.

GEOLOGICAL TIME SCALE

ERA	PERIOD	BEGAN (MILLIONS OF YEARS AGO)	DURATION (MILLIONS OF YEARS)	TYPICAL FOSSILS
Cenozoic ('recent life')	Quaternary	2	2	Man
	Tertiary	62	60	Mammals
Mesozoic ('middle life')	Cretaceous	130	68	Toothed birds, dinosaurs, ammonites
	Jurassic	180	50	Dinosaurs, ammonites, gastropods, crinoids
	Triassic	230	50	Dinosaurs, ammonites, crinoids, cycads and conifers
Upper Palaeozoic ('ancient life')	Permian	280	50	Reptiles
	Upper Carboniferous (Pennsylvanian)	320	40	Giant conifers, ferns, giant dragonflies, oldest reptiles, corals, molluscs, crinoids
	Lower Carboniferous (Mississippian)	345	25	Corals, brachiopods, crinoids, amphibians
	Devonian	400	55	Fishes, sharks, the oldest insects, tree ferns
	Silurian	425	25	Early land plants, corals, brachiopods, crinoids, trilobites
Lower Palaeozoic	Ordovician	500	75	The oldest vertebrates (fish-like creatures), corals, crinoids, brachiopods, gastropods, cephalopods, trilobites, graptolites
	Cambrian	600	100	Trilobites, molluscs, worms, sponges
	Pre-Cambrian	4,500?	4,000?	Fossils very rare.

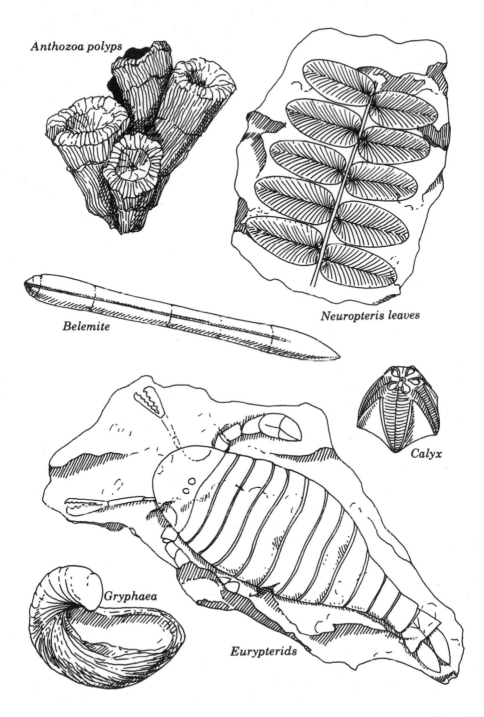

Anthozoa polyps

Neuropteris leaves

Belemite

Calyx

Gryphaea

Eurypterids

THE WORLD
AND ITS PEOPLE

North
America

Europe

Asia

South
America

Africa

Oceania

Countries of the World

Population figures in the following list cannot be absolutely accurate as there are many areas of the world where no census is taken. Furthermore, some countries have not been fully surveyed, so the areas given here may in some cases be only approximate.

An asterisk (*) denotes that the country is a member of the British Commonwealth.

AFGHANISTAN, Democratic Republic of　　　　population: 19,800,000
Capital: Kabul
Land area: 636,270 sq km (245,664 sq miles)
Principal languages: Pushtu, Dari (Persian), Turki
Currency: 100 puls = 1 afghani

ALBANIA　　　　population: 2,430,000
Capital: Tirana
Land area: 28,748 sq km (11,099 sq miles)
Principal languages: Gheg, Tosk
Currency: 100 qintars = 1 lek

ALGERIA　　　　population: 17,000,000
Capital: Algiers
Land area: 2,381,000 sq km (919,592 sq miles)
Principal languages: Arabic, French
Currency: 100 centimes = 1 dinar

ANDORRA　　　　population: 30,700
Capital: Andorra la Vella
Land area: 466 sq km (180 sq miles)
Principal languages: Catalan, French, Spanish
Currency: French and Spanish currency both in use

ANGOLA　　　　population: 5,400,000
Capital: Luanda
Land area: 1,246,700 sq km (481,351 sq miles)
Principal languages: Portuguese, tribal languages
Currency: 100 lwei = 1 kwanza

ARGENTINA　　　　population: 25,400,000
Capital: Buenos Aires
Land area: 2,777,815 sq km (1,072, 514 sq miles)
Principal language: Spanish
Currency: 100 centavos = 1 peso

*AUSTRALIA, Commonwealth of　　　　population: 14,070,000
Capital: Canberra
Land area: 7,686,884 sq km (2,967,906 sq miles)
Principal language: English
Currency: 100 cents = 1 Australian dollar

AUSTRIA   population: 7,460,000
Capital: Vienna
Land area: 83,853 sq km (32,376 sq miles)
Principal language: German
Currency: 100 groschen = 1 schilling

*BAHAMAS, Commonwealth of the   population: 218,000
Capital: Nassau
Land area: 13,864 sq km (5,353 sq miles)
Principal language: English
Currency: 100 cents = 1 Bahamas dollar

BAHRAIN   population: 275,600
Capital: Manama
Land area: 570 sq km (220 sq miles)
Principal languages: Arabic, Urdu
Currency: 1,000 fils = 1 dinar

*BANGLADESH (formerly the eastern province of   population: 80,500,000
Pakistan)
Capital: Dacca
Land area: 144,020 sq km (55,606 sq miles)
Principal language: Bengali
Currency: 100 paise = 1 taka

*BARBADOS   population: 258,000
Capital: Bridgetown
Land area: 430 sq km (166 sq miles)
Principal language: English
Currency: 100 cents = 1 Barbados dollar

BELGIUM   population: 9,800,000
Capital: Brussels
Land area: 30,513 sq km (11,781 sq miles)
Principal languages: Dutch (Flemish), French, German
Currency: 100 centimes = 1 franc

BENIN, People's Republic of (formerly Dahomey)   population: 3,200,000
Capital: Porto Novo
Land area: 112,622 sq km (43,483 sq miles)
Principal languages: French, tribal languages
Currency: 100 centimes = 1 franc CFA

*BERMUDA   population: 55,000
Capital: Hamilton
Land area: 53 sq km (20 sq miles)
Principal language: English
Currency: 100 cents = 1 Bermuda dollar

BHUTAN   population: 1,200,000
Capital: Thimphu
Land area: 46,600 sq km (18,000 sq miles)
Principal language: Dzongkha
Currency: 100 paise = 1 rupee

BOLIVIA
population: 4,700,000
Capital: La Paz
Land area: 1,098,580 sq km (424,160 sq miles)
Principal languages: Spanish, Quechua, Aymara
Currency: 100 centavos = 1 Bolivian peso

*BOTSWANA (formerly Bechuanaland Protectorate)
population: 800,000
Capital: Gaborone
Land area: 575,000 sq km (222,000 sq miles)
Principal languages: English, Setswana
Currency: 100 thebe = 1 pula

BRAZIL, Federative Republic of
population: 116,400,000
Capital: Brasilia
Land area: 8,511,965 sq km (3,286,470 sq miles)
Principal language: Portuguese
Currency: 100 centavos = 1 cruzeiro

*BRUNEI
population: 201,260
Capital: Bindar Seri Begawan
Land area: 5,800 sq km (2,226 sq miles)
Principal languages: Malay, English
Currency: 100 cents = 1 Brunei dollar

BULGARIA, People's Republic of
population: 8,760,000
Capital: Sofia
Land area: 110,912 sq km (42,823 sq miles)
Principal languages: Bulgarian, Turkish
Currency: 100 stotinki = 1 lev

BURMA, Socialist Republic of the Union of
population: 30,830,000
Capital: Rangoon
Land area: 678,000 sq km (262,000 sq miles)
Principal language: Burmese
Currency: 100 pyas = 1 kyat

BURUNDI (formerly part of Ruanda-Urundi)
population: 3,900,000
Capital: Bujumbura
Land area. 27,004 sq km (10,747 sq miles)
Principal languages: Kirundi, French
Currency: 100 centimes = 1 Burundi franc

CAMBODIA *see* Kampuchea

CAMEROON, United Republic of
population: 7,700,000
Capital: Yaoundé
Land area: 474,000 sq km (183,000 sq miles)
Principal languages: French, English
Currency: franc CFA

*CANADA, Dominion of
population: 23,500,000
Capital: Ottawa
Land area: 9,220,975 sq km (3,560,218 sq miles)
Principal languages: English, French
Currency: 100 cents = 1 Canadian dollar

CAPE VERDE
population: 360,000
Capital: Praia
Land area: 4,033 sq km (1,557 sq miles)
Principal languages: Portuguese, tribal languages
Currency: 100 centavos = 1 escudo

CENTRAL AFRICAN EMPIRE (formerly Central
African Republic)
population: 241,000
Capital: Bangui
Land area: 625,000 sq km (241,000 sq miles)
Principal languages: French, Sangho
Currency: franc CFA

CEYLON *see* Sri Lanka

CHAD
population: 3,870,000
Capital: N'djamena
Land area: 1,284,000 sq km (496,000 sq miles)
Principal languages: French, Arabic, tribal languages
Currency: franc CFA

CHILE
population: 10,400,000
Capital: Santiago
Land area: 741,767 sq km (286,396 sq miles)
Principal language: Spanish
Currency: 1,000 escudos = 6 Chilean peso

CHINA, People's Republic of
population: 900,000,000
Capital: Peking (Beijing)
Land area: 9,597,000 sq km (3,705,000 sq miles)
Principal language: Chinese (especially Mandarin and
Cantonese dialects)
Currency: 100 fens = 1 yuan (renminbi)

COLOMBIA
population: 26,500,000
Capital: Bogotá
Land area: 1,138,914 sq km (439,735 sq miles)
Principal language: Spanish
Currency: 100 centavos = 1 peso

COMOROS (Comoro Republic)
population: 290,000
Capital: Moroni
Land area: 1,862 sq km (719 sq miles)
Principal languages: Comoran, French
Currency: franc CFA

CONGO, People's Republic of the
population: 1,420,000
Capital: Brazzaville
Land area: 342,000 sq km (132,000 sq miles)
Principal languages: French, tribal languages
Currency: franc CFA

COSTA RICA
population: 2,000,000
Capital: San José
Land area: 51,100 sq km (19,730 sq miles)

Principal language: Spanish
Currency: 100 centimos = 1 colon

CUBA   population: 9,470,000
Capital: Havana
Land area: 114,524 sq km (44,218 sq miles)
Principal language: Spanish
Currency: 100 centavos = 1 Cuban peso

*CYPRUS   population: 639,000
Capital: Nicosia
Land area: 9,251 sq km (3,572 sq miles)
Principal languages: Greek, Turkish
Currency: 1,000 mils = 1 Cyprus pound

CZECHOSLOVAKIA (Czechoslovak Socialist Republic)   population: 14,970,000
Capital: Prague
Land area: 127,877 sq km (49,373 sq miles)
Principal languages: Czech, Slovak
Currency: 100 halers = 1 koruna

DENMARK   population: 5,100,000
Capital: Copenhagen
Land area: 43,075 sq km (16,631 sq miles)
Principal language: Danish
Currency: 100 öre = 1 krone

DJIBOUTI (formerly French Somaliland; Afars and   population: 125,000
Issas)
Capital: Djibouti
Land area: 23,000 sq km (9,000 sq miles)
Principal languages: French, Somali, Dankali, Arabic
Currency: 100 centimes = 1 Djibouti franc

*DOMINICA   population: 78,000
Capital: Roseau
Land area: 751 sq km (290 sq miles)
Principal language: English
Currency: The French franc, pound sterling and East
Caribbean dollar are all legal tender

DOMINICAN REPUBLIC   population: 4,700,000
Capital: Santo Domingo
Land area: 48,442 sq km (18,700 sq miles)
Principal language: Spanish
Currency: 100 centavos = 1 peso

ECUADOR   population: 6,500,000
Capital: Quito
Land area: 276,000 sq km (106,508 sq miles)
Principal languages: Spanish, Quechua and other
Amerindian languages
Currency: 100 centavos = 1 sucre

EGYPT, Arab Republic of (formerly United Arab Republic)
Capital: Cairo
Land area: 1,000,000 sq km (386,000 sq miles)
Principal language: Arabic
Currency: 100 piastres = 1 Egyptian pound

population: 40,000,000

EQUATORIAL GUINEA
Capital: Malabo
Land area: 28,050 sq km (10,830 sq miles)
Principal languages: Spanish, Arabic
Currency: ekpwele

population: 325,000

ETHIOPIA
Capital: Addis Ababa
Land area: 1,023,000 sq km (395,000 sq miles)
Principal language: Amharic
Currency: 100 cents = 1 birr

population: 30,180,000

*FIJI
Capital: Suva
Land area: 18,272 sq km (7,055 sq miles)
Principal languages: English, tribal languages
Currency: 100 cents = 1 Fiji dollar

population: 601,485

FINLAND
Capital: Helsinki
Land area: 305,475 sq km (118,000 sq miles)
Principal languages: Finnish, Swedish
Currency: 100 pennia = 1 markka

population: 4,740,000

FRANCE
Capital: Paris
Land area: 550,634 sq km (212,600 sq miles)
Principal language: French
Currency: 100 centimes = 1 franc

population: 53,200,000

GABON
Capital: Libreville
Land area: 267,667 sq km (103,346 sq miles)
Principal languages: French, Bantu dialects
Currency: franc CFA

population: 950,000

*GAMBIA, The
Capital: Banjul
Land area: 10,368 sq km (4,003 sq miles)
Principal languages: English, tribal languages
Currency: 100 bututs = 1 dalasi

population: 568,000

GERMAN DEMOCRATIC REPUBLIC (DDR)
Capital: Berlin (East)
Land area: 108,179 sq km (41,768 sq miles)
Principal language: German
Currency: 100 pfennig = 1 ostmark

population: 16,800,000

GERMANY, Federal Republic of
Capital: Bonn
Land area: 248,630 sq km (95,996 sq miles)
Principal language: German
Currency: 100 pfennig = 1 Deutsche mark

population: 61,350,000

*GHANA
Capital: Accra
Land area: 238,305 sq km (92,010 sq miles)
Principal languages: English, tribal languages
Currency: 100 pesewa = 1 cedi

population: 9,600,000

GILBERT ISLANDS *see* Kiribati

GREECE
Capital: Athens
Land area: 131,986 sq km (50,960 sq miles)
Principal language: Greek
Currency: 100 lepta = 1 drachma

population: 9,200,000

*GRENADA
Capital: St George's
Land area: 344 sq km (133 sq miles)
Principal language: English
Currency: 100 cents = 1 East Caribbean dollar

population: 108,000

GUATEMALA
Capital: Guatemala City
Land area: 108,889 sq km (42,042 sq miles)
Principal languages: Spanish, Amerindian languages
Currency: 100 centavos = 1 quetzal

population: 6,800,000

GUINEA
Capital: Conakry
Land area: 245,857 sq km (95,000 sq miles)
Principal languages: French, tribal languages
Currency: 100 cauris = 1 syli

population: 5,140,000

GUINEA-BISSAU (formerly Portuguese Guinea)
Capital: Bissau
Land area: 36,125 sq km (13,948 sq miles)
Principal languages: Portuguese, tribal languages
Currency: 100 centavos = 1 escudo

population: 800,000

*GUYANA (formerly British Guiana)
Capital: Georgetown
Land area: 210,000 sq km (81,000 sq miles)
Principal languages: English, Amerindian languages
Currency: 100 cents = 1 Guyana dollar

population: 800,000

HAITI
Capital: Port-au-Prince
Land area: 27,750 sq km (10,700 sq miles)
Principal languages: French, Creole
Currency: 100 centimes = 1 gourde

population: 4,580,000

HONDURAS
Capital: Tegucigalpa
Land area: 112,088 sq km (43,227 sq miles)
Principal languages: Spanish, tribal languages
Currency: 100 centavos = 1 lempira

population: 2,831,000

HUNGARY
Capital: Budapest
Land area: 93,032 sq km (35,920 sq miles)
Principal language: Hungarian (Magyar)
Currency: 100 filler = 1 forint

population: 10,670,000

ICELAND
Capital: Reykjavik
Land area: 103,000 sq km (39,768 sq miles)
Principal language: Icelandic
Currency: 100 aurar = 1 krona

population: 221,000

*INDIA
Capital: New Delhi
Land area: 3,166,828 sq km (1,222,712 sq miles)
Principal languages: Pushtu, Hindi, Baluchi, Bengali,
Pali, Urdu, Hindustani, Assamese, Oriya, Bihari,
Rajasthani, Gujarati, Punjabi, Kashmiri, Tamil, Telegu,
Gondi and many others
Currency: 100 paise = 1 rupee

population: 610,000,000

INDONESIA
Capital: Djakarta
Land area: 1,903,650 sq km (735,000 sq miles)
Principal language: Bahasa Indonesia
Currency: 100 sen = 1 rupiah

population: 141,600,000

IRAN (formerly Persia)
Capital: Teheran
Land area: 1,648,000 sq km (636,000 sq miles)
Principal languages: Persian (Farsi), Kurdish
Currency: 100 dinars = 1 rial

population: 34,000,000

IRAQ
Capital: Baghdad
Land area: 438,446 sq km (169,284 sq miles)
Principal languages: Arabic, Kurdish
Currency: 1,000 fils = 1 dinar

population: 12,200,000

IRELAND, Republic of
Capital: Dublin
Land area: 68,893 sq km (26,600 sq miles)
Principal languages: English, Irish (Gaelic)
Currency: 100 pence = 1 Irish pound

population: 3,220,000

ISRAEL
Capital: Jerusalem
Land area: 20,700 sq km (8,000 sq miles)

population: 3,600,000

Principal languages: Hebrew, Yiddish, Arabic and several European languages
Currency: 100 new agorot = 1 shekel

ITALY
population: 56,500,000
Capital: Rome
Land area: 301,245 sq km (116,300 sq miles)
Principal language: Italian
Currency: 100 centesimi = 1 lira

IVORY COAST
population: 7,300,000
Capital: Abidjan
Land area: 322,500 sq km (124,500 sq miles)
Principal languages: French, tribal languages
Currency: franc CFA

*JAMAICA
population: 2,110,000
Capital: Kingston
Land area: 10,991 sq km (4,244 sq miles)
Principal language: English
Currency: 100 cents = 1 Jamaican dollar

JAPAN
population: 114,200,000
Capital: Tokyo
Land area: 370,370 sq km (143,000 sq miles)
Principal language: Japanese
Currency: 100 sen = 1 yen

JORDAN
population: 3,000,000
Capital: Amman
Land area: 101,140 sq km (39,050 sq miles)
Principal language: Arabic
Currency: 1,000 fils = 1 dinar

KAMPUCHEA, Democratic (formerly Cambodia and Khmer Republic)
population: 7,700,000 (?)
Capital: Phnom Penh
Land area: 181,000 sq km (70,000 sq miles)
Principal language: Khmer
Currency: money officially abolished since 1978

*KENYA
population: 14,340,000
Capital: Nairobi
Land area: 582,600 sq km (224,960 sq miles)
Principal languages: Arabic, Swahili, Bantu and other tribal languages
Currency: 100 cents = 1 Kenya shilling

*KIRIBATI (formerly Gilbert Islands)
population: 52,000
Capital: Tarawa
Land area: 956 sq km (369 sq miles)
Principal languages: English, Gilbertese
Currency: 100 cents = 1 Australian dollar

KOREA, Democratic People's Republic of (North Korea)   population: 16,000,000
Capital: Pyongyang
Land area: 122,370 sq km (47,250 sq miles)
Principal language: Korean
Currency: 100 jun = 1 won

KOREA, Republic of (South Korea)   population: 36,400,000
Capital: Seoul
Land area: 98,447 sq km (38,002 sq miles)
Principal language: Korean
Currency: 100 chon = 1 won

KUWAIT   population: 1,130,000
Capital: Kuwait
Land area: 24,280 sq km (9,375 sq miles)
Principal language: Arabic
Currency: 1,000 fils = 1 dinar

LAOS (Lao People's Democratic Republic)   population: 2,900,000
Capital: Vientiane
Land area: 235,700 sq km (91,000 sq miles)
Principal languages: Lao, French
Currency: 100 ats = 1 kip

LEBANON   population: 3,060,000
Capital: Beirut
Land area: 10,400 sq km (4,000 sq miles)
Principal language: Arabic
Currency: 100 piastres = 1 Lebanese pound

*LESOTHO (formerly Basutoland)   population: 1,250,000
Capital: Maseru
Land area: 30,340 sq km (11,715 sq miles)
Principal languages: English, Sesotho
Currency: 100 cents = 1 South African rand

LIBERIA   population: 1,500,000
Capital: Monrovia
Land area: 112,600 sq km (43,500 sq miles)
Principal languages: English, tribal languages
Currency: 100 cents = 1 Liberian dollar

LIBYA (Popular Socialist Libyan Arab Jamahiriyah)   population: 2,630,000
Capital: Tripoli
Land area: 1,759,540 sq km (679,358 sq miles)
Principal language: Arabic
Currency: 1,000 dirhams = 1 dinar

LIECHTENSTEIN   population: 24,715
Capital: Vaduz
Land area: 160 sq km (62 sq miles)
Principal language: German
Currency: 100 centimes = 1 Swiss franc

LUXEMBOURG　　　　　　　　　　　　　　　population: 360,200
Capital: Luxembourg
Land area: 2,586 sq km (998 sq miles)
Principal languages: Letzeburgesch; French, German
and English are widely used
Currency: 100 centimes = 1 Luxembourg franc

MADAGASCAR, Democratic Republic of　　　population: 8,000,000
Capital: Antananarivo
Land area: 594,180 sq km (229,400 sq miles)
Principal languages: Malagasy, French, English
Currency: 100 centimes = 1 Malagasy franc

*MALAWI, Republic of (formerly Nyasaland)　　population: 5,310,000
Capital: Lilongwe
Land area: 117,614 sq km (45,411 sq miles)
Principal languages: English, Chinyanya,
Chitumbukaere
Currency: 100 tambala = 1 kwacha

*MALAYSIA　　　　　　　　　　　　　　population: 12,530,000
Capital: Kuala Lumpur
Land area: 334,110 sq km (129,000 sq miles)
Principal languages: Malay, English, Chinese, Tamil
Currency: 100 cents = 1 Malaysian dollar (ringgit)

MALDIVES, The　　　　　　　　　　　　　population: 143,500
Capital: Malé
Land area: 298 sq km (115 sq miles)
Principal language: Divehi
Currency: 100 laris = 1 rupee

MALI　　　　　　　　　　　　　　　　　population: 6,030,000
Capital: Bamako
Land area: 1,204,021 sq km (464,873 sq miles)
Principal languages: French, Bambara
Currency: 100 centimes = 1 Mali franc

*MALTA　　　　　　　　　　　　　　　　population: 309,000
Capital: Valletta
Land area: 246 sq km (95 sq miles)
Principal languages: Maltese, English
Currency: 100 cents = 1 Maltese pound

MAURITANIA (Mauritanian Islamic Republic)　population: 1,480,000
Capital: Nouakchott
Land area: 1,030,700 sq km (398,000 sq miles)
Principal languages: Arabic, French
Currency: 5 khoums = 1 ougiya

*MAURITIUS　　　　　　　　　　　　　　population: 880,800
Capital: Port Louis
Land area: 1,865 sq km (720 sq miles)
Principal languages: English, French, Creole, Hindi
Currency: 100 cents = 1 rupee

MEXICO (United Mexican States)   population: 62,330,000
Capital: Mexico City
Land area: 1,967,183 sq km (759,530 sq miles)
Principal languages: Spanish, Amerindian languages
Currency: 100 centavos = 1 peso

MONACO   population: 25,050
Capital: Monaco
Land area: 190 hectares (467 acres)
Principal languages: French, Monegasque
Currency: 100 centimes = 1 French franc

MONGOLIA (Mongolian People's Republic)   population: 1,500,000
Capital: Ulan Bator
Land area: 1,565,000 sq km (604,247 sq miles)
Principal language: Mongol
Currency: 100 möngö = 1 tugrik

MOROCCO   population: 18,340,000
Capital: Rabat
Land area: 659,970 sq km (254,814 sq miles)
Principal languages: Arabic, Berber, French, Spanish
Currency: 100 francs = 1 dirham

MOZAMBIQUE, People's Republic of   population: 11,000,000
Capital: Maputo
Land area: 784,961 sq km (303,073 sq miles)
Principal language: Portuguese
Currency: 100 centavos = 1 escudo

*NAURU   population: 7,254
Capital: Makwa
Land area: 2,130 hectares (5,263 acres)
Principal language: English
Currency: 100 cents = 1 Australian dollar

NEPAL   population: 11,700,000
Capital: Katmandu
Land area: 141,400 sq km (54,600 sq miles)
Principal languages: Nepali, Maithir, Bhojpuri
Currency: 100 pice (paisa) = 1 Nepalese rupee

NETHERLANDS, The   population: 13,880,000
Seat of government: The Hague
Capital: Amsterdam
Land area: 41,160 sq km (15,892 sq miles)
Principal language: Dutch
Currency: 100 cents = 1 guilder (florin)

*NEW ZEALAND   population: 3,130,000
Capital: Wellington
Land area: 268,704 sq km (103,747 sq miles)
Principal language: English
Currency: 100 cents = 1 NZ dollar

NICARAGUA
Capital: Managua
Land area: 148,000 sq km (57,000 sq miles)
Principal language: Spanish
Currency: 100 centavos = 1 cordoba

population: 2,240,000

NIGER
Capital: Niamey
Land area: 1,187,000 sq km (458,300 sq miles)
Principal languages: French, Arabic, tribal languages
Currency: Franc CFA

population: 4,990,000

*NIGERIA, Federal Republic of
Capital: Lagos
Land area: 923,770 sq km (356,670 sq miles)
Principal languages: English, Hausa, Ibo, Yoruba
Currency: 100 kobo = 1 naira

population: 73,000,000

NORWAY
Capital: Oslo
Land area: 323,895 sq km (125,056 sq miles)
Principal language: Norwegian
Currency: 100 öre = 1 krone

population: 4,050,000

OMAN (formerly Muscat and Oman)
Capital: Muscat
Land area: 212,380 sq km (82,000 sq miles)
Principal language: Arabic
Currency: 100 baiza = 1 riyal

population: 750,000

PAKISTAN
Capital: Islamabad
Land area: 803,943 sq km (310,403 sq miles)
Principal languages: Urdu, Punjabi, Sindhi, Pushtu,
Baluchi, Brahvi
Currency: 100 paisa = 1 rupee

population: 75,600,000

PANAMA
Capital: Panama City
Land area: 75,650 sq km (29,210 miles)
Principal language: Spanish
Currency: 100 centesimos = 1 balboa

population: 1,780,000

*PAPUA NEW GUINEA
Capital: Port Moresby
Land area: 462,840 sq km (178,700 sq miles)
Principal language: English
Currency: 100 toea = 1 kina

population: 2,960,000

PARAGUAY
Capital: Asuncion
Land areas: 406,752 sq km (157,047 sq miles)
Principal languages: Spanish, Guarani
Currency: 100 centimos = 1 guarani

population: 2,750,000

PERU
population: 15,500,000
Capital: Lima
Land area: 1,285,215 sq km (496,223 sq miles)
Principal languages: Spanish, Quechua, Aymara
Currency: 100 centavos = 1 sol

PHILIPPINES, The
population: 45,030,000
Capital: Quezon City (a suburb of Manila)
Land area: 300,000 sq km (115,830 sq miles)
Principal languages: Filipino, English, Spanish and over 70 Malayo-Polynesian languages
Currency: 100 centavos = 1 peso

POLAND
population: 34,900,000
Capital: Warsaw
Land area: 312,683 sq km (120,727 sq miles)
Principal language: Polish
Currency: 100 groszy = 1 zloty

PORTUGAL
population: 8,750,000
Capital: Lisbon
Land area: 91,631 sq km (35,379 sq miles)
Principal language: Portuguese
Currency: 100 centavos = 1 escudo

QATAR
population: 200,000
Capital: Doha
Land area: 11,000 sq km (4,247 sq miles)
Principal language: Arabic
Currency: 100 dirham = 1 riyal

ROMANIA
population: 21,650,000
Capital: Bucharest
Land area: 237,500 sq km (91,700 sq miles)
Principal language: Romanian
Currency: 100 bani = 1 leu

RWANDA
population: 4,400,000
Capital: Kigali
Land area: 26,330 sq km (10,170 sq miles)
Principal languages: Kinyarwanda, French
Currency: 100 centimes = 1 Rwanda franc

*ST LUCIA
population: 113,000
Capital: Castries
Land area: 616 sq km (238 sq miles)
Principal language: English
Currency: 100 cents = 1 East Caribbean dollar

SALVADOR, EL
population: 4,000,000
Capital: San Salvador
Land area: 21,393 sq km (8,260 sq miles)
Principal language: Spanish
Currency: 100 centavos = 1 colon

SAN MARINO
population: 19,200
Capital: San Marino
Land area: 61 sq km (24 sq miles)
Principal language: Italian
Currency: Italian and Vatican City currencies are in general use

SÃO TOMÉ AND PRINCIPE
population: 82,750
Capital: São Tomé
Land area: 964 sq km (372 sq miles)
Principal language: Portuguese
Currency: 100 centavos = 1 escudo

SAUDI ARABIA
population: 9,160,000
Capital: Riyadh
Land area: 2,400,000 sq km (927,000 sq miles)
Principal language: Arabic
Currency: 100 halalas = 1 riyal

SENEGAL
population: 5,090,000
Capital: Dakar
Land area: 197,720 sq km (76,340 sq miles)
Principal language: French
Currency: franc CFA

*SEYCHELLES
population: 62,000
Capital: Victoria (on island of Mahé)
Land area: 404 sq km (156 sq miles)
Principal languages: English, French, Creole
Currency: 100 cents = 1 rupee

*SIERRA LEONE
population: 3,470,000
Capital: Freetown
Land area: 73,326 sq km (28,311 sq miles)
Principal languages: English, tribal languages
Currency: 100 cents = 1 leone

*SINGAPORE
population: 2,310,000
Capital: Singapore
Land area: 616 sq km (238 sq miles)
Principal languages: Malay, Chinese, Tamil, English
Currency: 100 cents = 1 Singapore dollar

*SOLOMON ISLANDS
population: 196,850
Capital: Honiara (on Guadalcanal Island)
Land area: 29,785 sq km (11,500 sq miles)
Principal languages: English, Melanesian languages
Currency: Australian dollar, Solomon Islands dollar

SOMALIA (Somali Democratic Republic)
population: 3,200,000
Capital: Mogadishu
Land area: 630,000 sq km (243,000 sq miles)
Principal languages: Somali, Arabic, Italian, English
Currency: 100 cents = 1 Somali shilling

SOUTH AFRICA, Republic of
Administrative capital: Pretoria
Legislative capital: Cape Town
Judicial capital: Bloemfontein
Land area: 1,140,519 sq km (440,354 sq miles)
Principal languages: Afrikaans, English, Xhosa,
Zulu, Sesotho
Currency: 100 cents = 1 rand

population: 26,000,000

SPAIN
Capital: Madrid
Land area: 504,879 sq km (194,934 sq miles)
Principal languages: Spanish (Castilian), Catalan,
Galician, Basque
Currency: 100 centimos = 1 peseta

population: 35,700,000

*SRI LANKA (formerly Ceylon)
Capital: Colombo
Land area: 65,610 sq km (25,332 sq miles)
Principal languages: Sinhala, Tamil
Currency: 100 cents = 1 rupee

population: 13,940,000

SUDAN
Capital: Khartoum
Land area: 2,500,000 sq km (967,500 sq miles)
Principal language: Arabic
Currency: 100 piastres = 1 Sudan pound

population: 17,000,000

SURINAM
Capital: Paramaribo
Land area: 163,000 sq km (63,000 sq miles)
Principal languages: Sranan (Taki Taki), Dutch,
English, Spanish, Hindi, Javanese, Chinese
Currency: 100 cents = 1 Surinam guilder

population: 450,000

*SWAZILAND
Capital: Mbabane
Land area: 17,400 sq km (6,700 sq miles)
Principal languages: English, Siswati
Currency: 100 cents = 1 lilangeni (plural, emalangeni);
South African rand also in use

population: 528,000

SWEDEN
Capital: Stockholm
Land area: 411,479 sq km (158,872 sq miles)
Principal language: Swedish
Currency: 100 öre = 1 krona

population: 8,200,000

SWITZERLAND
Capital: Bern
Land area: 41,288 sq km (15,941 sq miles)
Principal languages: German, French, Italian,
Romansch
Currency: 100 centimes = 1 franc

population: 6,300,000

SYRIA (Syrian Arab Republic)　　　　　　population: 8,300,000
Capital: Damascus
Land area: 185,680 sq km (71,690 sq miles)
Principal language: Arabic
Currency: 100 piastres = 1 Syrian pound

TAIWAN (formerly Formosa)　　　　　　population: 15,000,000
Capital: Taipei
Land area: 35,989 sq km (13,895 sq miles)
Principal language: Chinese (Mandarin and Amoy dialects)
Currency: 100 cents = 1 new Taiwan dollar

*TANZANIA (a union formed in 1964 between　　population: 17,500,000
Tanganyika, Zanzibar and Pemba)
Capital: Dar es Salaam (moving to Dodoma)
Land area: 939,706 sq km (363,708 sq miles)
Principal languages: Swahili, English
Currency: 100 cents = 1 Tanzanian shilling

THAILAND　　　　　　　　　　　　population: 45,000,000
Capital: Bangkok
Land area: 514,000 sq km (198,500 sq miles)
Principal language: Thai
Currency: 100 satang = 1 baht (tical)

TOGO　　　　　　　　　　　　　　population: 2,200,000
Capital: Lomé
Land area: 56,000 sq km (22,000 sq miles)
Principal languages: Ewe, Mina, Dajomba, Tim,
Cabrais and other tribal languages
Currency: franc CFA

*TONGA (Friendly Islands)　　　　　　population: 90,150
Capital: Nuku'alofa (on the island of Tongatapu)
Land area: 700 sq km (270 sq miles)
Principal languages: Polynesian, English
Currency: 100 seniti = 1 pa'anga

*TRINIDAD AND TOBAGO　　　　　　population: 1,070,000
Capital: Port-of-Spain
Land area: 4,828 sq km (1,864 sq miles)
Principal language: English
Currency: 100 cents = 1 Trinidad and Tobago dollar

TUNISIA　　　　　　　　　　　　population: 6,030,000
Capital: Tunis
Land area: 164,150 sq km (63,380 sq miles)
Principal languages: Arabic, French
Currency: 1,000 millimes = 1 dinar

TURKEY　　　　　　　　　　　　population: 40,200,000
Capital: Ankara
Land area: 779,452 sq km (300,946 sq miles)

Principal language: Turkish
Currency: 100 kurus = 1 Turkish pound (lira)

*TUVALU (formerly Ellice Islands)   population: 5,900
Capital: Funafuti
Land area: 24 sq km (9 sq miles)
Principal languages: English, Ellice
Currency: 100 cents = 1 Australian dollar

*UGANDA   population: 11,170,000
Capital: Kampala
Land area: 236,860 sq km (91,430 sq miles)
Principal languages: English, Bantu languages, Kiswahili
Currency: 100 cents = 1 Uganda shilling

USSR (Union of Soviet Socialist Republics)   population: 260,000,000
Capital: Moscow
Land area: 22,400,000 sq km (8,650,000 sq miles)
Principal languages: Russian, Ukrainian, Uzbek and several others
Currency: 100 kopeks = 1 rouble

UNITED ARAB EMIRATES (a federation consisting   population: 652,900
of the former Trucial States; Abu Dhabi, Dubai,
Sharjah, Ajman, Umm al Qawain and Fujairah joined
in 1971, Ras al Khaimah joined in 1972)
Capital: Abu Dhabi
Land area: 92,100 sq km (35,560 sq miles)
Principal language: Arabic
Currency: 100 fils = 1 dirham

UNITED KINGDOM OF GREAT BRITAIN AND   population: 56,000,000
NORTHERN IRELAND (Comprises England, Scotland,
Wales and Northern Ireland. It does not include the
Channel Islands or the Isle of Man, which are
dependencies of the Crown, but have their own
legislative and taxation systems.)
Capital: London
Land area:
  England: 130,362 sq km (50,333 sq miles)
  Wales: 20,761 sq km (8,016 sq miles)
  Scotland: 78,772 sq km (30,414 sq miles)
  Northern Ireland: 14,121 sq km (5,452 sq miles)
Total land area: 244,016 sq km (94,205 sq miles)
Principal languages: English, Welsh, Gaelic
Currency: 100 pence = 1 pound sterling

USA (United States of America)   population: 218,060,000
Capital: Washington DC
Land area: 9,363,169 sq km (3,615,120 sq miles)
Principal language: English
Currency: 100 cents = 1 dollar

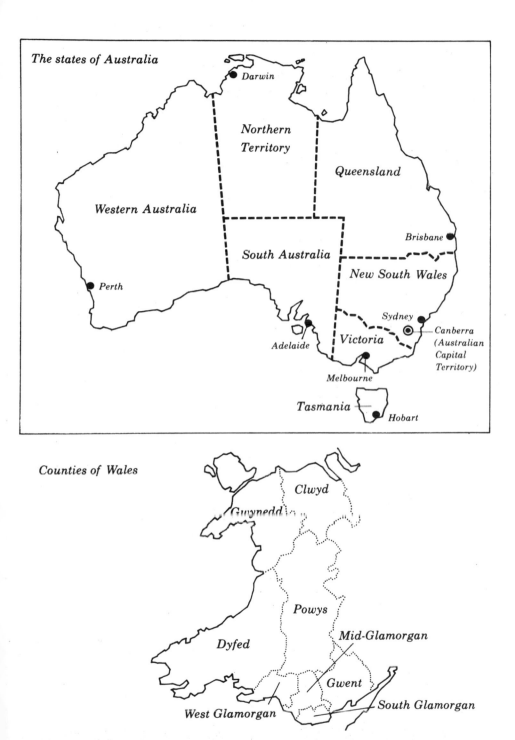

The states of Australia

Darwin

Northern Territory

Queensland

Western Australia

Brisbane

South Australia

New South Wales

Perth

Sydney

Adelaide

Victoria

Canberra (Australian Capital Territory)

Melbourne

Tasmania

Hobart

Counties of Wales

Clwyd

Gwynedd

Powys

Mid-Glamorgan

Dyfed

Gwent

West Glamorgan

South Glamorgan

ENGLISH COUNTIES AND SHIRES

NON-METROPOLITAN COUNTIES	AREA SQ KM	POPULATION	ADMINISTRATIVE HEADQUARTERS
Avon (1)	1,338	921,900	Bristol
Bedfordshire (2)	1,235	494,700	Bedford
Berkshire (3)	1,256	672,600	Reading
Buckinghamshire (4)	1,883	525,100	Aylesbury
Cambridgeshire (5)	3,409	570,200	Cambridge
Cheshire (6)	2,322	919,800	Chester
Cleveland (7)	583	568,200	Middlesbrough
Cornwall and Scilly Isles (8)	3,546	416,700	Truro
Cumbria (9)	6,809	472,400	Carlisle
Derbyshire (10)	2,631	896,200	Matlock
Devon (11)	6,715	948,000	Exeter
Dorset (12)	2,654	586,500	Dorchester
Durham (13)	2,436	603,800	Durham
Essex (14)	3,674	1,435,600	Chelmsford
Gloucestershire (15)	2,638	495,300	Gloucester
Hampshire (16)	3,772	1,453,400	Winchester
Hereford and Worcester (17)	3,927	610,100	Worcester
Hertfordshire (18)	1,634	947,100	Hertford
Humberside (19)	3,512	844,900	Hull
Kent (20)	3,732	1,449,000	Maidstone
Lancashire (21)	3,043	1,369,600	Preston
Leicestershire (22)	2,553	833,300	Leicester
Lincolnshire (23)	5,884	530,100	Lincoln
Norfolk (24)	5,355	679,800	Norwich
Northamptonshire (25)	2,367	516,400	Northampton
Northumberland (27)	5,033	289,200	Newcastle-upon-Tyne
Nottinghamshire (27)	2,164	982,000	Nottingham
Oxfordshire (28)	2,611	973,700	Oxford
Salop (Shropshire) (29)	3,490	540,600	Shrewsbury
Somerset (30)	3,458	365,900	Taunton
Staffordshire (31)	2,716	411,100	Stafford
Suffolk (32)	3,800	592,700	Ipswich
Surrey (33)	1,655	995,400	Kingston-upon-Thames
Sussex, East (34)	1,795	652,500	Lewes
Sussex, West (35)	2,016	633,600	Chichester
Warwickshire (36)	1,981	469,500	Warwick
Wight, Isle of (37)	381	114,300	Newport, IOW
Wiltshire (38)	3,481	516,200	Trowbridge
Yorkshire, North (39)	8,317	661,300	Northallerton

(Numbers and letters in brackets refer to map position)

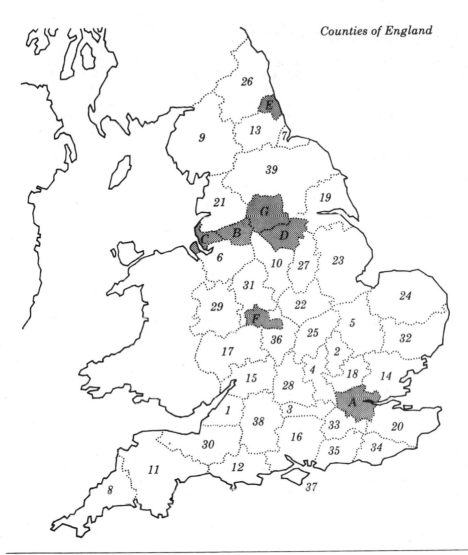

METROPOLITAN COUNTIES	AREA SQ KM	POPULATION	ADMINISTRATIVE HEADQUARTERS
Greater London (A)	1,580	7,379,014	London
Greater Manchester (B)	1,286	2,674,800	Manchester
Merseyside (C)	652	1,561,800	Liverpool
South Yorkshire (D)	1,560	1,304,000	Barnsley
Tyne and Wear (E)	540	1,174,000	Newcastle-upon-Tyne
West Midlands (F)	899	2,729,900	Birmingham
West Yorkshire (G)	2,039	2,072,500	Wakefield

THE SCOTTISH REGIONS

REGION	AREA SQ KM	POPULATION	ADMINISTRATIVE HEADQUARTERS
Borders	4,670	100,540	Newtown St Boswells
Central	2,621	271,800	Stirling
Dumfries and Galloway	6,369	143,469	Dumfries
Fife	1,305	338,700	Glenrothes, Fife
Grampian	8,702	464,194	Aberdeen
Highland	25,141	189,752	Inverness
Lothian	1,753	750,308	Edinburgh
Orkney	905	18,197	Kirkwall
Shetland	1,429	21,050	Lerwick
Strathclyde	13,849	2,445,283	Glasgow
Tayside	7,501	402,000	Dundee
Western Isles	2,898	29,665	Stornoway

THE PROVINCES OF IRELAND

PROVINCE	AREA SQ KM	POPULATION	COUNTIES AND COUNTY BOROUGHS
Connacht	17,775	390,900	Galway, Leitrim, Mayo, Roscommon, Sligo
Leinster	19,736	1,498,150	Carlow, Dublin County Borough, Dublin, Dun Laoghaire Borough, Kildare, Kilkenny, Laoighis, Longford, Louth, Meath, Offaly, Westmeath, Wexford, Wicklow
Munster	24,540	882,000	Clare, Cork County Borough, Cork, Kerry, Limerick County Borough, Limerick, Tipperary – North Riding, Tipperary – South Riding, Waterford County Borough, Waterford
Ulster (part of)	8,011	207,200	Cavan, Donegal, Monaghan

NORTHERN IRELAND

Northern Ireland consists of the major portion of the province of Ulster and is part of the United Kingdom. It is divided into 26 district and borough councils: Antrim, Ards, Armagh, Ballymena, Ballymoney, Banbridge, Belfast City, Carrickfergus, Castlereagh, Coleraine, Cookstown, Craigavon, Down, Dungannon, Fermanagh, Larne, Limavady, Lisburn, Londonderry City, Magherafelt, Moyle, Newry and Mourne, Newtownabbey, North Down, Omagh, Strabane.

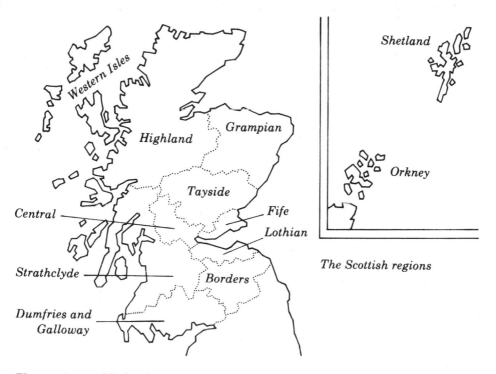

Central

Strathclyde

Dumfries and
Galloway

Western Isles

Highland

Grampian

Tayside

Fife

Lothian

Borders

Shetland

Orkney

The Scottish regions

The provinces of Ireland

Ulster

Northern
Ireland
(Ulster)

Connacht

Ulster

Munster

Leinster

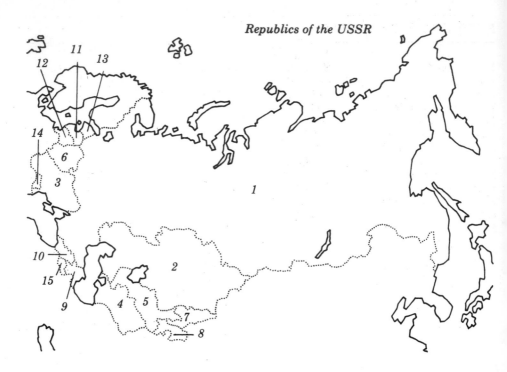

Republics of the USSR

THE 15 UNION REPUBLICS OF THE USSR

REPUBLIC	AREA SQ KM	POPULATION	CAPITAL
Russian Socialist Federal Soviet Republic (RSFSR) (1)	16,838,885	137,552,000	Moscow
Kazakhstan (2)	2,778,544	14,685,000	Alma-Ata
Ukraine (3)	582,750	49,757,000	Kiev
Turkmenistan (4)	491,072	2,759,000	Ashkhabad
Uzbekistan (5)	412,250	15,391,000	Tashkent
Belorussia (6)	209,790	9,559,000	Minsk
Kirghizia (7)	196,581	3,529,000	Frunze
Tadzhikistan (8)	144,263	3,801,000	Dushanbe
Azerbaijan (9)	86,661	6,028,000	Baku
Georgia (10)	69,671	5,016,000	Tbilisi
Latvia (11)	66,278	2,521,000	Riga
Lithuania (12)	65,201	3,339,000	Vilnius
Estonia (13)	45,610	1,466,000	Tallinn
Moldavia (14)	34,188	3,948,000	Kishinev
Armenia (15)	30,821	3,031,000	Erevan

PROVINCES OF CANADA

PROVINCE	AREA SQ KM	POPULATION	CAPITAL
Alberta (1)	661,188	1,950,300	Edmonton
British Columbia (2)	948,600	2,530,000	Victoria
Manitoba (3)	650,000	1,032,000	Winnipeg
New Brunswick (4)	72,481	695,000	Fredericton
Newfoundland and Labrador (5)	404,519	568,900	St John's
Nova Scotia (6)	54,556	841,200	Halifax
Ontario (7)	1,068,587	8,443,800	Toronto
Prince Edward Island (8)	5,657	122,000	Charlottetown
Quebec (9)	1,540,687	6,285,000	Quebec
Saskatchewan (10)	651,903	947,100	Regina
TERRITORY			
Yukon Territory (11)	536,327	21,700	Whitehorse
Northwest Territories (12)	3,379,711	43,500	Yellowknife

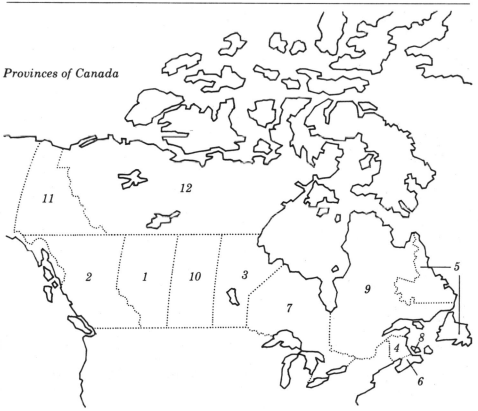

Provinces of Canada

THE UNITED STATES OF AMERICA

STATE	AREA SQ KM	POPULATION	CAPITAL
Alabama (1)	133,667	3,665,000	Montgomery
Alaska (2)	1,518,776	382,000	Juneau
Arizona (3)	295,024	2,270,000	Phoenix
Arkansas (4)	137,534	2,109,000	Little Rock
California (5)	411,014	21,520,000	Sacramento
Colorado (6)	270,000	2,583,000	Denver
Connecticut (7)	12,973	3,117,000	Hartford
Delaware (8)	6,138	582,000	Dover
Florida (9)	151,670	8,421,000	Tallahassee
Georgia (10)	152,489	4,970,000	Atlanta
Hawaii (11)	16,638	887,000	Honolulu
Idaho (12)	216,413	831,000	Boise
Illinois (13)	146,076	11,229,000	Springfield
Indiana (14)	93,994	5,302,000	Indianapolis
Iowa (15)	145,791	2,870,000	Des Moines
Kansas (16)	213,095	2,310,000	Topeka
Kentucky (17)	104,623	3,428,000	Frankfort
Louisiana (18)	125,675	3,841,000	Baton Rouge
Maine (19)	86,027	1,070,000	Augusta
Maryland (20)	27,394	4,144,000	Annapolis
Massachusetts (21)	21,386	5,809,000	Boston
Michigan (22)	150,779	9,104,000	Lansing
Minnesota (23)	217,736	3,965,000	St Paul
Mississippi (24)	123,584	2,354,000	Jackson
Missouri (25)	180,456	4,778,000	Jefferson City
Montana (26)	377,456	753,000	Helena
Nebraska (27)	200,147	1,553,000	Lincoln
Nevada (28)	286,299	610,000	Carson City
New Hampshire (29)	24,097	822,000	Concord
New Jersey (30)	20,295	7,336,000	Trenton
New Mexico (31)	315,115	1,168,000	Santa Fé
New York (32)	128,402	18,084,000	Albany
North Carolina (33)	136,524	5,469,000	Raleigh
North Dakota (34)	183,022	643,000	Bismarck
Ohio (35)	106,608	10,690,000	Columbus
Oklahoma (36)	181,090	2,766,000	Oklahoma City
Oregon (37)	250,948	2,329,000	Salem
Pennsylvania (38)	117,412	11,862,000	Harrisburg
Rhode Island (39)	3,144	927,000	Providence
South Carolina (40)	80,432	2,848,000	Columbia
South Dakota (41)	199,552	686,000	Pierre
Tennessee (42)	109,412	4,214,000	Nashville
Texas (43)	692,408	12,487,000	Austin
Utah (44)	219,932	1,228,000	Salt Lake City
Vermont (45)	24,887	476,000	Montpelier
Virginia (46)	105,711	5,032,000	Richmond

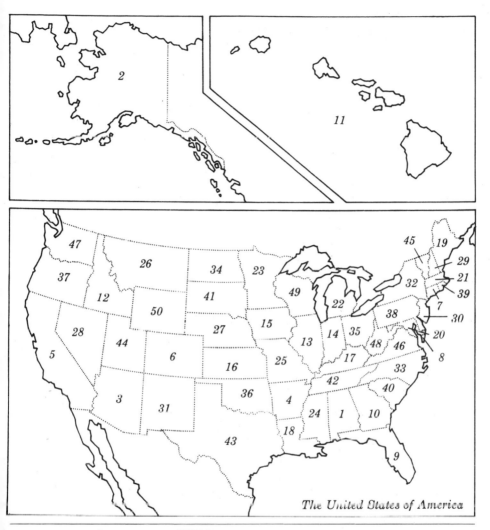

The United States of America

STATE	AREA SQ KM	POPULATION	CAPITAL
Washington (47)	176,617	3,612,000	Olympia
West Virginia (48)	62,629	1,821,000	Charleston
Wisconsin (49)	145,439	4,609,000	Madison
Wyoming (50)	253,597	390,000	Cheyenne
Dist. of Columbia (D.C.)	179	916,000	The capital territory is governed by Congress through a Commissioner and City Council

The Population of the World

Between 1750 and 1850 the world's population increased from 750,000,000 to well over 1,000,000,000. This was largely the result of technological progress. An English clergyman, Thomas Malthus (1766–1834), noted in his famous *Essay on Population* that the rate of growth of food production could not keep pace with the rate of increase of population. Ultimately, he wrote, disease and malnutrition among the poorer peoples was the only foreseeable check on population growth.

Since Malthus's time, great advances in medical science have further reduced the death rate (which used to roughly balance the birth rate), swelling the world's population to an even greater degree. At the same time there has been enormous progress in technology and greater use of resources. But it is now becoming increasingly clear that the world's resources are not limitless. As the human population increases, new ways have to be devised to support the growing numbers.

Many millions are undernourished and living in extremely poor conditions. In the developing countries of Africa, Asia and Latin America the birthrate is far higher than in the industrialized countries of Europe, North America, the USSR, parts of South America, Japan, Australia and New Zealand. Unfortunately, the countries where the population growth is highest are the least able to provide enough food for the many extra mouths.

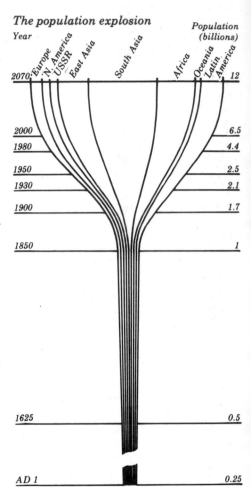

In 1850, the world's population was over 1,000,000,000. By 1930 the figure had doubled. Only 30 years later, another 1,000,000,000 were added. By the end of this century, if the present pattern of growth continues, a population of 7,500,000,000 will be reached. Even if the rate of growth declines to a considerable extent, the world's population is certain to exceed 6,500,000,000 unless war or some other catastrophe intervenes.

The World's Principal Political, Economic and Military Organizations

United Nations Organization
This worldwide association of almost all independent countries came into being on 26 June 1945 with the signing of the UN Charter – as World War II drew to its close – with the primary aim of ensuring that no further global conflicts ever take place. With the exception of a small number of countries which are not fully independent, or whose status is in dispute, the organization includes every sovereign state, although Switzerland has not become a member in order to preserve her neutrality.

The United Nations has four main purposes: the preservation of security, the administration of justice, the provision of welfare and the guardianship of human rights. Members pledge themselves to settle their disputes without resort to force, and to support the Charter's terms at all times.

Six major organs are contained within the UN:

1 **The General Assembly** Meeting annually, the representatives of all the member countries consider matters concerned with world peace and security and make recommendations to the Security Council. The Assembly also elects the Economic and Social Council and supervises its work, besides controlling the financial affairs of the UN.

2 **The Security Council** The Security Council, which sits continuously, has the responsibility of arranging peaceful settlement of international disputes, and of stopping wars when they occur. Five of the Council's 15 seats are held permanently by Britain, China, France, the USSR and the USA. The other ten are occupied, temporarily, by countries elected periodically in the General Assembly. The Council can take no action in an emergency, however, if any one of its permanent members uses the veto (the right to forbid the Council taking action).

3 **The Economic and Social Council** The purpose of this body is to help raise the standards of life all over the world. The Council concerns itself with matters of health, education, employment, human rights and all the economic and social problems to be found everywhere, but more particularly in the underdeveloped, and often poverty-stricken, areas of the world. Regional and functional commissions have been set up to deal with these affairs, plus four special bodies: UN Children's Fund (UNICEF), Commissioner for Refugees (UNHCR), Conference on Trade and Development (UNCTAD) and Industrial Development Organization (UNIDO). In addition, the Council has fifteen intergovern-

ment agencies for special purposes as follows: International Atomic Energy Agency (IAEA), International Labour Organization (ILO), Food and Agriculture Organization (FAO), UN Educational, Scientific and Cultural Organization (UNESCO), World Health Organization (WHO), World Bank, International Finance Corporation (IFC), International Monetary Fund (IMF), International Development Association (IDA), International Civil Aviation Organization (ICAO), Universal Postal Union (UPU), International Telecommunications Union (ITU), World Meteorological Organization (WMO), Intergovernmental Maritime Consultative Organization (IMCO) and General Agreement on Tariffs and Trade (GATT).

4 **The Trusteeship Council**
5 **The International Court of Justice**
6 **The Secretariat**

Since 1945 the United Nations Organization has stationed military peace forces, composed of detachments from various member countries, in a number of places where fighting has either broken out or is threatened. These have helped to keep warring nations apart, and have given time for peace talks and negotiations to be arranged.

The Commonwealth
The British Commonwealth of Nations is composed of fully independent countries from all over the world. It arose out of the former British Empire and was legalized

1946	Trygve Lie (Norway)
1951	Trygve Lie (resigned in 1952)
1953	Dag Hammarskjöld (Sweden)
1957	Dag Hammarskjöld (killed in an air crash in 1961)
1961	Sithu U Thant (Burma)
1966	Sithu U Thant
1972	Kurt Waldheim (Austria)
1977	Kurt Waldheim

by the Statute of Westminster (1931) by Australia, Canada, New Zealand and the United Kingdom. Member nations of this organization and their dependencies associate freely together in the work of the Commonwealth. They attend conferences, co-operating to promote the best interests of the countries concerned, and also try to help the causes of peace and development in the world at large. The members all regard Queen Elizabeth II of the United Kingdom as Head of the Commonwealth, and many of them acknowledge her as Head of State also. The Commonwealth countries, in order of joining, are as follows: United Kingdom, Canada, Australia, New Zealand, India, Sri Lanka, Ghana, Nigeria, Cyprus, Sierra Leone, Jamaica, Trinidad and Tobago, Uganda, Kenya, Malaysia, Malawi, Malta, Tanzania, Zambia, Gambia, Singapore, Barbados, Botswana, Guyana, Lesotho, Mauritius, Nauru (limited membership), Swaziland,

Fiji, Tonga, Western Samoa, Bangladesh, Bahamas, Grenada, Papua New Guinea, Seychelles, Dominica, Tuvalu Islands and St Lucia.

Co-ordination Bureau of the Non-aligned Countries

This is a rather loosely-knit association of 'Third World' countries and those desiring to steer clear of committed organizations supported by either the Western powers or the Soviet bloc. It largely derived from the Belgrade Conference of 1961, attended by 25 nations. Yugoslavia has continued to play a leading role in strengthening the Non-aligned Co-ordination Bureau, which came into being in 1973. A conference of non-aligned countries, held at Havana in 1979, made a controversial decision to adopt Cuba, a communist state, as current leader of the group.

Organization of American States (OAS)

A pan-American regional alliance, founded in 1948, to assist American nations towards greater understanding and co-operation. Its members are:
Argentina, Barbados, Bolivia, Brazil, Chile, Colombia, Costa Rica, Dominican Republic, Ecuador, El Salvador, Guatemala, Haiti, Honduras, Mexico, Nicaragua, Panama, Paraguay, Peru, Trinidad and Tobago, USA, Uruguay and Venezuela.

Organization of Central American States (OCAS)

Founded in 1951, with aims similar to those of OAS, by the Central American countries of Costa Rica, El Salvador, Guatemala, Honduras and Nicaragua.

Organization of African Unity (OAU)

Another regional alliance, covering Africa, and embracing all fully independent countries in that continent with the exception of the Republic of South Africa. Founded at Addis Ababa in 1963, OAU seeks to bring member countries together for the mutual advantage of all concerned, and to solve disputes among them or with nations outside the organization.

League of Arab States (Arab League)

An association of Arab countries in North Africa and Southwest Asia, founded in 1945. The Arab League includes in its membership: Algeria, Egypt, Iraq, Jordan, Kuwait, Lebanon, Libya, Morocco, Saudi Arabia, Sudan, Syria, Tunisia and Yemen. Disagreements between the members have caused problems, particularly with regard to Egyptian membership.

Council of Europe

The Council comprises a Consultative Assembly and a Committee of Ministers. Founded in 1949, it comprises 19 member nations and has its headquarters at Strasbourg. The Council of Europe is greatly concerned with human rights and the growth of international cooperation in areas such as social services, law-making, and the problems of refugees.

European Economic Community (EEC)

Created by the Treaty of Rome in 1957, the EEC, or 'Common Market', originally comprised six members – Belgium, France, Italy, Luxembourg, the Netherlands and West Germany. It was enlarged in 1973 when Denmark, the Republic of Ireland and the United Kingdom joined. Greece, Portugal and Spain are also negotiating entry into the EEC.

The EEC consists of a Commission, Council of Ministers, Parliament (Assembly) and Court of Justice. It was founded to create a common market by gradually adjusting all aspects of the economies of the member countries until they operate as a whole, with no great economic differences between one country and the next. At the same time, social and commercial activities are to be harmonized, and 'closer relations established between its member states' in every sphere.

The EEC has its headquarters in Brussels. The Assembly, made up of elected members from constituencies in the nine countries, meets regularly to debate major policy issues, study legislation and control part of the Community's budget.

European Free Trade Association (EFTA)

Although Britain and Denmark left EFTA on joining the EEC, the other EFTA members have continued to operate the free trade area created since 1958 while, at the same time, concluding co-operative agreements with the Community. The EFTA countries are: Austria, Iceland, Norway, Portugal, Sweden, Switzerland and Finland (an associated member). EFTA objectives include an end to tariff restrictions. Industrial customs barriers between EFTA and the EEC were removed in 1976.

Council for Mutual Economic Assistance (COMECON)

Established in 1949, Comecon represents the East European counterpart to the EEC. It brings together, through economic co-operation, Bulgaria, Cuba, Czechoslovakia, East Germany, Hungary, Mongolia, Poland, Romania and the USSR.

Association of Southeast Asian Nations (ASEAN)

This organization was formed in 1967 to promote economic and political co-operation amongst the non-Communist countries of Southeast Asia: Indonesia, Malaysia, the Philippines, Singapore and Thailand.

Latin American Free Trade Association (LAFTA)

Comprising 11 nations, LAFTA was set up in 1960 to bring about closer economic association among its members: Argentina, Bolivia, Brazil, Chile, Colombia, Ecuador, Mexico, Paraguay, Peru, Uruguay and Venezuela.

Organization for Economic Co-operation and Development (OECD)

Stemming from the OEEC (Organization for European Economic Co-operation), this body was formed in 1961. Canada and the

USA, plus Japan, joined the 18 OEEC members in OECD's work of promoting economic growth and development, and in expanding world trade. OECD has been particularly concerned recently with the worldwide energy crisis and in helping to ease its effects.

Organization of Petroleum Exporting Countries (OPEC)

This association of countries concerned with large-scale petroleum exports was founded in Caracas, the capital of Venezuela, in 1961. Member nations from various parts of the world meet regularly to agree upon the price and quantities of oil to be made available for sale to importing countries. The power and importance of OPEC have grown enormously recently, with the development of the world's energy crisis.

North Atlantic Treaty Organization (NATO)

NATO represents a defensive alliance covering Europe, the North Atlantic and North America. It arose from a pact, made in 1949, between Belgium, Canada, Denmark, France, Iceland, Italy, Luxembourg, the Netherlands, Norway, Portugal, the United Kingdom and the USA. Later, Greece and Turkey joined NATO,

but France withdrew militarily in 1966, though not from the alliance as a whole. Since then, Greece and Turkey have both introduced reservations about the commitment of their forces to NATO.

Warsaw Treaty Organization (Warsaw Pact)

In effect, the Warsaw Pact is the East European equivalent of NATO in the West. Formed in 1955, it is a military mutual assistance organization. Its members are Bulgaria, Czechoslovakia, East Germany, Hungary, Poland, Romania and the USSR.

Anzus Pact

Also known as the Pacific Security Treaty, this tripartite alliance dates from 1951, when Australia, New Zealand and the USA agreed to align themselves to preserve the security of the Pacific area and to seek peaceful settlement of disputes arising in that region.

Southeast Asia Treaty Organization (SEATO)

Another regional defensive organization, set up in 1954 for the better security of Southeast Asia. The eight members of this alliance are Australia, France, New Zealand, Pakistan, the Philippines, Thailand, the United Kingdom and the USA.

Man-made Structures

LARGEST CITIES OF THE WORLD

The following cities are ranked according to the size of population in their metropolitan areas. The figures are taken from the most recent censuses.

CITY	POPULATION
New York	11,572,000
Tokyo	11,403,744
Shanghai	10,820,000
Mexico City	8,589,630
Buenos Aires	8,352,900
Peking (Beijing)	7,570,000
London	7,379,014
Moscow	7,061,000
Los Angeles	6,974,103
Chicago	6,892,509
Bombay	5,970,575
Seoul	5,536,000
Cairo	5,384,000
São Paulo	5,186,752
Philadelphia	4,777,414
Djakarta	4,576,009
Tientsin (Tianjin)	4,280,000
Rio de Janeiro	4,252,009
Detroit	4,163,517
Delhi	3,647,023

THE WORLD'S TALLEST INHABITED BUILDINGS

BUILDING	HEIGHT METRES	FEET	NUMBER OF STOREYS	WHEN BUILT	LOCATION
Sears Tower	443	1,454	110	1974	Chicago, Illinois
World Trade Center	411	1,350	110	1973	New York City
Empire State Building	381	1,250	102	1930	New York City
Standard Oil Building	346	1,136	80	1973	Chicago, Illinois
John Hancock Center	343	1,127	100	1968	Chicago, Illinois
Chrysler Building	319	1,046	77	1930	New York City

The tallest man-made structure in the world is the Warsaw Radio Mast, 646 m (2,120 ft) high.

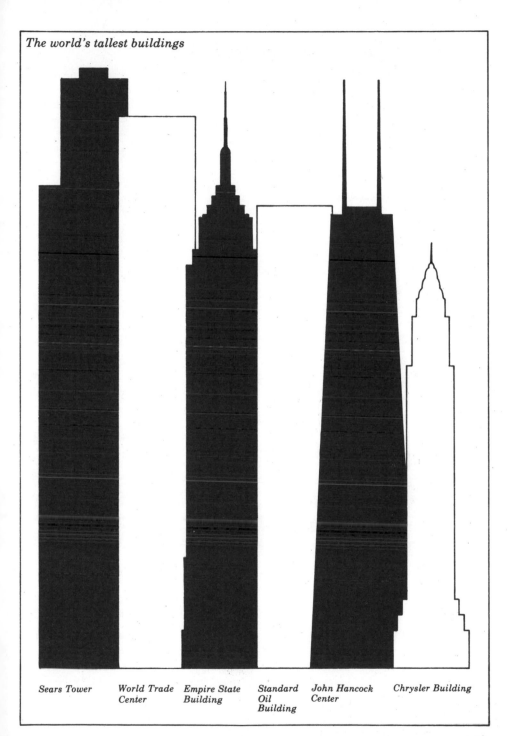

The world's tallest buildings

Sears Tower

World Trade
Center

Empire State
Building

Standard
Oil
Building

John Hancock
Center

Chrysler Building

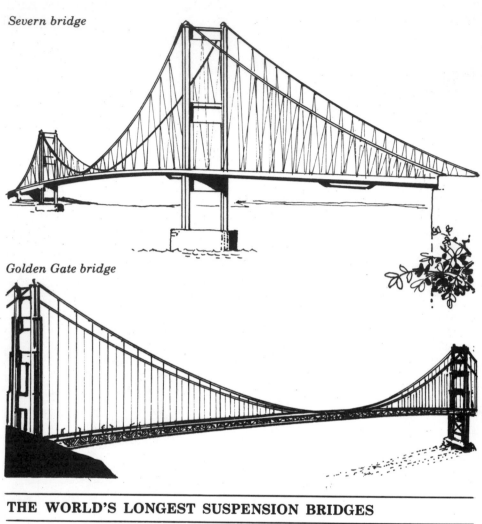

Severn bridge

Golden Gate bridge

THE WORLD'S LONGEST SUSPENSION BRIDGES

BRIDGE	LENGTH METRES	FEET	YEAR OF COMPLETION	LOCATION
Akashi-Kaikyo	1,780	5,840	Under construction	Honshu–Shikoku, Japan
Humber Estuary	1,410	4,626	Under construction	Humber, England
Verrazano Narrows	1,298	4,260	1964	Brooklyn–Staten Island, USA
Golden Gate	1,280	4,200	1937	San Francisco Bay, USA

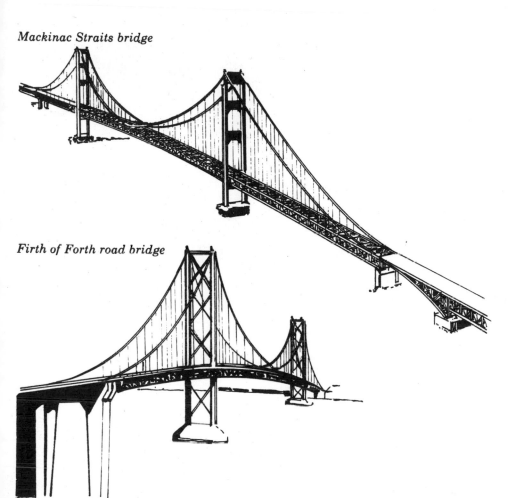

Mackinac Straits bridge

Firth of Forth road bridge

Mackinac Straits	1,158	3,800	1957	Mackinac Straits, Michigan, USA
Ataturk	1,074	3,524	1973	Bosporus, Turkey
George Washington	1,067	3,500	1931	Hudson River, New York City, USA
Ponto do 25 Abril	1,013	3,323	1966	Tagus River, Lisbon, Portugal
Firth of Forth (road bridge)	1,006	3,300	1964	Firth of Forth, Scotland
Severn	988	3,240	1966	Severn Estuary, England

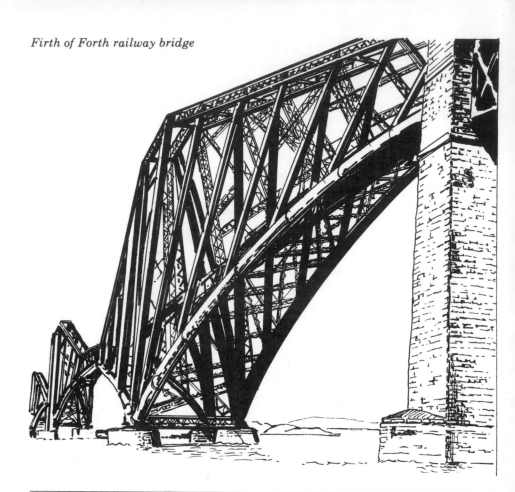

Firth of Forth railway bridge

THE WORLD'S LONGEST CANTILEVER BRIDGES

BRIDGE	LENGTH METRES	FEET	YEAR OF COMPLETION	LOCATION
Quebec (railway bridge)	549	1,800	1917	St Lawrence River, Canada
Firth of Forth (railway bridge)	521	1,710	1889	Firth of Forth, Scotland
Delaware River	501	1,644	1971	Chester, Pennsylvania, USA
Greater New Orleans	480	1,575	1958	Algiers, Mississippi River, Louisiana, USA

THE WORLD'S GREATEST STEEL ARCH BRIDGES

BRIDGE	LENGTH METRES	FEET	YEAR OF COMPLETION	LOCATION
New River Gorge	518	1,700	1977	Fayetteville, West Virginia, USA
Bayonne	504	1,652	1931	Bayonne, New Jersey–Staten Island, New York, USA
Sydney Harbour	503	1,650	1932	Sydney, Australia
Fremont	383	1,255	1971	Portland, Oregon, USA

Sydney Harbour bridge

THE WORLD'S LONGEST RAIL TUNNELS

TUNNEL	LENGTH KM	MILES	LOCATION	DATE OF CONSTRUCTION
Seikan	54	33.5	Tsugaru Channel, Japan	1972–
Northern Line – Morden to East Finchley (underground)	28	17	London, England	1939
Simplon II	20	12	Brig, Switzerland, to Iselle, Italy	1918–22
Simplon I	20	12	Brig, Switzerland, to Iselle, Italy	1898–1906
Great Apennine	18.5	11.5	Vernio, Italy	1923–34

GREAT SHIP CANALS OF THE WORLD

CANAL	COUNTRY	LENGTH KM	MILES	DEPTH METRES	FEET	YEAR OPENED
Amsterdam	Netherlands	26.5	16.5	7	23	1876
Corinth	Greece	6.5	4	8	26	1893
Elbe and Trave	Germany	66	41	3	10	1900
Gota	Sweden	185	115	3	10	1832
Houston (Texas)	USA	92	57	10	34	1940
Kiel	Germany	98	61	13.5	45	1895
Manchester	England	57	35.5	8.5	28	1894
Panama	Panama	81	50.5	13.5	45	1914
Princess Juliana	Netherlands	32	20	5	16	1935
Saulte Ste Marie	Canada	1.8	1.1	7	22	1895
Saulte Ste Marie	USA	2.6	1.6	7	22	1855
Suez	Egypt	162.5	101	12	39	1869
V.I. Lenin Volga–Don	USSR	100	62	—	—	1952
Welland	Canada	43.5	27	7.5	25	1887
White Sea–Baltic (formerly Stalin Canal)	USSR	227	141	5	16.5	1933

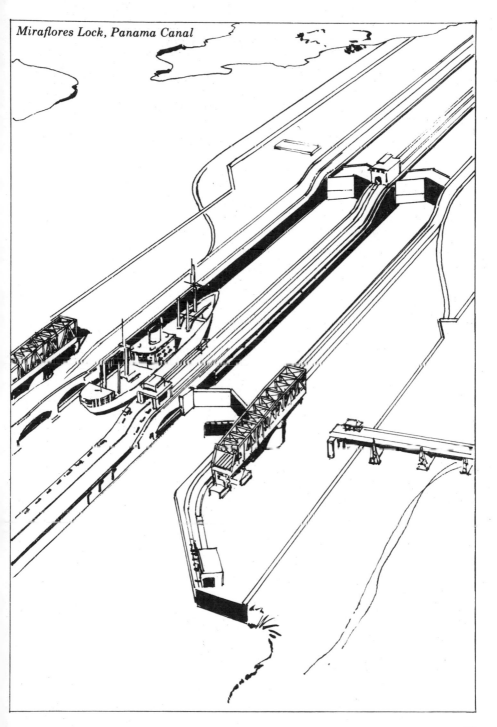

Miraflores Lock, Panama Canal

THE WORLD OF SCIENCE

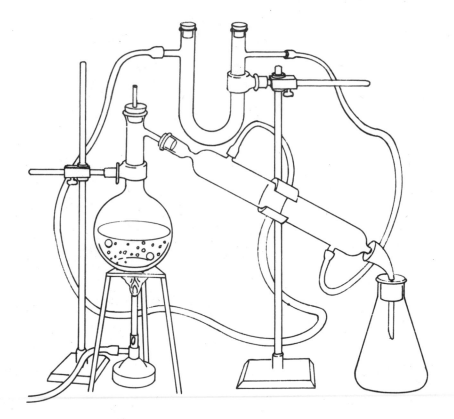

Recent Developments in Science and Technology

In 18th-century England, machinery was invented to perform various kinds of work which, until then, people had always done by hand. The goods manufactured with the use of machines were produced faster and were often better in quality than those hitherto made by country craftsmen. This was the beginning of what is known as the Industrial Revolution. Today there are machines that can do what people cannot do mentally (at least, not without an enormous amount of effort). We might call this development the Electronics Revolution.

Electronics

Electronics is a branch of science and engineering closely related to the science of electricity. It started with the discovery of the electron by Sir J. J. Thomson in 1897. Every atom has one or more electrons, particles which carry an electric charge. In materials called conductors (which include most metals) the atoms have electrons that can flow freely from atom to atom. Such a flow forms an electric current. An electric current is utilized in all electrical equipment, such as electric lights and electric motors. Electric power is controlled by varying the voltage or the current. Electronic equipment, such as TV sets and computers, on the other hand, mostly uses minute voltages and current from specialized devices producing pulses of

Transistor

electrons. One such device is the transistor.

Transistors can perform many of the functions of thermionic valves, which they have largely replaced. They can be made very small and are more reliable than valves. Both valves and transistors amplify (increase) small voltages and currents to control a much larger one. The transistor is made of a solid, semiconductor material. A semiconductor is neither a good conductor of electricity nor a good insulator. The materials commonly used in transistors are germanium or silicon. When 'doped', i.e. treated with impurities such as arsenic or phosphorus, they can conduct electricity.

The invention of the transistor in 1949 led immediately to the transistor radio. It also marked the beginning of the computer industry as computers could at last be made cheaper and less prone to breaking down. However, transistors were to be replaced by even more amazing devices called integrated circuits. The weakness of the transistor system was the circuit of wires joining the individual transistors, resistors and other components. As electronic circuits became more complicated, this wiring took more and more time to assemble. During the 1950s the problem was overcome by the use of printed circuits.

A printed circuit is made from an insulating board with a layer of copper on one side. The copper is dissolved away except along the paths which connect the components mounted on the board. These conducting pathways are thus chemically 'printed'. The basic principles underlying the printed circuit were used in the development of integrated circuits. The wires and components of integrated circuits are manufactured as a single unit by the treatment of different areas of the material.

Microelectronics

Most integrated circuits consist of an entire electronic circuit fitted on to a minute sliver of silicon. In its pure state, silicon does not conduct electricity but when slightly contaminated it becomes a semiconductor. Part of the tiny 'chip' of pure silicon is made electrically positive and therefore capable of conducting signals. This is achieved by 'doping' pathways in the silicon with impurities. Negative areas are created by charging the rest of the silicon with electrons. How is such an intricate job done? A full-scale circuit diagram is drawn and then photo-reduced to the size of the chip. This is then used as a photo-mask. It is placed over the chip and the network is etched into it by exposure to ultra-violet light. The areas shielded from the rays remain soft and are washed away with acid. The areas exposed to the rays, on the other hand, harden and resist the acid.

The techniques of silicon chip manufacture are still being developed. Electron and laser beams may be used as alternative means of making the masks. Some factories now 'shoot' atoms of impurity directly into the silicon. Although the development and machinery costs of silicon chip production are extremely high, the cost of the raw materials used in making a chip is almost negligible. Furthermore, the density of the circuits that can be placed on a chip is increasing all the time. A 3mm by 3mm chip (or microprocessor) can perform all the calculations that a large computer can do, just as fast and at much less cost. Data (information) can be stored in microelectronics memory circuits, just as in a computer. And just as our brain can store up past experiences, electronic machines are able to call upon stored data in their 'memory' when it is needed.

Since the mid-1970s microprocessors have been used in pocket calculators, digital watches, video games and some household appliances. They are so reliable that they are used in the flight control devices on aircraft. Soon we can expect to see many more gadgets and machines under the control of microprocessors. For example, microcircuits that are sensitive to temperature will be placed between the panes of double-glazed windows or in strategic parts of a room to feed back information on temperature and humidity. The information will be processed by a microcomputer which will calculate what the rate of heat production of the central heating system should be to make up for the heat loss if it is a cold day. On hot days the cooling rate will be calculated.

Similar circuits can be used to control the amount of lighting in a room. Light-sensitive microcircuits can cause blinds to open and close and electric lights to switch on and off as needed. Mechanical door locks may become old-fashioned as electronic ones take over. Micro-processors programmed to recognize magnetically coded patterns on keys will cause the door to be opened. Even control by voice is a possibility. Simple as the action of opening or closing a door is, microprocessors will be cheap enough to make their use feasible for this function.

Tasks involving calculations of great complexity can only be carried out by microprocessors that work with *digital* instructions and are linked to a more powerful memory. This is the type of microprocessor used in a computer.

Computers
There are two kinds of computer. Analogue computers are normally used to monitor and control changes in quantity or conditions, in an industrial process for example. Essentially, they deal with quantities of things, measured in terms of other quantities rather than numbers – just as a bathroom scale indicates your weight by the distance the dial moves.

Digital computers solve problems by counting with numbers, using what is called a *binary* code. Ordinary, or decimal, numbers have the symbols 0, 1, 2, 3, 4, 5, 6, 7, 8 and 9, i.e. the base is 10. Binary numbers have the base 2. There are only two symbols, or *bits*: 0 and 1. They correspond with the only two positions an electrical switch can have: 'on' or 'off'.

Before a digital computer can solve a problem it must have a set of instructions called a *program* that tells it what to do with the facts and figures put into it by a human operator. The programmer writes a program in a special computer language consisting of certain words or symbols. The language used depends on what sort of job has to be done and the particular computer that is being used. One computer language is called COBOL (*CO*mmon *B*usiness *O*rientated *L*anguage). It is used for processing business data. Another language is FORTRAN (*FOR*mula *TRAN*slation) which is used in solving algebraical problems. Both these languages use words for the instructions but the computer can only deal with the instructions by changing the words into numbers.

The information put into a computer is often in the form of tiny magnetic spots on a plastic tape. A machine 'reads' the tape and sends the information into

BINARY CONVERSION SCALE

DECIMAL (OR DENARY) NUMBERS	BINARY NUMBERS	DECIMAL (OR DENARY) NUMBERS	BINARY NUMBERS
1	1	16	10000
2	10	17	10001
3	11	18	10010
4	100	19	10011
5	101	20	10100
6	110	32	100000
7	111	64	1000000
8	1000	100	1100100
9	1001	128	10000000
10	1010	144	10010000
11	1011	150	10010110
12	1100	200	11001000
13	1101	250	11111111
14	1110	500	111110100
15	1111	1,000	1111101000

the computer in the form of electric signals. Automatic typewriters and printing machines electrically connected to computers record the information they produce at high speed. Computers can work at a speed only a little less than the speed of light and can perform about one million operations in one second.

All sorts of people use computers for all kinds of purposes. Scientists have many uses for them. For example, computers keep spacecraft on course during interplanetary missions. Business people use computers for bookkeeping and accounting, for keeping track of sales, payments by customers and the amount of stock in warehouses. Banks use computers to keep a check on the money deposited and withdrawn by each of their customers. In some industries computers are used to control the quality of their products.

Word processors
A time can be foreseen when few people need go to an office to do their work because office services will be computerized. The time-consuming tasks of dictating, drafting, typing and mailing letters

Integrated circuit (actual size)

Computer terminal and print-out

Pocket calculator

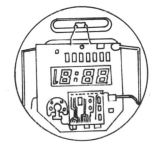

Inside an electronic watch.
The integrated circuit can be seen at the bottom

may be eliminated. Electronic machines called word processors take a good deal of work out of these processes. The text of standard letters is stored in the memory of a word processor. A draft of this may go to the business executive from a normal typewriter, or it may be shown on a visual display screen where it can be altered as required. Any words, lines or paragraphs that have to be altered, deleted or moved on the draft can be marked. The operator then types the instructions to the microprocessor. The letter is printed by a high-speed automatic printer that prints at the rate of 60 characters a second. As many copies as the boss needs can be produced, each with minor alterations if necessary.

What about the labour of mailing all those letters? 'Electronic mail' can now handle them. This is how it's done. A machine reduces the image on the printed page into digital code, then transmits that code down the telephone line to anyone with a suitable receiver at the end of their phone. This produces a facsimile (exact copy) of the original letter. Even facsimile transmission may become outdated if everyone has a computer receiver-transmitter in their home. There would be no need to put the message on paper at all. The text would be shown directly on a video screen. Think of all the paper that would be saved!

Telecommunications

Telegraph, telephone, radio, television and radar are all means of sending messages over a long distance. In other words, they are all forms of telecommunications. New developments in tele-communications have followed developments in electronic computer control.

The means of transmitting telephone calls is generally through copper cables. This involves unsightly pylons and the digging of holes to bury the cables under-ground. However, a new way of transmitting telephone calls without the use of cables has been adopted. This is by means of microwaves, beamed from the tops of tall towers.

There are some problems in microwave transmission, however. The expense of building the towers, which must be no more than 25 km (15½ miles) apart, offsets the savings made in not having to install cables. Furthermore, all radio transmissions are affected by bad weather and various kinds of interference.

Yet another means of telephone transmission is now being developed by the use of cables of glass fibres. An optical fibre will be able to carry 10,000 simultaneous telephone conversations in less space than is taken today by a copper cable whose limit is 5,000.

How can telephone conversations

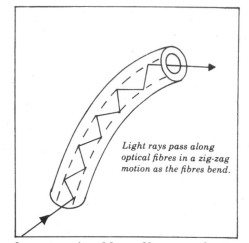

Light rays pass along optical fibres in a zig-zag motion as the fibres bend.

be transmitted by a filament of glass? Optical fibres (they may be glass or plastic) are so-called because they transfer light. Rays of light are reflected on the inner surface of the glass instead of passing through it. In other words, the light in the centre core cannot break out to the outer layer but bounces along it in zig-zag fashion as the fibre bends and turns. Signals are sent along the fibres by a light source flashing on and off. Each flash represents a pulse in the digital code. The light source is a laser, which produces an intense narrow beam of light.

Television programmes can also be transmitted through glass cables. A receiver at the end of the fibres changes the light signals into copies of the original sounds and pictures.

Teletext

People in Britain and America (and soon many other countries) can link up their telephones and television sets to certain computers to obtain all kinds of information. For

Teletext system

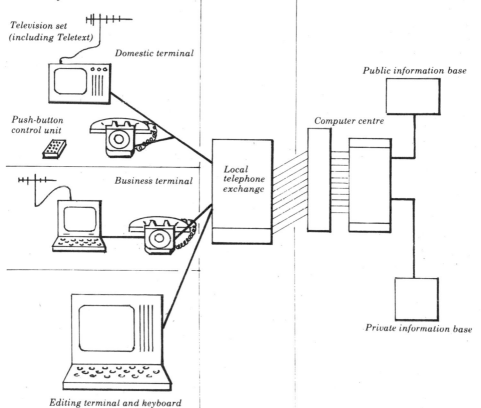

Television set (including Teletext)

Domestic terminal

Public information base

Push-button control unit

Computer centre

Business terminal

Local telephone exchange

Private information base

Editing terminal and keyboard

example, a horse-racing enthusiast does not need to wait for the day's racing results to appear in the newspapers if he has a teletext system in his home. With a push-button control unit about the size of a pocket calculator he can call up the information, which has been stored on a computer, and have it immediately displayed in words and simple diagrams on his television screen.

There are numerous other kinds of information available on different television channels. These cover national and international news, weather, sports, finance, travel information, entertainment, recipes and a multitude of other items.

In the future it may be common-place for people to have direct contact with a public computer linked to their telephone. They will be able to ask the computer for advice on various matters and, if they wish, play games with it.

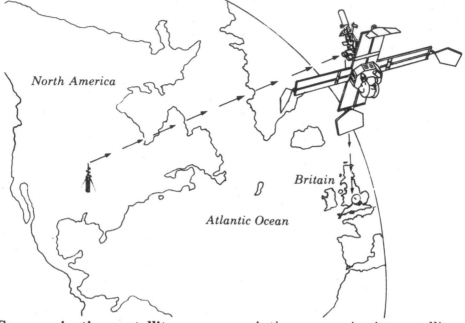

An active communications satellite linking North America and Britain

North America

Atlantic Ocean

Britain

Communications satellites

When we receive immediate television pictures of events that are occurring in far distant countries, these pictures are beamed to us by artificial satellite. How is this possible?

A communications satellite is either passive or active, depending on the way it sends signals back to Earth. A passive satellite reflects signals, just as a mirror reflects light. The first passive communications satellite, launched in 1960, was *Echo 1*, a huge 30 m (100 ft) plastic balloon coated with a thin layer of metal. Signals sent to passive satellites must be strong because radio waves weaken as they travel to the satellite and back to Earth. The satellite must be large, too, so that it can reflect the radio waves back to ground stations.

Active communications satellites carry a radio receiver and transmitter. The signals received from transmitting stations on Earth are amplified (strengthened) and retransmitted to Earth. The electronic equipment is powered by solar cells (batteries) which harness energy from the Sun.

Because a single satellite can serve less than a third of the Earth's surface, a series of satellites is necessary to provide global coverage. Usually a communications satellite is launched to a height of 35,890 km (22,340 miles). At this altitude it takes 24 hours to complete an orbit round the Earth. Because the Earth takes 24 hours to rotate once, the satellite appears to be staying in the same place. *Telstar*, the first active telecommunications satellite (launched in

1962) took a mere 2½ hours to complete an orbit. It was therefore within range of the ground stations in Europe and North America for very short periods. In 1964 the International Telecommunications Satellite Organization (Intelsat) was founded to create an inter-national system. By 1978 over 100 countries had joined.

Theoretically, three satellites only, properly placed, can now link stations in any two parts of the world. For example, television pictures are sent to Britain from the USA through a satellite over the Atlantic Ocean. The other two satellites to complete the system are positioned over the Indian Ocean and the Pacific Ocean. Sending and receiving stations must point their antennae at the satellites.

Communications satellites carry a wider range of wave lengths than ordinary short-wave radio and the quality of reception is better. With advancing technology, satellites have been developed to carry telephone, telex and computer data as well as television.

The Earth's dwindling resources
All the exciting technological achievements mentioned above, and many others, may well encourage us to look towards the future with cheerful optimism. Given time, science seems to come up with the answers to a good many problems. Nevertheless, there are mounting world problems that present a great challenge to scientists and technologists, and time is not on our side. For

example, millions of people in the world today do not have enough to eat. Will we have to find new kinds of food? Can the deserts be made fertile?

Many of our raw materials are in short supply. How will we manage when the fossil fuels (petroleum, coal and natural gas) run out? Already there is great concern about the shortage of oil. At the present rate of consumption, the world's fossil fuels and the radio-active materials used in the present types of nuclear power station will be exhausted within a few decades. Public anxiety about possible accidents at nuclear power stations, and the dangers from their radio-active byproducts, has furthermore led to a virtual halt in the building of new power stations. So how shall we obtain our power?

Many people hope that we shall soon find a means to obtain energy by atomic fusion, the same process that makes the Sun burn. Research groups throughout the world are working towards this aim. To bring about a fusion reaction, very light atomic nuclei, such as those of hydrogen, deuterium and tritium, must be brought together and fused into a single nucleus. This would release a great quantity of nuclear energy. To achieve fusion of the nuclei, they would have to be forced together for long periods of time at an extremely high temperature – about one million degrees centi-grade. Even if the necessary requirements for fusion can be met, it would still take many years for a commercial reactor to be designed and built.

The great advantage of nuclear

fusion is that the materials for making the reaction possible, heavy hydrogen, deuterium and tritium, are all readily obtainable. The environmental hazards from these materials if an accident should occur are considerably less than in the case of plutonium, the byproduct of the fast breeder type of reactor.

What alternatives are there to nuclear energy? Solar energy is one. It is used already in many small devices. Solar cells, made from thin slices of semiconductor materials, convert light into electricity. They have been used in artificial satellites. Another solar device is the flat-plate collector which is used to heat houses. It consists of a metal plate painted black which is placed where it faces the Sun. (Black absorbs sunlight more than any other colour.) The plate absorbs sunlight and becomes hot. The heat is kept in by one or more layers of glass that cover the plate. A system of pipes is used to distribute the heat through the house. Solar energy could produce a clean and almost limitless supply of power but unfortunately it is spread so thinly that a huge land area would be required to harness it on a large scale.

Wind power can turn windmills to produce energy but they are practicable only on a very small scale. Tidal energy can be utilized wherever there happens to be a high tide in a bay that can be closed by a dam. During high tide the bay fills with water. At low tide the level of the sea drops below the level of the water held behind the

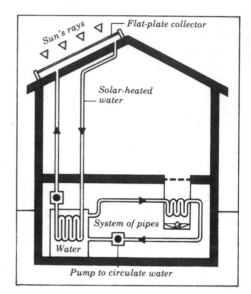

dam. When the water is released it drives turbines that generate power. A disadvantage of tidal power is that it can produce electricity only at certain times and for rather short periods. Another disadvantage is that there are very few places where such plants can be built.

Capturing the heat trapped in the core of the Earth may be one of the answers to our energy needs. When water comes into contact with hot underground rocks it turns to steam. The steam can be directed against the blades of a steam turbine to produce electricity.

Fuel cells are kinds of battery in which gas or liquid fuels combine chemically to generate electricity. Their disadvantage is that they are expensive to make. Garbage in the form of plant or animal waste can be a quite valuable source of energy. It can be burnt to produce electrical power, or converted to a fuel such as methanol.

A great deal of money will be

spent in the future on research into new ways of obtaining energy. As oil becomes scarcer and more expensive, the schemes mentioned above and many others, such as wave power and energy from fast-growing plants, will have to be considered seriously.

Progress in Space Research

The 1960s and 1970s will be famous for centuries to come as a time when tremendous advances were made in space technology, and exciting discoveries about the Moon and planets took place.

The V2 rocket of World War II was the direct ancestor of modern space probes. But rocket speeds many times faster than that of the V2 had to be developed before a satellite could be placed in orbit. The Soviet *Sputnik 1*, whose launch in 1957 surprised the world, marked the beginning of the Space Age.

While a satellite needs a launching speed of about 29,000 km/h to place it in orbit several hundred kilometres above the Earth, a rocket must travel at over 40,000 km/h to escape from the Earth's gravitational pull and set course for the planets.

Before human beings were risked on space missions, unmanned crafts containing instruments were used, and sometimes animals were sent into space. The design of manned spacecraft incorporates control systems to regulate cabin temperature, pressure and atmospheric conditions, food and waste-handling equipment, and other equipment needed by the crew to sustain them during periods of rapid acceleration on the one hand and weightlessness on the other. There are guidance and navigation systems for keeping on course and making manoeuvres, and communications receivers and transmitters. Some of the hazards of space travel proved not to be as great as had been feared. The effects of weightlessness were not as severe as had been first thought, and the risks of collision with meteorites not high.

Space exploration reached a climax when man first landed on the Moon in 1969. However, almost all of the really significant scientific discoveries have been obtained through the use of robot spacecraft. Some of these discoveries have been most astonishing. On Mars there are huge volcanoes and canyons which dwarf any on Earth, even though Mars is a smaller planet. There are also sandstorms approaching the speed of sound. The chemistry of the soil is so puzzling that the presence of micro-organisms in it has not been discounted.

Surprisingly, Jupiter is now known to have a thin flat ring encircling it. Two of its moons, Europa and Ganymede, show remarkable networks of straight and curved surface markings, while on Io active volcanoes have been seen. Titan's clouds containing organic substances are another extraordinary sight. It seems, though, that manned flight to Jupiter is unlikely because of the belts of high radiation found there.

Equally inhospitable is Venus, with its clouds of sulphuric acid and high surface temperatures. Probes have revealed continuous thunder and lightning and strange chemical fires on the planet.

IMPORTANT DATES IN SPACE RESEARCH

1957   October 4   *Sputnik 1* put in orbit (USSR).

November 3   *Sputnik 2* launched carrying dog, Laika (USSR).

1958   January   *Explorer 1* put into orbit. Provided first information about radiation zones around the Earth now known as the Van Allen belts (USA).

1959   January   *Luna 1* bypassed Moon at 6,400 km (4,000 miles) (USSR).

September   *Luna 2* crash-landed on Moon (USSR).

October   *Luna 3* made first circumlunar flight; first pictures of hidden side of Moon (USSR).

1960   March   *Pioneer 5* measured solar system and returned data on solar wind (USA).

August   *Discoverer 13* launched. First successful recovery of a capsule from orbit (USA).

Echo 1 launched. First successful voice and picture transmission by reflection off satellite (USA).

Sputnik 5 launched. Two dogs, six mice and insects returned safely (USSR).

1961   April 12   Yuri Gagarin made full circuit of Earth in *Vostok 1* (USSR).

May 5   Alan Shepard became first American in space in *Freedom 7*; the suborbital flight lasted about 15 minutes.

August   Gherman Titov made 17 orbits (USSR).

1962   February   John Glenn made three orbits in *Friendship 7* (USA).

December   *Mariner 2*, first successful planetary probe, bypassed Venus at 35,000 km (22,000 miles); sent back valuable data (USA).

1963   June 16   Valentina Tereshkova became first woman in space. She made 48 orbits in *Vostok 6* (USSR).

1964   July   *Ranger 7*, first of three successful Ranger probes, took close-range pictures of the Moon's surface before crash-landing (USA).

1965	March	Alexei Leonov became the first man to venture outside an orbiting space capsule, the two-man *Voskhod 2* (USSR).
	June	Edward White walked in space during Gemini programme (USA).
	July	*Mariner 4* bypassed Mars and transmitted close-range pictures of the surface (USA).
	December	Manned spacecraft *Gemini 6* and *Gemini 7* met in space, coming within 30 cm (1 ft) of each other. This was a rehearsal of the docking procedure to be used in future Moon landings (USA).
1966	January	*Luna 9* made first successful soft landing on Moon; several pictures of the surface (USA).
	February	*Venera 2*, first successful Soviet planetary probe, bypassed Venus at 24,000 km (15,000 miles).
	March	*Venera 3* soft-landed on Venus (USSR). *Luna 10* became first spacecraft to orbit Moon (USSR).
	May	*Surveyor 1* made first American soft landing on Moon; transmitted pictures of surface.
1966–7		*Orbiters 1* to *5* put into orbit round Moon. Thousands of pictures transmitted, enabling whole lunar surface to be mapped (USA).
1967	October	*Venera 4* soft-landed on Venus; transmitted data during descent (USSR). *Mariner 5* bypassed Venus at 4,000 km (2,500 miles) and sent back data (USA).
1968	January	*Surveyor 7* soft-landed on Moon near crater Tycho; sent back high-quality pictures of crater wall (USA).
	October	*Soyuz 2* used in docking manoeuvres with *Soyuz 3* (USSR).
	December	*Apollo 8* made ten orbits of the Moon with crew: Frank Borman, James Lovell and William Anders (USA).
1969	May	*Veneras 5* and *6* soft-landed on Venus; data transmitted from surface (USSR).
	July 20	*Apollo 11* Moon mission. Neil Armstrong was the first man to set foot on the Moon; with him was Edwin Aldrin. Michael Collins piloted the command module orbiting above (USA). *Mariners 6* and *7* bypassed Mars. High-quality pictures transmitted (USA).
	November	*Apollo 12* Moon mission. Landed close to an earlier probe, *Surveyor 3*. Astronauts Charles Conrad and Alan Bean brought parts of it back together with rock samples (USA).
1970	September	*Luna 16* landed on Moon. Sample of Moon rocks gathered

by robot and returned to Earth (USSR).

	November	*Luna 17* landed on Moon in Mare Imbrium. Automated machine 'Lunokhod' crawled along for months sending back information to Earth (USSR).
	December	*Apollo 13* Moon mission was unlucky. An explosion on the outward journey put the main propulsion unit out of action and the Moon landing was called off. Astronauts used motors of lunar module to pass around Moon and return to Earth (USA).
1971	February	*Apollo 14* Moon mission; landing by astronauts Shepard and Mitchell; Roosa was in the command module. Rock samples brought back (USA).
	June	*Soyuz 10* docked with *Salyut* space station. Three Russian cosmonauts became the first crew to transfer from an orbiting spacecraft to an orbiting space station.
	July	First joint US–USSR space project; crews of *Soyuz* craft and specially modified *Apollo* capsule were able to enter each others' craft after docking in space.
	August	*Apollo 15* Moon landing with lunar rover vehicle; rock samples brought back (USA).
	November	*Mariner 9* put into orbit around Mars. Thousands of high-quality pictures transmitted of Mars and its satellites (USA). *Mars 2* put in orbit around Mars (USSR).
	December	*Mars 3* made soft landing on Mars (USSR).
1972	February	*Luna 20* soft-landed on Mars and returned to Earth with rock samples (USSR).
	March	*Pioneer 10*, first Jupiter probe, launched (USA).
	April	*Apollo 16* Moon mission; landing by Young and Duke, with Mattingly in command module (USA).
	July	*Venera 8* landed on Venus (USSR).
	December	*Apollo 17* Moon mission; landing by Cernan and Schmitt with Evans in command module (USA).
1973	January	*Luna 21* Moon landing; 'Lunokhod 2' gathered and analyzed specimens (USSR).
	March	*Pioneer 11* launched towards Jupiter (USA).
	May	*Skylab*, first American space station, was launched. Three successive crews spent a total of 171 days on the craft.
	December	*Pioneer 10* reached Jupiter, passing within 132,000 km (182,000 miles). It then moved away to begin a journey without end into space (USA).

1974	February	*Mariner 10* bypassed Venus before swinging towards Mercury; sent back data and photographs (USA).
	March	*Mariner 10* made close contact with Mercury (USA).
	May	*Luna 22* soft-landed on the Moon (USSR).
	September	*Mariner 10* made second contact with Mercury after orbiting the Sun (USA).
	October	*Luna 23* soft-landed on Moon (USSR).
	December	*Pioneer 11* reached Jupiter; further data obtained. Afterwards it flicked away towards Saturn, when it was renamed *Pioneer Saturn* (USA).
1975	March	*Mariner 10* bypassed Mercury for third time (USA).
	October	*Venera 9* soft-landed on Venus. Pictures transmitted for about one hour, after which the cameras were put out of action by extreme heat and pressure on planet. *Venera 10* followed shortly afterwards, but cameras again soon ceased functioning (USSR).
1976	July	*Viking 1* landed on Mars. Soil analyzed (USA).
	August	*Luna 24* landed on Moon. Soil samples taken and returned to Earth (USSR).
	September	*Viking 2* landed on Mars (USA).
1977	August	*Voyager 2* launched towards Jupiter (USA).
	September	*Voyager 1* launched. On the way to Jupiter, it overtook *Voyager 2* which was launched 16 days earlier (USA).
1978	December	Two space probes which had been launched close together, *Pioneer Venus 1* and *2*, reached the atmosphere of Venus. The first probe went into orbit round the planet. The other, consisting of a battery of probes, crash-landed two probes which continued to send data for a short time (USA). *Veneras 11* and *12* reached Venus (USSR).
1979	February	*Voyager 1* reached Jupiter (USA).
	July	*Voyager 2* reached Jupiter (USA).
	September	*Pioneer Saturn* reached Saturn. Afterwards it drifted off into the solar system (USA).

Future planetary programmes

Will there be great advances in space research in the 1980s? Cutbacks in expenditure could threaten future plans.

The United States is now concentrating on developing the space shuttle in an effort to cut costs. Hitherto, craft ferrying crew to a space station have been powered by expendable rockets. The space shuttle, however, will be reusable. It consists of a winged Orbiter, intended to be used at least 100 times, two solid rocket boosters which are discarded when the craft has reached an altitude of 45 km (28 miles), and a large fuel tank which is cast off just before the Orbiter goes into orbit. When re-entering the Earth's atmosphere, the Orbiter, whose hull is built to withstand very high temperatures, uses its manoeuvring engine as retro-rockets. It then returns to base.

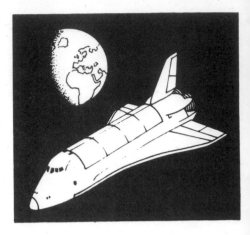

The Elements

An element is a substance which cannot be split up into simpler substances by chemical means. There are 92 naturally occurring elements. Some elements have been made artificially in nuclear reactors or machines called cyclotrons; these are known as the *transuranic* elements.

The smallest whole unit of an element which cannot be subdivided by chemical means is the atom. An atom of any element consists of a positively charged nucleus orbited by electrons. The electrons have a negative charge which exactly balances that of the nucleus. The nucleus is composed of two types of particle – protons and neutrons. The proton is positively charged; the neutron has no charge but it has slightly more mass than that of a proton. The simplest atom is that of hydrogen, consisting of one proton and one electron only. A carbon atom has six orbiting electrons, six protons and six neutrons.

The *atomic number* of an element indicates the number of protons in the nucleus of an atom, which is also equivalent to the number of orbiting electrons.

The atomic weight is the weight of an element compared with that of a carbon atom whose weight is taken as exactly 12.

The atoms of the various elements differ only in the number and arrangement of their protons, neutrons and electrons. Atoms of the same element, i.e. of identical atomic number, but differing in the number of neutrons present in the nucleus, are called *isotopes*. If the number of outer electrons of an atom is altered then it becomes an *ion*. The addition of electrons creates negative ions; the removal of electrons creates positive ions. Chemical combination takes place by the transfer or sharing of electrons between combining atoms.

THE NATURAL ELEMENTS

ATOMIC NUMBER	ELEMENT	SYMBOL	ATOMIC WEIGHT
1	Hydrogen	H	1.008
2	Helium	He	4.003
3	Lithium	Li	6.939
4	Beryllium	Be	9.012
5	Boron	B	10.811
6	Carbon	C	12.011
7	Nitrogen	N	14.007
8	Oxygen	O	15.999
9	Fluorine	F	18.998
10	Neon	Ne	20.183
11	Sodium	Na	22.990
12	Magnesium	Mg	24.312
13	Aluminium	Al	26.982
14	Silicon	Si	28.086
15	Phosphorus	P	30.974
16	Sulphur	S	32.064
17	Chlorine	Cl	35.453
18	Argon	A	39.948
19	Potassium	K	39.102
20	Calcium	Ca	40·08
21	Scandium	Sc	44.956
22	Titanium	Ti	47.90
23	Vanadium	V	50.94
24	Chromium	Cr	52.00
25	Manganese	Mn	54.94
26	Iron	Fe	55.85
27	Cobalt	Co	58.93
28	Nickel	Ni	58.71
29	Copper	Cu	63.54
30	Zinc	Zn	65.37
31	Gallium	Ga	69.72
32	Germanium	Ge	72.59
33	Arsenic	As	74.92
34	Selenium	Se	78.96
35	Bromine	Br	79.909
36	Krypton	Kr	83·80
37	Rubidium	Rb	85.47
38	Strontium	Sr	87.62
39	Yttrium	Y	88.905
40	Zirconium	Zr	91.22
41	Niobium	Nb	92.906
42	Molybdenum	Mo	95.94
43	Technetium	Tc	99.00
44	Ruthenium	Ru	101.07
45	Rhodium	Rh	102.91

ATOMIC NUMBER	ELEMENT	SYMBOL	ATOMIC WEIGHT
46	Palladium	Pd	106.4
47	Silver	Ag	107.87
48	Cadmium	Cd	112.40
49	Indium	In	114.82
50	Tin	Sn	118.69
51	Antimony	Sb	121·75
52	Tellurium	Te	127.60
53	Iodine	I	126.904
54	Xenon	Xe	131.30
55	Caesium	Cs	132.905
56	Barium	Ba	137.34
57	Lanthanum	La	138.91
58	Cerium	Ce	140.12
59	Praseodymium	Pr	140.907
60	Neodymium	Nd	144.24
61	Prometheum	Pm	147
62	Samarium	Sm	150.35
63	Europium	Eu	151.96
64	Gadolinium	Gd	157.25
65	Terbium	Tb	158.92
66	Dysprosium	Dy	162.50
67	Holnium	Ho	164.93
68	Erbium	Er	167.26
69	Thulium	Tm	168.93
70	Ytterbium	Yb	173.04
71	Lutecium	Lu	174.97
72	Hafmium	Hf	178.49
73	Tantalum	Ta	180.95
74	Wolfram	W	183.85
75	Rhenium	Re	186.2
76	Osmium	Os	190.2
77	Iridium	Ir	192.2
78	Platinum	Pt	195.09
79	Gold	Au	196.97
80	Mercury	Hg	200.59
81	Thallium	Tl	204.37
82	Lead	Pb	207.19
83	Bismuth	Bi	208.98
84	Polonium	Po	210
85	Astatine	At	211
86	Radon	Rn	222
87	Francium	Fr	223
88	Radium	Ra	226.05
89	Actinium	Ac	227.05
90	Thorium	Th	232.12
91	Protactinium	Pa	231.05
92	Uranium	U	238.07

THE TRANSURANIC ELEMENTS

ATOMIC NUMBER	ELEMENT	SYMBOL	ATOMIC WEIGHT
93	Neptunium	Np	237
94	Plutonium	Pu	239
95	Americum	Am	241
96	Curium	Cm	242
97	Berkelium	Bk	243–250
98	Californium	Cf	251
99	Einsteinium	Es	246, 247
100	Fermium	Fm	250, 252–256
101	Mendelevium	Md	256
102	Nobelium	No	254
103	Lawrencium	Lr	257
*104	—	—	—
*105	—	—	—
*106	—	—	—

*Names proposed for elements 104, 105 and 106 have been Kurchatovium, Ruther-
fordium (and Hahnium) and Nielsbohrium respectively.

Hydrogen atom

Carbon atom

THE ARTS

Who Wrote That?

General Literature

Bevis, Richard Jefferies (1848–87)
Billy Bunter books, C. H. St John Hamilton (1875–1961)
Blue Boat, The, William Mayne (b. 1928)
Bobbsey Twins, The, Laura Lee Hope
Boney was a Warrior, Rosemary Manning (b. 1911)
Borrowers, The, Mary Norton (b. 1903)
Broom Stages, Clemence Dane
Carrots: Just a Little Boy, Mrs M. L. Molesworth (1839–1921)
Children of Green Knowe, Lucy M. Boston (b. 1892)
Christmas Carol, A, Charles Dickens (1812–70)
Circus Boy, Ruth Manning-Saunders (b. 1895)
Clunie, Hugh Charteris
Cowboy Small, Lois Lenski (1893–1974)
Darkie & Co., Howard Spring (1889–1965)
David Copperfield, Charles Dickens (1812–70)
Eric, or Little by Little, F. W. Farrar (1831–1903)
Family at Misrule, The, Ethel Turner (1872–1958)
Family from One End Street, The, Eve Garnett
Famous Five, The (Secret Seven etc.), Enid Blyton (1897–1968)
Five Proud Riders, Ann Stafford
Freckles, Gene Stratton-Porter (1868–1924)
Golden Shore, The, Elinor Lyon (b. 1921)
Grass Rope, A, William Mayne (b. 1928)
Green Dolphin Country, Elizabeth Goudge (b. 1900)
Green Mansions, W. H. Hudson (1841–1922)
Hans Brinker; or The Silver Skates, Mary Mapes Dodge (1831–1905)
Harlequin Corner, Pamela Brown (b. 1924)
Hartwarp books, The, John Pudney (1909–77)
House in Turner Square, Ann Thwaite (b. 1932)
House of the Pelican, The, Elizabeth Kyle
Human Boy books, The, Eden Phillpotts (1862–1960)
Impractical Chimney Sweep, The, Rosemary Anne Sisson (b. 1923)
I Will Tell You of a Town, Alastair Reid (b. 1926)
Jeremy stories, Sir Hugh Walpole (1884–1941)
Just William books, Richmal Crompton (1890–1969)
Lark in the Morn, The, Elfrida Vipont (b. 1902)
Little House in the Big Woods, Laura Ingalls Wilder (1867–1957)
Little Lord Fauntleroy, Frances Hodgson Burnett (1849–1924)
Little Tim and the Brave Sea Captain, Edward Ardizzone (1900–79)
Lorna Doone, R. D. Blackmore (1825–1900)
Lovely Summer, Barbara Ker Wilson (b. 1929)
Marlows and the Traitor, The, Antonia Forest
Martin Pippin in the Daisy Field, Eleanor Farjeon (1882–1965)
Minnow on the Say, Ann Philippa Pearce (b. 1920)
Mystery at Witchend, Malcolm Saville (b. 1901)
Not Scarlet but Gold, Malcolm Saville (b. 1901)
Paddington Bear books, Michael Bond (b. 1926)

Parcel of Trees, A, William Mayne (b. 1928)
Path Through the Woods, Barbara Ker Wilson (b. 1929)
Pigeon Post, Arthur Ransome (1884–1967)
Polly & Oliver books, David Scott Daniell (1906–65)
Prize Essay, The, Kathleen Wallace
Punchbowl Farm books, Monica Edwards (b. 1912)
Raffles books, Ernest Hornung (1866–1921)
Redcap Runs Away, Rhoda Power (1890–1957)
Romany books, The, G. Bramwell Evans (1884–1943)
Ryan's Fort, Patricia Lynch (1898–1972)
Sampson's Circus, Howard Spring (1889–1965)
Sandford of Merton, Desmond Coke (1879–1940s)
Saturdays, The, Elizabeth Enright (1909–68)
Secret Garden, The, Frances Hodgson Burnett (1849–1924)
Showboat Summer, Pamela Brown (b. 1924)
Silver Curlew, The, Eleanor Farjeon (1882–1965)
Stalky & Co., Rudyard Kipling (1865–1936)
Stig of the Dump, Clive King (b. 1924)
Story of Holly and Ivy, The, Rumer Godden (b. 1907)
Summer with Spike, The, Barbara Willard (b. 1909)
Susan and Bill stories, Malcolm Saville (b. 1901)
Swish of the Curtain, The, Pamela Brown (b. 1924)
Teddy Robinson books, Joan G. Robinson (b. 1910)
Thimble Summer, Elizabeth Enright (1909–68)
Thumbstick, The, William Mayne (b. 1928)
We Couldn't Leave Dinah, Mary Treadgold (b. 1910)
We Didn't Mean to Go to Sea, Arthur Ransome (1884–1967)
Wintle's Wonders, Noel Streatfeild (b. 1897)
Wooroo, Joyce Gard (b. 1911)

Animal Stories

At the Back of the North Wind, George MacDonald (1824–1905)
Bambi, Felix Salten (1869–1945)
Black Beauty, Anna Sewell (1820–78)
Born Free, Joy Adamson (1910–80)
Call of the Wild, Jack London (1876–1916)
Dog Crusoe, R. M. Ballantyne (1825–94)
Dog Toby, Richard Church (1893–1972)
Jungle Book, The, Rudyard Kipling (1865–1936)
Just-so Stories, Rudyard Kipling (1865–1936)
Mousewife, The, Rumer Godden (b. 1907)
One Hundred and One Dalmatians, Dodie Smith
Orlando books, Kathleen Hale (b. 1898)
Rufty Tufty books, Ruth Ainsworth (b. 1908)
Snow Goose, The, Paul Gallico (1897–1976)
Soapbox Derby, The, Rosemary Weir (b. 1905)
Tarka the Otter, Henry Williamson (b. 1897)
Uncle Remus books, Joel Chandler Harris (1848–1908)
Watership Down, Richard Adams (b. 1920)
White Fang, Jack London (1876–1916)
White Stag, The, Kate Seredy (1899–1975)

Whoo Whoo, the Wind Blew, Diana Ross (b. 1910)
Wind in the Willows, Kenneth Grahame (1859–1932)

Fantasy and Fairy Stories

Alice's Adventures in Wonderland, Lewis Carroll (1832–98)
Blue Fairy Book, The, Andrew Lang (1844–1912)
Book of Discoveries, A, John Masefield (1878–1967)
Box of Delights, The, John Masefield (1878–1967)
Cuckoo Clock, The, Mrs M. L. Molesworth (1839–1921)
Dragon of the Hill, The, Joyce Gard (b. 1911)
Enchanted Castle, The, E. Nesbit (1858–1924)
English Fairy Tales, Joseph Jacobs (1854–1916)
Five Children and It, E. Nesbit (1858–1924)
Granny's Wonderful Chair, Frances Browne (1816–c. 1879)
Happy Prince and Other Stories, The, Oscar Wilde (1854–1900)
Hobbit, The, J. R. R. Tolkien (1892–1973)
Invisible Man, The, H. G. Wells (1866–1946)
King of the Golden River, John Ruskin (1819–1900)
Lion, the Witch and the Wardrobe, The, C. S. Lewis (1898–1963)
Little Grey Men, The, 'B.B.' (b. 1905)
Lord of the Rings, The, J. R. R. Tolkien (1892–1973)
Lost World, The, Sir Arthur Conan Doyle (1859–1930)
Magic City, The, E. Nesbit (1858–1924)
Magic Finger, The, Roald Dahl (b. 1916)
Magic Walking Stick, The, John Buchan (1875–1940)
Mary Poppins books, Pamela L. Travers (b. 1906)
Midnight Folk, The, John Masefield (1878–1967)
Moon of Gomrath, The, Alan Garner (b. 1934)
Oz books, L. Frank Baum (1856–1919)
Peter Pan and Wendy, Sir James Barrie (1860–1937)
Phoenix and the Carpet, The, E. Nesbit (1858–1924)
Princess and the Goblin, The, George MacDonald (1824–1905)
Puck of Pook's Hill, Rudyard Kipling (1865–1936)
Rose and the Ring, The, William Makepeace Thackeray (1811–63)
Story of the Amulet, The, E. Nesbit (1858–1924)
Three Royal Monkeys, The, Walter de la Mare (1873–1956)
Through the Looking Glass, Lewis Carroll (1832–98)
Time Garden, The, Edward Eager (b. circa 1900–64)
Tom's Midnight Garden, Ann Philippa Pearce (b. 1920)
Twelve and the Genii, The, Pauline Clarke (b. 1921)
Weirdstone of Brisingamen, Alan Garner (b. 1934)
Witch Family, The, Eleanor Ruth Estes (b. 1906)
Wizard of Earthsea, Ursula Le Guin (b. 1929)

Adventure Stories

Adventures of Huckleberry Finn, The, Mark Twain (1835–1910)
Adventures of Tom Sawyer, The, Mark Twain (1835–1910)
Biggles books, Captain W. E. Johns (1893–1968)
Coral Island, The, R. M. Ballantyne (1825–94)
Gulliver's Travels, Jonathan Swift (1667–1745)

Hill, The, H. A. Vachell (1861–1955)
Hornblower books, C. S. Forester (1899–1966)
Howard Pyle's book of Pirates, Howard Pyle (1853–1911)
Kidnapped, Robert Louis Stevenson (1850–94)
King Solomon's Mines, Sir Henry Rider Haggard (1856–1925)
Martin Rattler, R. M. Ballantyne (1825–94)
Moby Dick, Herman Melville (1819–91)
Pilgrims of the Wild, 'Grey Owl' (1885–1937)
Pirates in the Deep Green Sea, Eric Linklater (1899–1974)
Prisoner of Zenda, The, Anthony Hope (1863–1933)
Robinson Crusoe, Daniel Defoe (1660–1731)
Scarlet Pimpernel, The, Baroness Orczy (1865–1947)
Swiss Family Robinson, W. H. G. Kingston (1814–80)
Treasure Island, Robert Louis Stevenson (1850–94)
Twenty Thousand Leagues Under the Sea, Jules Verne (1828–1905)
Uncle Tom's Cabin, Harriet Beecher Stowe (1811–96)

Humorous Stories

Bad Child's Book of Beasts, The, Hilaire Belloc (1870–1953)
Book of Nonsense, A, Edward Lear (1812–88)
Charlie and the Chocolate Factory, Roald Dahl (b. 1916)
Dr Doolittle books, Hugh Lofting (1886–1947)
Father Christmas, Raymond Briggs (b. 1934)
Magic Pudding, The, Norman Lindsay (1879–1969)
My Friend Mr Leakey, J. B. S. Haldane (1892–1964)
Nonsense Novels, Stephen Leacock (1869–1944)
North Winds Blow Free, Elizabeth Howard
Now We are Six, A. A. Milne (1882–1956)
Old Possum's Book of Practical Cats, T. S. Eliot (1888–1965)
Professor Branestawm books, Norman Hunter (b. 1899)
Three Men in a Boat, Jerome K. Jerome (1859–1927)
Wind on the Moon, The, Eric Linklater (1899–1974)
Winnie-the-Pooh, A. A. Milne (1882–1956)
Wombles books, Elisabeth Beresford (b. circa 1890)
Worzel Gummidge books, Barbara E. Todd (d. 1976)

Historical Stories

Children of the New Forest, Captain Marryat (1792–1848)
Daisy Chain, The, Charlotte M. Yonge (1823–1901)
Eagle of the Ninth, Rosemary Sutcliff (b. 1920)
Fearless Treasure, The, Noel Streatfeild (b. 1897)
Hereward the Wake, Charles Kingsley (1819–75)
House of Arden, The, E. Nesbit (1858–1924)
Knight Crusader, Ronald Welch (b. 1909)
Land the Ravens Found, The, Naomi Mitchison (b. 1897)
Lantern Bearers, The, Rosemary Sutcliff (b. 1920)
Load of Unicorn, The, Cynthia Harnett (b. 1893)
Men of the Hills, Henry Treece (1911–66)
Otto of the Silver Hand, Howard Pyle (1853–1911)
Peacock House, The, Gillian Avery (b. 1926)

Traveller in Time, A, Alison Uttley (1884–1976)
Wool-pack, The, Cynthia Harnett (b. 1893)
Word to Caesar, Geoffrey Trease (b. 1909)

Myths and Legends
Heroes of Greece and Troy, The, Roger Lancelyn Green (b. 1918)
Mystery at Mycenae, Roger Lancelyn Green (b. 1918)
Sword in the Stone, The, T. H. White (1906–64)
Tales of Troy and Greece, Andrew Lang (1844–1912)
Tanglewood Tales, Nathaniel Hawthorne (1804–64)

Composers and Their Works

ADAM, Adolphe Charles (1803–56), French. Composed light operas. He is best known today for the classical ballet *Giselle.*

ALBÉNIZ, Isaac (1860–1909), Spanish. Best-known composition is *Iberia.* Also wrote operas and songs.

ALBINONI, Tommaso (1671–1750), Italian. Operas and instrumental music.

ARNE, Thomas (1710–78), English. Best-known works are his songs, including 'Rule Britannia' and 'Where the Bee Sucks'.

ARNOLD, Malcolm (b. 1921), English. Compositions include incidental music to Shakespeare's *The Tempest,* the overture *Beckus the Dandipratt,* symphony for strings, and concertos for horn, clarinet and oboe.

BACH, Johann Christian (1735–82), German. He composed many operas and cantatas, and much orchestral music, chamber music and keyboard music.

BACH, Johann Sebastian (1685–1750), German. Composed an enormous amount of sacred choral music, including 200 cantatas, the St Matthew and St John Passions and the Mass in B Minor. Bach's orchestral music includes the six Brandenberg Concertos, a number of concertos for violin and clavier, and four orchestral suites. There is a number of important keyboard works for clavier and organ including the collection of 48 preludes and fugues known as *The Well-tempered Clavier.*

BACH, Karl Philipp Emanuel (1714–88), German. Composed about 200 pieces for clavier. His church music includes the oratorio *The Israelites in the Wilderness,* a Magnificat and 22 Passions. Also symphonies, concertos, organ sonatas, chamber music and songs.

BALAKIREV, Mily Alexeievich (1837–1910), Russian. Works include two symphonies, incidental music to Shakespeare's *King Lear,* overtures, piano music and songs.

BALFE, Michael (1808–70), Irish. Works include 29 operas, such as *The Bohemian Girl,* the ballet *La Pérouse,* three cantatas and many songs.

Bach

Beethoven

BARBER, Samuel (b. 1910), American. Operas *Antony and Cleopatra, Vanessa,* and *A Hand of Bridge*. Two symphonies, concertos for piano, violin and cello, *Capricorn* Concerto for flute, oboe, trumpet and strings. Chamber music and songs.

BARTÓK, Béla (1881–1945), Hungarian. His numerous works include violin and piano concertos, orchestral suites, the Concerto for Orchestra, the opera *Bluebeard's Castle* and string quartets.

BEETHOVEN, Ludwig van (1770–1827), German. Works include two masses (in C Major and *Missa Solemnis*), the *Choral Fantasia*, the opera *Fidelio*, nine symphonies, five piano concertos, one violin concerto, a concerto for piano, violin and cello, and several concert overtures such as *Egmont*. Beethoven's chamber music includes a septet, a string quintet, 16 string quartets, six piano trios, four string trios, ten violin sonatas and five cello sonatas. His piano music includes 32 sonatas, 22 sets of variations, and three sets of bagatelles.

BELLINI, Vincenzo (1801–35), Italian. Operas, including *Norma* and *La Somnambula*.

BERG, Alban (1885–1935), Austrian. A well-known work is his opera *Wozzeck*. He also wrote one violin concerto and several instrumental pieces and songs.

BERLIOZ, Hector (1803–69), French. Works include the operas *Benvenuto Cellini, Les Troyens* and *Béatrice et Bénédict*; programme symphonies *Symphonie Fantastique, Harold in Italy* and *Roméo et Juliette* (with voices); *Symphonie Funèbre et Triomphale*; six concert overtures; choral works including a Requiem, *La Damnation de Faust, Te Deum* and *L'Enfance du Christ*; as well as several songs.

BIZET, Georges (1838–75), French. Operas include *Carmen, The Pearl Fishers, The Fair Maid of Perth* and *Djamileh*. Orchestral works include Symphony in C, the suite *Jeux d'Enfants* (Children's Games) and incidental music to Daudet's *L'Arlésienne*.

BOCCHERINI, Luigi (1743–1805), Italian. His works include oratorios, a mass, cantatas, motets, 20 symphonies, four cello concertos, concertos for flute, violin, harpsichord, much chamber music and one opera.

BOITO, Arrigo (1842–1918), Italian. Operas *Mefistofele* and *Nerone*.

BORODIN, Alexander (1833–87), Russian. Opera *Prince Igor* (unfinished). Orchestral works include *In the Steppes of Central Asia, Scherzo* for orchestra, and three symphonies. Chamber music and songs.

BOULEZ, Pierre (b. 1925), French. Avant-garde compositions include *Le Marteau sans Maître* for alto and six instruments, *Sonatine* for flute, and *Structures* for two pianos.

BRAHMS, Johannes (1833–97), German. Orchestral works include four symphonies, two piano concertos, a concerto for violin and a concerto for violin and cello, *Academic Festival Overture, Tragic Overture,* and the *St Anthony Chorale (Variations on a Theme by Haydn)*. The best known of Brahms's choral works is the *German Requiem*. His chamber music includes three string quartets, two string quintets, a clarinet quintet, two string sextets, five piano trios (one with clarinet, one with horn), three piano quartets and a piano quintet.

BRIDGE, Frank (1879–1941), English. Works include the orchestral suite *The Sea*, a symphonic poem *Isabella*, rhapsody *Enter Spring*, and tone poem *Summer*, as well as chamber music.

BRITTEN, Sir Benjamin (1913–77), English. Works include three symphonies, two piano concertos, *War Requiem, Hymn to St Cecilia, Young Person's Guide to the Orchestra, Variations on a Theme of Frank Bridge, Serenade for Tenor, Horn and Strings, Sinfonia da Requiem,* and two string quartets. Operas include *Peter Grimes, The Rape of Lucretia, Albert Herring, Billy Budd, Gloriana* and *Noye's Fludde*.

BRUCH, Max (1838–1920), German. Works include three symphonies, two violin concertos, *Scottish Fantasia*, and the *Serenade* for violin, harp and orchestra.

BRUCKNER, Anton (1824–96), Austrian. Works include nine symphonies (the last unfinished), four masses, a Requiem and a Te Deum.

BUSONI, Ferruccio Benvenuto (1866–1924), Italian. Composed mostly piano music but also several operas, the *Fantasia Contrappuntistica* on an unfinished fugue by Bach, and an immense piano concerto with chorale finale.

BUTTERWORTH, George (1885–1916), English. Works include the rhapsody *A Shropshire Lad*, an idyll *The Banks of Green Willow*, and two song cycles on Housman's *A Shropshire Lad*.

BUXTEHUDE, Dietrich (1637–1707), Danish. Church cantatas, sonatas for strings, organ music including chorale preludes, and suites for harpsichord.

BYRD, William (1543–1623), English. Church music, madrigals, virginal pieces, etc.

CAGE, John (b. 1912), American. Music for 'prepared piano', i.e. where different objects are inserted between the strings to alter the tone; electronic music.

CAVALLI, Pietro Francesco (1602–76), Italian. Many operas, masses, motets, psalms, vespers, a Requiem, etc.

CHABRIER, Alexis Emmanuel (1841–94), French. His works include the operas *Le Roi Malgré Lui*, the rhapsody *España* and *Marche Joyeuse*.

CHERUBINI, Luigi (1760–1842), Italian. Operas include *The Water Carrier, Médée* and *Les Deux Journées*. Church music includes Mass in F and Requiem in D Minor.

CHOPIN, Frédéric (1810–49), Polish. Piano music includes three sonatas, 14 waltzes, 26 preludes, 27 études, 19 nocturnes, four ballades, four impromptus, four scherzos, three rondos, 16 polonaises and 50 mazurkas. Chopin also composed two piano concertos.

COPLAND, Aaron (b. 1900), American. Ballets *Billy the Kid, Rodeo* and *Appalachian Spring*. Orchestral works include three symphonies, *El Salon Mexico* and *Danzon Cubano*. Also some chamber music.

CORELLI, Arcangelo (1653–1713), Italian. Works include violin sonatas and a set of concerti grossi.

COUPERIN, François (1668–1733), French. Over 200 harpsichord pieces, 42 organ pieces, several works for chamber orchestra, church music, motets, etc.

CZERNY, Karl (1791–1857), Austrian. Czerny's best-known works today are his piano studies.

DEBUSSY, Claude (1862–1918), French. Numerous piano pieces, chamber music, songs and ballet music. Opera *Pelléas et Mélisande*. Orchestral pieces include *L'Après-midi d'un Faune, La Mer*, three *Images, Printemps*, and *Danse Sacré et Danse Profane* for harp and strings.

DELIBES, Léo (1836–91), French. Ballets include *Coppélia* and *La Source*. Also comic operas such as *Le Roi l'a Dit* and *Lakmé*.

DELIUS, Frederick (1862–1934), English. Operas such as *Irmelin, Koanga, A Village Romeo and Juliet* and *Fennemore and Gerda*. Choral works include *Sea Drift, Song of the High Hills, Appalachia, Songs of Sunset* and *Requiem*. Orchestral works include *Brigg Fair, In a Summer Garden, Over the Hills and Far Away, On Hearing the First Cuckoo in Spring* and *A Song Before Sunrise*. Delius also composed chamber music and songs.

DONIZETTI, Gaetano (1797–1848), Italian. Many operas, the best-known being *Lucrezia Borgia, Lucia di Lammermoor, La Fille du Régiment, La Favorita* and *Don Pasquale*.

DUKAS, Paul (1865–1935), French. Works include the popular orchestral piece *The Sorcerer's Apprentice*, and a successful opera *Ariane et Barbe-Bleue*.

DVOŘÁK, Antonin (1841–1904), Czech. Nine symphonies, including *From The New World* (the 9th), one piano concerto, one violin concerto, one cello concerto. Five concert overtures include *Carnival, Amid Nature* and *Othello*. Other orchestral works include *Scherzo Capriccioso*, two sets of Slavonic dances, Slavonic rhapsodies and five symphonic poems: *The Water Sprite, The Noon-Day Witch, The Golden Spinning Wheel, The Wood-Dove* and *Hero's Song*. Ten operas, including *Rusalka*; a Mass in D Major, Requiem, *Te Deum*, chamber music and many songs.

ELGAR, Sir Edward (1857–1934), English. Works include two symphonies, one violin and one cello concerto, concert overtures *Froissart, Cockaigne, In the South,*

Chopin

Dvořák

Polonia. Orchestral pieces include *Enigma Variations, Introduction and Allegro for Strings*, symphonic study *Falstaff*, and the five *Pomp and Circumstance* marches. His four oratorios include *The Dream of Gerontius*.

FALLA, Manuel de (1876–1946), Spanish. Opera *La Vida Breve*; ballets *El Amor Brujo* and *The Three-cornered Hat*; orchestral piece *Nights in the Gardens of Spain*, and *Master Peter's Puppet Show* (with solo voice). Also several songs and works for piano and guitar.

FAURÉ, Gabriel (1845–1924), French. Orchestral works include *Pavane* and suite *Masques et Bergamasques*; incidental music *Pelléas et Mélisande*; Requiem for solo voices, chorus and orchestra. Songs and chamber music.

FINZI, Gerald (1901–56), English. Works include cantata *Dies Natalis*, festival anthem *Intimations of Immortality*, and *For St Cecilia* for chorus and orchestra.

FRANCK, César (1822–90), Belgian. Symphony in D Minor, *Symphonic Variations* for piano and orchestra; oratorios, organ pieces, church music and songs.

GABRIELI, Andrea (c. 1520–86), Italian. Works include masses, madrigals, motets and church music.

GABRIELI, Giovanni (c. 1555–1612), Italian. Works include church music for voices and instruments, organ music and various instrumental pieces.

GERSHWIN, George (1898–1937), American. Popular songs and musical comedies. More serious music includes *Rhapsody in Blue*, the opera *Porgy and Bess* and a piano concerto.

GESUALDO, Carlo (c. 1560–1613), Italian. Works include madrigals and church music for voices.

GLAZUNOV, Alexander Constantinovich (1865–1936), Russian. Works include eight symphonies, two piano concertos, a violin concerto, a concerto for saxophone, flute and strings, ballets *Raymonda, Ruses d'Amour* and *Les Saisons*, and some chamber music.

GLIÈRE, Reinhold (1875–1956), Russian of Belgian descent. Three symphonies, three symphonic poems, several operas and patriotic songs. Ballets include *The Red Poppy*.

GLINKA, Mikhail (1804–57), Russian. Two operas: *A Life for the Tsar* and *Russlan and Ludmilla*. Orchestral pieces include *Kamarinskaya* and *Festival Polonaise*.

GLUCK, Christoph (1714–87), German. Several operas including *Orfeo, Alceste, Iphigénie en Aulide* and *Iphigénie en Tauride*.

GOUNOD, Charles (1818–93), French. Sacred songs, masses and an oratorio *The Redemption*. Operas include *Sappho, Faust, Philémon et Baucis, Mireille* and *Roméo et Juliette*.

GRÉTRY, André Ernest Modeste (1741–1813), French. His many operas include *Richard Coeur-de-Lion* and *Zémire et Azor*.

GRIEG, Edvard (1843–1907), Norwegian. Works include a piano concerto, incidental music for *Peer Gynt* and *Sigurd Jorsalfar, Holberg Suite* for string orchestra, concert overture *In Autumn*, chamber music and songs. Grieg's piano music includes the collection of Lyric Pieces.

HANDEL, George Frideric (1685–1759), German. About 40 operas, including *Rinaldo*. Oratorios include *Messiah, Samson, Belshazzar*, the *Occasional Oratorio, Israel in Egypt, Judas Maccabaeus* and *Jephtha*. Secular choral works include *Alexander's Feast, Acis and Galatea, Ode for St Cecilia's Day* and *L'Allegro*. The *Water Music* and *Music for the Royal Fireworks* are among Handel's most popular works.

HARTY, Sir Hamilton (1879–1941), Irish. Works include the tone poem *With the Wild Geese* and *Irish Symphony*, together with many songs.

HAYDN, Franz Joseph (1732–1809), Austrian. A prolific composer of 104 symphonies, chamber music including 84 string quartets, piano sonatas, operas, church music and oratorios. *The Creation* and *The Seasons* are among his best-known works.

HENZE, Hans Werner (b. 1926), German. Works include several operas, six symphonies, concertos for piano and violin, an oratorio and chamber music.

HINDEMITH, Paul (1897–1963), German. Several operas, including *Mathis der Maler*, a violin concerto, a cello concerto, the *Sinfonia Serena, Symphonic Metamorphosis on a Theme by Weber* and chamber music.

HOLST, Gustav (1874–1934), English. Best-known work is the orchestral suite *The Planets*. Choral works include *Hymns from the Rig-Veda* and *The Hymn of Jesus*. Operas include *Savitri* and *The Perfect Fool*. Two more popular works are *St Paul's Suite* for strings and the orchestral piece *Egdon Heath*.

HONEGGER, Arthur (1892–1955), Swiss. Operas, such as *Antigone*; five symphonies, a cello concerto, symphonic poems, ballets *Skating Rink* and *Sémiramis*, orchestral pieces *Pacific 231* and *Pastorale d'été*; stage oratorios including *King David* and *Judith*, and chamber music.

HUMMEL, Johann Nepomuk (1778–1837), German. Most important compositions are piano works consisting of trios, sonatas, rondos and six concertanti.

HUMPERDINCK, Engelbert (1854–1921), German. Best-known opera is *Hansel and Gretel*.

d'INDY, Vincent (1851–1931), French. Works include symphonies, chamber music, symphonic variations, *Istar*, operas such as *Fervaal* and *Le Chant de la Cloche*, *Quintette* suite for flute, string trio and harp and arrangements for hundreds of songs.

IPPOLITOV-IVANOV, Mikhail (1859–1935), Russian. Most popular work is *Caucasian Sketches*.

IRELAND, John (1879–1962), English. One piano concerto; choral work *These Things Shall Be*; orchestral works including *The Forgotten Rite* and *Mai-Dun*; songs, such as the setting of Masefield's 'Sea Fever', and Songs Sacred and Profane.

IVES, Charles (1874–1954), American. Orchestral work includes five symphonies, *Three Places in New England* and *July 4th*. Also chamber music and over 200 songs.

JANÁČEK, Leoš (1854–1928), Czech. Several operas including *Jenufa*, *Katya Kabanova* and *The Cunning Little Vixen*. A popular orchestral work is *Sinfonietta*. Janáček also composed numerous choral works, some chamber music and organ pieces.

KABALEVSKY, Dmitri Borisovich (b. 1904), Russian. Works include several operas, four symphonies, three piano concertos, a violin concerto, chamber music, piano music and songs.

KHACHATURIAN, Aram (b. 1903), Russian of Armenian descent. Works include ballets *Happiness* and *Gayaneh*, two symphonies, concertos for piano, violin, cello, and violin and cello, and incidental music such as that for *Macbeth*.

KODÁLY, Zoltán (1882–1967), Hungarian. Much chamber and instrumental music. Comic opera *Háry János*. Orchestral works include *Dances of Galánta* and *Dances of Marosszék*, and Symphony in C Major. Choral works include *Psalmus Hungaricus* and *Missa Brevis*.

LALO, Edouard (1823–92), French. Operas, including *Le Roi d'Ys*, Symphony in G Minor, *Symphonie Espagnole*, concertos for piano, violin and cello, the ballet *Namouna* and several chamber works.

LAMBERT, Constant (1905–51), English. Ballet music *Romeo and Juliet*, *Pomona* and *Horoscope*; cantata *Summer's Last Will and Testament*, a piano concerto, *Music for Orchestra*, and song setting for Sacheverell Sitwell's poem 'The Rio Grande'.

LEONCAVALLO, Ruggiero (1858–1919), Italian. Operas, the most successful being *Pagliacci*.

LIADOV, Anatol (1855–1914), Russian. Works include symphonic poems *Baba Yaga*, *The Enchanted Lake* and *Kikimora*, two orchestral scherzos and a number of piano pieces.

LIGETI, György (b. 1923), Hungarian. Electronic music such as *Artikulation* and other avant-garde music, including *Poème Symphonique* for 100 metronomes, *Apparitions*, *Atmosphères* and *Aventures* for orchestra.

LISZT, Franz (1811–86), Hungarian. *Faust* and *Dante* symphonies. Several masses and oratorios. Numerous songs and piano pieces, including Liebesträume

Mendelssohn

Mozart

and Hungarian Rhapsodies. Orchestral music includes symphonic poems such as *Mazeppa* and *Totentanz (Dance of Death)*.

LULLY, Jean-Baptiste (1632–87), French. Sacred music, including the famous *Miserere*, 49 ballets and 15 operas including *Les Fêtes de l'Amour et de Bacchus*.

MAHLER, Gustav (1860–1911), Austrian. Ten symphonies and *Song of the Earth* (six songs with orchestra). Various song cycles, such as *Songs of a Wayfarer*.

MARTINU, Bohuslav (1890–1959), Czech. Numerous works include ballet *Istar*, symphonic poem *Vanishing Midnight*, concerto grosso for chamber orchestra and the Double Concerto for two string orchestras.

MASCAGNI, Pietro (1863–1945), Italian. Best-known of his several operas is *Cavalleria Rusticana*.

MASSENET, Jules (1842–1912), French. Many operas including *Hérodiade (Salomé), Manon, Le Cid*, and *Thaïs*. Incidental music including *The Furies*. Massenet also composed over 200 songs, a piano concerto and several orchestral suites and oratorios.

MENDELSSOHN, Felix (1809–47), German. Incidental music to *A Midsummer Night's Dream*, five symphonies, six concert overtures including *The Hebrides (Fingal's Cave)*, a violin concerto and two piano concertos. Oratorios: *St Paul* and *Elijah*. Chamber music includes seven string quartets, three piano quartets, two string quintets, two piano trios, an octet and a sextet. Piano pieces include *Songs without Words* and *Rondo Capriccioso*. Also wrote numerous songs.

MESSIAEN, Olivier (b. 1908), French. Much religious music. Orchestral works include *Turangalila Symphony, Chronochromie* and *The Awakening of the Birds*.

MEYERBEER, Giacomo (1791–1864), German. Many operas, including *Robert the Devil, The Huguenots, The North Star, The Prophet*, and *L'Africaine*. Meyerbeer also wrote an oratorio, church music and songs.

MIASKOVSKY, Nikolai (1881–1950), Russian. Works include the oratorio *Kirov Is With Us*, 27 symphonies, a violin concerto, symphonic poems, chamber music and songs.

MILHAUD, Darius (1892–1974), French. Operas, such as *Bolivar*; the oratorio *Christopher Columbus*; ballets *The Creation of the World* and *The Nothing-doing*

Bar; orchestral works *Suite Provençale* and *Saudades do Brazil*; piano duet *Scaramouche*, chamber music and songs.

MONTEVERDI, Claudio (1567–1643), Italian. Operas such as *The Coronation of Poppea*, sacred and secular madrigals, masses, magnificats and psalms.

MOZART, Wolfgang Amadeus (1756–91), Austrian. Orchestral works include 49 symphonies, *Sinfonia Concertante*, 25 piano concertos, five violin concertos, concertos for flute, horn, clarinet, etc. Chamber music includes 25 string quartets and 40 violin sonatas. Operas include *Idomeneo, Il Seraglio, The Marriage of Figaro, Don Giovanni, Cosi fan tutte* and *The Magic Flute*. Mozart's *Requiem* was left unfinished.

MUSSORGSKY, Modest Petrovich (1839–81), Russian. Orchestral pieces: *Pictures at an Exhibition; Night on the Bare Mountain.* Operas: *Boris Godunov, Khovanshtchina* and *Sorochintsy Fair.* Many songs.

NICOLAI, Otto (1810–49), German. Mainly operas, including *The Merry Wives of Windsor.*

NIELSEN, Carl (1865–1931), Danish. Six symphonies, one violin concerto and concertos for flute and clarinet, several overtures, such as *Helios*, and various instrumental works. Chamber music includes four string quartets. Operas: *Saul and David; Maskarade.*

OFFENBACH, Jacques (1819–80), German-French. Light operas, the best-known being *Orpheus in the Underworld, La Belle Hélène* and *La Vie Parisienne.* One grand opera: *Tales of Hoffmann* (unfinished). A popular orchestral work, *Gaîté Parisienne*, a suite of Offenbach's music, was arranged by Manuel Rosenthal.

ORFF, Carl (b. 1895), German. Mainly operas and dramatic works. The secular oratorio *Carmina Burana* has achieved great popularity.

PAGANINI, Niccolo (1782–1840), Italian. Two violin concertos, three string quartets with a guitar part, 12 sonatas for violin or guitar and 24 *capricci* for violin.

PALESTRINA, Giovanni Pierluigi de (1525–94), Italian. Masses, motets, hymns, litanies and magnificats.

PERGOLESI, Giovanni Battista (1710–36), Italian. Several operas, oratorios, masses and other church music.

POULENC, Francis (1899–1963), French. Three operas, including *Les Dialogues des Carmélites*, ballets *Les Biches (The House Party)* and *Les Animaux Modèles*, several religious works and over 100 songs. Orchestral works include *Concert Champêtre* for harpsichord and orchestra, concerto for two pianos and orchestra and an organ concerto.

PROKOFIEV, Sergei (1891–1953), Russian. Seven symphonies, including the Classical (No. 1), five piano concertos, two violin concertos and two cello concertos. Six ballets and music for films. Operas such as *The Love for Three Oranges.* Orchestral works, *Scythian Suite* and *Peter and the Wolf.* Chamber music includes two string quartets, two violin sonatas and nine piano sonatas.

PUCCINI, Giacomo (1858–1924), Italian. Operas, including *Manon Lescaut, La Bohème, Madame Butterfly, Tosca* and *Turandot* (unfinished).

PURCELL, Henry (1659–95), English. Opera *Dido and Aeneas*, 62 settings for anthems and much incidental music.

RACHMANINOFF, Sergei (1873–1943), Russian. Three operas, including *Francesca da Rimini*, three symphonies, four published piano concertos, a number of piano and chamber works, and *Rhapsody on a Theme by Paganini* for orchestra.

RAMEAU, Jean-Philippe (1683–1764), French. Operas and opera-ballets. Best-known today is Rameau's music for harpsichord.

RAVEL, Maurice (1875–1937), French. Works include two piano concertos (one for the left hand) orchestral pieces *Rapsodie Espagnole* and *Boléro*; an opera *L'Heure Espagnole*; an opera-ballet *L'Enfant et les Sortilèges*, and the ballet *Daphnis and Chloé*. Chamber music includes a string quartet, a piano trio and three violin sonatas. Piano works include *Gaspard de la Nuit*, five *Miroirs*, and the suite *Le Tombeau de Couperin*.

RESPIGHI, Ottorino (1879–1936), Italian. Several operas. Orchestral works include *The Fountains of Rome, The Pines of Rome* and the suite *The Birds*.

RIMSKY-KORSAKOV, Nikolai (1844–1908), Russian. Operas include *The Maid of Pskov, The Snow Maiden* and *The Golden Cockerel*. Orchestral pieces include *Sheherazade, Easter Festival* Overture and *Capriccio Espagnol*.

ROSSINI, Gioacchino (1792–1868), Italian. Operas *Tancredi, The Barber of Seville, William Tell, Semiramide, Cinderella, The Italian Girl in Algiers* and *The Thieving Magpie*.

ROUSSEL, Albert (1869–1937), French. Works include four symphonies, chamber music, songs and choral works. Stage works include the opera *Padmavâti* and the ballet *The Spider's Feast*. Orchestral works include *For a Festival of Spring*.

SAINT-SAËNS, Camille (1835–1921), French. Three symphonies, five piano concertos, three violin concertos. Operas include *Samson et Dalila*. Four symphonic poems, including *La Danse Macabre. Carnival of Animals* for small orchestra. Chamber music, church music and many songs.

SALIERI, Antonio (1750–1825), Italian. About 40 operas, some orchestral and church music.

SARASATE, Pablo (1844–1908), Spanish. Works include romances, fantasies and Spanish dances for violin.

SATIE, Erik (1866–1925), French. Works include the symphonic drama *Socrate*, ballets, including *Parade* scored for typewriters, sirens, airplane propellers, ticker tape and a lottery wheel. Several piano pieces and songs.

SCARLATTI, Alessandro (1660–1725), Italian. Works include 115 operas, over 600 chamber cantatas, and church music.

SCARLATTI, Domenico (1685–1757), Italian. Best-known works today are his keyboard sonatas.

SCHOENBERG, Arnold (1874–1951), Austrian. Two symphonies, one piano concerto, one violin concerto and chamber music. Other works include the symphonic poem *Pelleas und Melisande; Five Orchestral Pieces*. Drama with

Sibelius

Strauss

music: *The Hand of Fate*. Vocal music: *Gurrelieder; Pierrot Lunaire* for voice and chamber orchestra.

SCHUBERT, Franz (1797–1828), Austrian. Nine symphonies including the *Unfinished* (No. 8), and seven masses. Incidental music to *Rosamunde*. He wrote over 600 songs, including three great song cycles. Chamber music includes an octet, a piano quintet (*The Trout*), a string quintet, 15 string quartets and two piano trios. Piano music includes *Moments Musicaux*.

SCHUMANN, Robert (1810–56), German. Works include four symphonies, concertos for piano, violin and cello, incidental music to Byron's *Manfred*, much chamber music (piano sonatas 11 and 22 are particularly famous), and songs.

SCRIABIN, Alexander Nicolas (1871–1915), Russian. Three symphonies, tone poems *Prometheus*, etc., *Rêverie* and *Poem of Ecstasy* for orchestra. A piano concerto and many works for piano.

SHOSTAKOVICH, Dmitri (1906–75), Russian. Works include 15 symphonies, two piano concertos, two violin concertos and two cello concertos. Operas include *The Nose*, and ballets include *The Golden Age*. Shostakovich also composed a good deal of chamber music.

SIBELIUS, Jean (1865–1957), Finnish. Seven symphonies including the *Kullervo* Symphony. Symphonic tone poems: *En Saga, The Swan of Tuonela, Finlandia, Pohjola's Daughter, The Bard* and *Tapiola*. Other orchestral pieces include *Valse Triste*, the *Karelia Suite*, violin concerto, and incidental music *Pelléas et Mélisande* and *The Tempest*.

SMETANA, Bedřich (1824–84), Czech. Symphonic suite *Ma Vlast (My Country)*. Operas include *The Bartered Bride* and *Dalibor*. He also wrote the quartet *From My Life*.

SOUSA, John Philip (1854–1932), American. Many marches for brass bands, such as *Washington Post* and *The Stars and Stripes Forever*.

SPOHR, Ludwig (1784–1859), German. Works include nine symphonies, 17 violin concertos, four clarinet concertos and several operas. Oratorios: *Calvary* and *The Last Judgement*. Chamber music, piano music and songs.

STOCKHAUSEN, Karlheinz (b. 1928), German. Rather unusual works include

Stravinsky

Wagner

Kontakte for electronic sounds, *Gruppen* for three orchestras and *Kontrapunkt* for ten instruments.

STRAUSS, Johann (1804–49), Austrian. Over 150 waltzes and other dance music.

STRAUSS, Johann (1825–99), Austrian. Operettas, such as *Die Fledermaus* and *The Gypsy Baron.* Many well-known waltzes such as *The Blue Danube, Morgenblatten (Morning Leaves), Wine, Women and Song* and *Tales from the Vienna Woods.*

STRAUSS, Richard (1864–1949), German. Symphonic tone poems include *Don Juan, Death and Transfiguration, Till Eulenspiegel, Don Quixote, Also Sprach Zarathustra* and *Ein Heldenleben.* Operas include *Salome, Elektra, Der Rosenkavalier, Ariadne auf Naxos, Arabella* and *Die Schweigsame Frau.*

STRAVINSKY, Igor (1882–1971), Russian. Many and varied works include the ballets *The Firebird, Petrushka, Pulcinella* and *The Rite of Spring.* Operas include *The Rake's Progress.* Orchestral works include four symphonies, concertos for piano and violin, concerto for 16 instruments (Dumbarton Oaks), and *Symphony of Psalms* for chorus and orchestra.

SUK, Josef (1874–1935), Czech. Orchestral works include symphonic poems *Prague* and *Maturity,* two symphonies, chamber music and piano pieces.

SULLIVAN, Sir Arthur (1842–1900), English. Light operas written in collaboration with Sir W. S. Gilbert, include *HMS Pinafore, The Pirates of Penzance, Patience, The Mikado, The Yeomen of the Guard, The Gondoliers, Ruddigore, Iolanthe* and *Princess Ida.* One serious opera: *Ivanhoe.* The ballad *The Lost Chord* and other songs.

SUPPÉ, Franz von (1819–95), Austrian. Operettas include *Light Cavalry, Fatinitza* and *Boccaccio.* Ballets include *Poet and Peasant* and *Wallensteins Lager.* Also more than 200 stage works.

SZYMANOWSKY, Karol (1883–1937), Polish. Three symphonies, two operas, ballets, choral music, chamber music and songs.

TALLIS, Thomas (c. 1505–85), English. Masses, anthems and other church music.

TCHAIKOVSKY, Peter Ilyich (1840–93), Russian. Six symphonies, three piano concertos (the third unfinished), one violin concerto, four suites for orchestra, two serenades for strings, fantasy overture *Romeo and Juliet*, orchestral fantasies *Francesca da Rimini* and *Hamlet, Variations on a Rococo Theme* for cello and orchestra, *1812 Overture, Italian Caprice* and *Marche Slav*. Ballet music: *Swan Lake, The Sleeping Beauty* and the *Nutcracker*. Operas include *Eugene Onegin* and *The Queen of Spades*. Tchaikovsky's chamber music includes three string quartets, one trio and one sextet.

TELEMANN, George Philipp (1681–1767), German. His works include 46 operas, choral works, instrumental music and church music.

TIPPETT, Michael (b. 1905), English. Orchestral works include two symphonies. An oratorio: *A Child of Our Time*. Operas: *The Midsummer Marriage, King Priam* and *The Knot Garden*. Also chamber music and songs.

VAUGHAN WILLIAMS, Ralph (1872–1958), English. Operas, including *Hugh the Drover*. Orchestral works include nine symphonies, the *Fantasia on a Theme by Tallis*, concertos for piano, oboe and tuba, fantasy on *Greensleeves, The Lark Ascending*, and overture *The Wasps*. *On Wenlock Edge* for tenor, string quartet and piano.

VERDI, Giuseppe (1813–1901), Italian. Operas include *Rigoletto, Il Trovatore, La Traviata, Don Carlos, Aïda, Otello* and *Falstaff*. Religious music includes Verdi's *Requiem*.

VILLA-LOBOS, Heitor (1887–1959), Brazilian. Operas, ballets, 12 symphonies, symphonic suites and chamber music. A characteristic work is *Bachianas Brasileiras* (nine pieces for various instrumental and vocal groups).

VIVALDI, Antonio (1678–1741), Italian. Many operas and at least 450 concertos for various instruments, the best-known being *The Four Seasons*.

WAGNER, Richard (1813–83), German. Best known for his operatic works including *Rienzi, The Flying Dutchman, The Mastersingers, Tannhäuser, Lohengrin, Tristan and Isolde, The Ring of the Nibelungs* and *Parsifal*. A well-known piece for small orchestra is *Siegfried Idyll*.

WALTON, Sir William (b. 1902), English. Works include two operas, two symphonies, concertos for violin, viola and cello, overtures including *Doctor Syntax* and *Portsmouth Point*, a ballet *Façade*, music for the films *Henry V* and *Hamlet*, marches *Crown Imperial* and *Orb and Sceptre*, chamber music and songs.

WEBER, Carl Maria von (1786–1826), German. Romantic operas: *Abu Hassan, Der Freischütz, Euryanthe* and *Oberon*. Also symphonies, concertos, chamber music, piano music and masses.

WEBERN, Anton von (1883–1945), Austrian. One symphony, choral works, chamber music and instrumental pieces.

WEILL, Kurt (1900–50), German. Operas and operettas, such as *Mahagonny*. Orchestral music includes two symphonies and a concerto for violin and wind band.

WOLF, Hugo (1860–1903), Austrian. Many songs. Orchestral works include *Italian Serenade*. An opera: *Der Corregidor*.

Glossary of Styles in Art and Architecture

Abstract art A term usually applied to 20th-century art in which form and colour are all-important, being independent of any recognizable form of reality.

Baroque The flamboyant art style of the period c. 1600–1720. A characteristic of Baroque painting and sculpture is its strong drama and appeal to the emotions. Architecture in the Baroque style is heavily ornate.

Classicism A form of art which emphasizes the characteristic qualities of Greek and Roman art, such as restraint, simplicity of form and harmony. The paintings of Ingres (1780–1867) are examples of Classicism. *See* neo-Classicism.

Cubism A movement created in the years 1907–9 by the painters Picasso (1881–1973) and Braque (1882–1963). Natural subjects were reduced to several interlocking planes, often seen from different perspectives.

Dadaism A forerunner of Surrealism, Dadaism was born of the disillusion induced by World War I. The Dadaists aimed to overthrow all standards and traditions in art and set out to outrage and scandalize. An example is a painting by Duchamp (1887–1968) of the Mona Lisa with a moustache.

Expressionism A 20th-century style of painting which does not imitate nature but tries to convey what the artist feels about a subject. The movement was influenced by the work of van Gogh and Munch. Important expressionist painters include Klee, Kandinsky and Kokoschka.

Fauvism An art movement originating in Paris when a number of artists, including Matisse (1869–1954), exhibited their works in one room. The paintings were full of flat patterns, distortion and brilliant colour. A critic contemptuously described the artists collectively as *les fauves*, meaning 'the wild beasts'.

Gothic The predominant style of church architecture in northern Europe from the 12th to the 15th century. It is characterized by tall, pointed arches and pillars with fan vaulting, and flying buttresses supporting the building on the outside. Wall space was reduced to a minimum, giving a feeling of space and of striving upwards. The Gothic style was revived in Europe and the USA during the 18th and 19th centuries.

Impressionism A movement originating in France in the 1860s. Artists such as Monet, Manet, Sisley and Pissarro sought to capture the fleeting play of light, particularly in landscapes. The impressionists did not mix their paints but dabbed them side by side in the pure state on the canvas. The shadows of objects were represented in the complementary colours. For example, an orange object would have a purple shadow. In the widest sense, Turner and Constable were impressionists, and in fact the French impressionists were much inspired by these artists. The artists Cézanne, van Gogh and Gauguin, once associated with impressionism, were later labelled 'post-impressionists'.

Mannerism The art style of the period 1530–1600, principally in Italy. A characteristic of mannerist paintings is the emphasis on the human figure, often frenziedly twisted and gesticulating. Emotional effects were heightened by vivid and sometimes harsh colours. Tintoretto and El Greco painted in this style.

Neo-Classicism A movement which originated in Rome in the middle of the 18th century and then spread rapidly in Europe. Painters and architects consciously

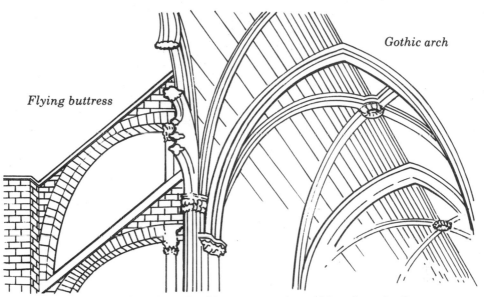

Gothic arch

Flying buttress

imitated antique art in style and subject matter. A notable painter in the neo-Classic style was the French artist David (1748–1825).

Pre-Raphaelites In 1848 a number of English artists revolted against the art of their time. They wished to make a return to the simple naturalism of the pre-Raphael Italian painters such as Botticelli, Fra Angelico and Filippo Lippi. The Pre-Raphaelite brotherhood used bright colour and great detail. The three founding members of the brotherhood were Dante Gabriel Rossetti, J. E. Millais and W. Holman Hunt.

Realism The frank and vigorous representation of the actuality of everyday life. The first Realist painter was Courbet (1819–77) who rejected idealized art and romanticism in the mid-19th century.

Renaissance The word means 'rebirth'. During the Renaissance (14th to early 16th century), art in Italy was revived or 'reborn' under the influence of Greek and Roman models. The Renaissance spread all over western Europe. At its height, *c.* 1600, the Renaissance produced artists of supreme skill including Leonardo da Vinci, Michelangelo and Raphael.

Rococo A style of architecture and decoration prevailing in France during the period 1720–70. The name comes from the French word *rocaille*, meaning 'shell-shaped'. The shell was a favourite motif in Rococo ornamentation. The style was more dainty and graceful than that of the more robust Baroque from which it grew. Paintings of the period, such as the works of Watteau (1684–1721), Boucher (1703–70) and Fragonard (1732–1806), show the same light-hearted vitality.

Romanticism A movement that began in France in 1830 as a reaction to Classicism. Romanticism put imagination before reason, expressing unbridled passion and a love for the exotic. A painter in the Romantic style was Delacroix (1798–1863).

Surrealism An art movement which developed from Dadaism in the 1920s. Surrealist painters aimed to create from the depths of the subconscious mind, free from the dictates of reason. Their works depict the weird and fantastic, such as Salvador Dali's trees with limp watches draped over their branches.

RELIGION

Main Religions of the World

Many world religions are in the process of rapid growth, perhaps as a response to the challenge of the technological revolution which is rapidly changing the face of the Earth.

Hinduism

This is the religion of the great majority of people in India. It has a number of religious books containing its main beliefs, especially the *Veda*, the *Brahmanas*, the *Upanishads* and the *Bhagavad-gita*.

Hinduism's two main doctrines are *karma* and reincarnation, or rebirth. A person's destiny is shaped by his deeds (*karma*). He can seek release from an endless succession of lives by living a hard, ascetic life, or through the discipline of yoga. If he fails to attain release, the person is reincarnated to a higher or lower form of life after he dies. Hinduism absorbs other beliefs into its system, no matter how contradictory they are.

Buddhism

Buddhism is a widespread religion of the Orient which grew out of a Hindu background. It takes its name from its founder, the Hindu prince Siddhartha Gautama, known as the Buddha ('the enlightened one'), who lived around the 6th century BC.

The Buddha was dissatisfied with Hinduism as he contemplated the human problem of suffering. His meditations fall into 'four noble truths' which are the basis of Buddhism:

1 Existence is a nightmare of unhappiness
2 Unhappiness is the result of selfish desire or craving
3 Selfish desire can be destroyed
4 It is destroyed by following an Eightfold Path involving morality and discipline

Islam

This is the religion of one out of every six people in the world, and today it is undergoing a great revival. It comes out of a Judaistic and Christian background, with prophets and a belief in one God who created the universe.

Islam's two main divisions are between the conservative Shi'ites and the Sunnis. The Shi'ites wish for a distinct Muslim culture based on the *Sharia*, the strict Muslim law. The Sunnis are more prepared to Westernize. Present-day Islam is a major world influence and its power is likely to increase in the future as an alternative to both Western values and Communism.

The importance of law and good behaviour is clear from the 'five pillars of Islam':

1 The confession: 'There is no God but Allah, and Muhammad is his prophet'
2 The ritual prayers
3 Ritual alms and offerings
4 The month-long annual fast of Ramadan
5 The pilgrimage to Mecca

Christianity

This religion is centred on Jesus of Nazareth, son of God and Messiah. Its beliefs are based upon the Bible, in particular the teachings of Jesus which are recorded in the New Testament. Christianity is statistically the world's largest religion, but there are many different branches within it.

Judaism

Judaism shares with Christianity the Old Testament but it rejects the Christian interpretation given by the New Testament. Nevertheless, Jews and Christians have much in common in their belief in a personal creator God. Jewish belief adds other sacred books to the Old Testament.

There is a special 'covenant' relationship between God and his chosen people, the Jews. Judaism is a social and family religion and its observances concern every aspect of ordinary daily life.

THE TEN COMMANDMENTS

Jesus Christ summarized the Ten Commandments – central to Old Testament teaching – as loving God with all your heart, soul, mind and strength, and loving your neighbour as you love yourself. Christianity teaches that a person's relationship with God determines his relationship with other people.

The commandments may be simplified as follows:

1 Worship only the true God
2 Worship no idols
3 Don't misuse God's name
4 Keep the seventh day as a day of rest from work
5 Respect your parents
6 Don't murder
7 Don't commit adultery
8 Don't steal
9 Don't falsely accuse anybody
10 Don't desire someone else's possessions

THE TWELVE APOSTLES

These people were specially chosen by Jesus Christ to spread his message (Paul later replaced the traitor Judas):

Andrew, brother of Peter
Peter
Bartholomew, also called Nathanael
Philip
James the Elder, son of Zebedee, and brother of John
John
James the Younger, son of Alphaeus
Judas, also called Thaddeus or Lebbaeus
Matthew, also called Levi
Simon the Zealot
Thomas
Judas Iscariot, the betrayer of Jesus
Paul, called Saul before his conversion

MAIN CHRISTIAN FESTIVALS

Advent	The fourth Sunday before Christmas
Christmas Day	25 December, celebrating Jesus' birth
Ash Wednesday	The first day of Lent
Lent	The fast of forty days before Easter
Palm Sunday	Celebrating Christ's triumphant entry into Jerusalem a few days before he died
Good Friday	The day of Christ's death (originally probably called God's Friday)
Easter	Celebrating the resurrection of Christ. The date varies annually between 22 March and 25 April
Ascension Day	The withdrawal of Christ to Heaven. Celebrated on the sixth Thursday (the fortieth day) after Easter
Whitsunday	The second Sunday after Ascension Day, celebrating the coming of the Holy Spirit to the Church at Pentecost

Most of the festivals depend upon the date of Easter for their timing each year. Easter is the Christian Passover, as Christ's death and resurrection occurred during the Jewish Passover. In fact, Christ celebrated the Passover before he died. There was much controversy within the Church over when Easter's date should be fixed but finally agreement was reached.

Britain, for example, followed the practice of the rest of Europe after the Synod of Whitby in 664. Easter falls on one of 35 days between 22 March and 25 April. Throughout Christendom various Easter celebrations take place such as lighting fires and giving Easter eggs – eggs being symbols of resurrection, life and fruitfulness.

Events in the Bible

The Bible is a collection of 66 books spanning thousands of years. It claims to give a true picture of human history from beginning to end. This is from the start of mankind in the deep past to some-time in our future when Christ, the true king of men, will return.

The religion of the Bible is based upon a God who made the entire universe. This God is a person who deals with man in history, and who himself became a man – Jesus Christ. Christians long ago divided

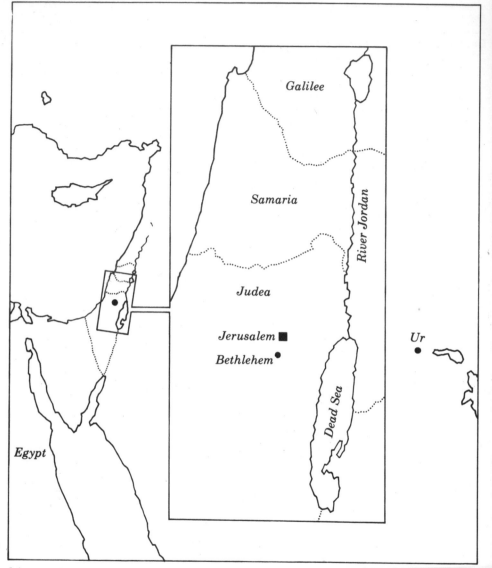

history into BC and AD – *Before Christ* and *Anno Domini* (literally, 'in the year of the Lord') referring to the years since his birth. A slight computing error was made; Christ in fact was born several years BC, probably 6 BC.

In the following chronology, dates are often given in round figures, or are approximate. When speaking of very ancient times, this doesn't usually mean that the record of events is inaccurate. The main Bible books which relate to each period appear in brackets at the end of each entry.

Before 2000   The early history of man from his beginnings. Man disobeys God and brings a curse upon himself and upon his environment. This is called 'the fall of man'. From early times the twin themes of history's pattern begin to work out – man's quest for salvation (and God's provision for this) and his cruelty as the result of his disobedience to God. These are seen in the murder of Abel by his brother Cain, in catastrophic judgement (as the early civilization is destroyed by the great flood) and in the breaking up of society (after Babel, standing for man's pride). The world then increasingly takes the form of a variety of nations and civilizations. (The Book of Genesis, which means 'beginning' or 'origin')

2000   The Age of the Patriarchs begins (the age of Abraham, his son Isaac, Isaac's son Jacob and Jacob's son Joseph). Abraham migrates from the civilized centre, Ur of Sumeria, to Canaan. He is called by God to forsake polytheism (the worship of many gods) and return to the original monotheism (worship of one god) of the human race. Abraham is chosen to be the founder of a new nation, which God promises will one day have the blessing of his salvation. The new nation is promised the land of Palestine as its eventual home. During this time Palestine, in its Bronze Age, is inhabited by the Canaanites. (Genesis)

1900–1750   Isaac, Abraham's son, long promised by God, is born when his parents are old. When Abraham is about to sacrifice the young Isaac, God provides a substitute – a ram – to die in his place. (Genesis)

1800–1700   Jacob, Isaac's son. Traditionally, the family inheritance is passed to the eldest son, but Jacob tricks his big brother into selling his birthright for a bowl of lentils one day when he is very hungry. Jacob is notorious for his trickery, and this leads him into a lot of trouble. He is eventually renamed 'Israel' by God. His new name is passed down to his descendants and finally the new nation. (Genesis)

1750–1650   Joseph. Jacob's favourite son, Joseph, is secretly sold as a slave in Egypt because of his brothers' jealousy. In a classic case of 'rags to riches', he rises to the top of Egyptian society. Joseph is reunited with his family after many years, and they settle in Egypt. (Genesis)

1700–1280   Israel in Egypt. During Egypt's New Kingdom, the Israelites stay several centuries. Finally, increasing oppression forces them to leave as refugees. Permission for their exodus is not granted until after a series of ten increasingly fearful plagues. (Exodus)

1280   The exodus from Egypt is led by Moses, a great leader. This is the central event of the Old Testament. The leaving of Egypt and migration to Palestine is an act of faith that God will fulfil his promise of a national territory for the growing body of Israelite people. (Exodus, Numbers, Deuteronomy)

1240   After many years in the desert, the Israelites cross the River Jordan. This is the natural geographical boundary of Palestine to the east. The nation is now led by Moses' successor, Joshua. This is the beginning of the gradual occupation of Palestine. The time roughly corresponds with the beginning of the Iron Age in Palestine. (Joshua)

1220?–1050/45?   The period of the 'judges'. These are military leaders, usually local, who lead the resistance – both physical and spiritual – to the Philistines and other warlike neighbouring nations. The 'judges' include Samson, who has a disastrous affair with the beautiful Philistine, Delilah. The final 'judge' is Samuel, under whom the nation has its first king. (Judges, Ruth, 1 Samuel)

1050/45?–931/30   The New Kingdom. In this period there are three kings, all of them national heroes – Saul, David and Solomon. This is the time of Israel's Golden Age, and Solomon builds a magnificent temple in the capital, Jerusalem. It is dedicated to the one, true, unseen God. Loving dedication to God is seen as the basis of a good national life which provides peace, security and quality of living. (1 and 2 Samuel, 1 Kings, 1 Chronicles, 2 Chronicles)

From 931/30   The nation falls into disunity and rivalry. The kingdom is divided into a Northern Kingdom and the Southern Kingdom of Judah. In both kingdoms prophets appear, interpreting political and historical events in terms of God's blessing and judgement upon nations, depending upon whether they obey or disobey Him. The greatest judgement prophesied upon the Jews is the loss of their national territory. In 722 Samaria, the northern capital, falls to the Assyrians. This marks the end of the Northern Kingdom. Many of the inhabitants are taken into captivity. In 587 a similar fate overtakes Jerusalem, the capital of Judah, this time by Assyria's successors, the Babylonians. In this and earlier conquests a great number of Judeans are taken into exile in Babylon. (1 Kings, 2 Kings, 2 Chronicles)

539   Babylon falls to the Persians.

538   Zerubbabel and other Jews return to Jerusalem. He helps lay the foundations of a new temple to replace the destroyed one. (Ezra)

520   Temple rebuilding is resumed after hindrances.

516   The temple is completed.

458   The scribe Ezra goes to Jerusalem, leading a party from captivity. (Ezra)

445–433   Nehemiah is given permission by the Persian king to go to Jerusalem to rebuild the walls and set up new gates. He is appointed governor of Judah. (Nehemiah)

The period from this time up to the birth of Jesus Christ is not recorded in the Old Testament. But full historical records of much of the period are to be found in apocryphal (non-canonical) books such as 1 and 2 Maccabees, which are included in many editions of the Bible. During this period Greece, Egypt, Syria and finally Rome are dominant influences upon Palestine.

331–323	Alexander the Great conquers many lands and founds the Egyptian city of Alexandria where many Jews settle. His empire includes Palestine.
323–63	The Age of the Ptolemies and Seleucids. After Alexander's sudden death his empire is divided up. Ptolemy, one of his generals, rules Egypt, while Seleucus, another general, seizes Babylonia and Asia Minor. The Ptolemies of Egypt rule Palestine for a hundred years. Then in 198 Antiochus the Great, a Seleucid, occupies it for Syria until Roman rule is established in 63.
168	Antiochus Epiphanes, son of Antiochus, marches against Jerusalem, killing and looting. The temple is desecrated and is replaced by a statue of Zeus, outraging the Jews.
167	The Maccabean revolt begins in the tiny village of Modein, near Jerusalem. One of the greatest leaders of the revolt is Judas Maccabeus. The rebels conduct a successful guerrilla war.
164	Rededication of the temple.
63	Pompey establishes a Roman protectorate in Palestine.
40	Herod the Great is appointed king of Judea by Rome.
6?	Jesus Christ is born in Bethlehem in Judea. (Matthew, Luke)
4	Herod the Great dies.

AD

14–37	Reign of Tiberius Caesar.
26–36	Pontius Pilate is Roman Procurator, based in Jerusalem.
29?	Baptism of Jesus and the beginning of his public life as a travelling preacher and teacher. (the Gospels)
30	During the annual Passover, Jesus is in Jerusalem.
30–31	Jesus is in Samaria, a province lying between Judea and Galilee – Jesus' home area.
31	During the annual Feast of Tabernacles Jesus is in Jerusalem.
32	At the time of the Passover, Jesus feeds the five thousand.
32	During both the Feast of Tabernacles and the Feast of Dedication Jesus is in Jerusalem.

33	The annual Passover becomes the prelude for the first Christian Easter when Jesus is executed by crucifixion and rises from the dead on the third day.
34–5	Paul's conversion. (The Acts of the Apostles)
37–8	Paul's first visit to Jerusalem as a Christian.
37–41	Reign of Caligula Caesar.
41–54	Reign of Claudius Caesar.
45–6	The Church in Antioch makes a collection for a great famine.
46–7	Paul's first missionary journey.
48	The apostles hold a council in Jerusalem.
48–51	Paul's second missionary journey.
50	Paul reaches Corinth, the largest seaport in Greece.
53	The third missionary journey begins.
54–68	Reign of Nero Caesar.
54–7	Paul stays in Ephesus.
57	Departure for Troas.
58–9	Paul is in Macedonia and Achaia.
59	Paul returns to Jerusalem.
59–61	He is imprisoned in Caesarea.
61	He appeals directly to Nero Caesar and leaves for Rome.
62	Paul arrives at Rome after being shipwrecked.
62–4	Imprisonment in Rome. (His death there by execution is not recorded in the Bible)
62?	The martyrdom of James, brother of Jesus.
70	The fall of Jerusalem.
81–96	Persecution of Christians under Domitian Caesar.
c. 100	Death of John the apostle.

HISTORY

Main Events in World History

BC

c. 3500	Height of Sumerian civilization in central Asia.
c. 3200	First dynasty of Egypt.
c. 2650	The Great Pyramid is erected for Cheops (Khufu) at Gizeh.
c. 2205	Hsia dynasty founded in China.
c. 2000	Bronze Age in Britain and Northern Europe.
c. 1800	Hammurabi of Babylon sets the laws of his kingdom in order, providing the first known legal system.
1766	Founding of Shang dynasty in China.
c. 1650	Invasion of Egypt by the Hyksos tribes.
c. 1500	Ganges civilization in India.
c. 1400	Palace of Minos at Knossos destroyed.
c. 1360	In Egypt, Amenhotep IV (Akhnaton) discards the old gods to worship one god, Aton, the Sun god.
1300	Temple of Abu-Simbel built for Rameses II of Egypt.
c. 1184	Destruction of Troy.
1122	Beginning of the Chou dynasty in China.
c. 1120	Assyrian Empire set up in Mesopotamia.
c. 800	Building of Carthage.
776	First recorded Olympic Games.
753	City of Rome founded.
606	Nineveh captured by the Chaldeans and Medes. Chaldean Empire founded.
c. 550	Buddha and Lao-tze live about this time.
510	Rome is declared a republic; Tarquin, the last king, is expelled.
490	Greeks defeat Persian armies at Marathon.
480	Greek navy defeats Xerxes at Battle of Salamis.
460	Pericles rules in Athens.
431	Peloponnesian War between Athens and Sparta begins.
338	Philip of Macedon invades Greece.
335–23	Campaigns of Alexander the Great.
264–41	First Punic War between Rome and Carthage.
256	Ch'in dynasty begins in China.
218–01	Second Punic War; Hannibal makes surprise attack on Northern Italy (218).
214	Great Wall of China is begun.
206	Han dynasty begins in China.
149	Third Punic War.
146	Carthage is destroyed by Scipio.
60	Julius Caesar is elected Consul of Rome.
58–51	Caesar's conquest of Gaul.
55	Caesar invades Britain.
49–46	Civil war between Caesar and Pompey.
45	Caesar is virtually dictator of Rome.
44	Caesar is murdered.
36	Marriage of Mark Antony with Cleopatra VII.

31	Combined fleets of Antony and Cleopatra are defeated at Actium by Roman fleet of Octavian. Mark Antony and Cleopatra commit suicide. Egypt becomes a Roman province.
27	Octavian changes his name to Augustus and is given the title Princeps.
6	Probable year of the birth of Christ.

AD

14	Death of Augustus; Tiberius becomes Emperor.
37	Caligula succeeds Tiberius.
41	Claudius is made Emperor.
43	Roman conquest of Britain begins.
54	Nero becomes Emperor.
68	Suicide of Nero.
70	Destruction of Jerusalem.
79	Vesuvius erupts, destroying Pompeii and Herculaneum.
117	Under the Emperor Hadrian, the Roman Empire reaches its greatest extent.
122	Hadrian's Wall is built in Britain.
180	After the death of the Emperor Marcus Aurelius, nearly a century of war and disorder begins in the Roman Empire.
303	The Emperor Diocletian persecutes the Christians.
306	Constantine the Great becomes Emperor.
313	Constantine legalizes Christianity by the Edict of Milan.
354	St Augustine is born.
395	On the death of Theodosius the Great the Roman Empire is divided into two, a western, Latin-speaking half and an eastern (Byzantine), Greek-speaking half.
410	Alaric the Goth marches on Italy and captures Rome; Roman legions withdraw from Britain to protect Rome.
451	Attila the Hun raids Gaul but is defeated.
455	Rome is sacked by Vandals.
476	Fall of Roman Empire in the West.
493	Theodoric the Ostrogoth conquers Italy and becomes King of Italy.
529	Justinian becomes Emperor in the Eastern Roman Empire.
553	Goths expelled from Italy by Justinian.
565	Death of Justinian. Lombards conquer most of North Italy.
570	Muhammad is born in Mecca.
618	Tang dynasty begins in China.
632	Death of Muhammad. Abu Bekr becomes Caliph.
634	Omar becomes second Caliph.
638	Jerusalem surrenders to Omar.
711	Moors overrun Spain.
732	Moors driven from France.
786	Haroun al Raschid is Caliph in Bagdad (to 809).
800	Pope Leo III crowns Charlemagne Emperor of the West.
814	Death of Charlemagne.
823	Egbert becomes first King of England.
1016	Canute becomes King of England, Denmark and Norway.
1066	William, Duke of Normandy, conquers England.
1071	Jerusalem captured by Turks.

1095	First Crusade.
1147	Second Crusade.
1187	Saladin captures Jerusalem.
1189	Third Crusade.
1202	Fourth Crusade diverted to attack Constantinople; a Latin Empire is established there.
1214	The Mongols, under Genghis Khan, take Peking.
1215	Magna Carta is signed by King John in England.
1217	Failure of Fifth Crusade against Egyptian Sultanate.
1223	Mongols invade Russia.
1225	Thomas Aquinas is born.
1226	Death of St Francis of Assisi.
1228	Christians driven out of Jerusalem; Sixth Crusade.
1244	Egyptian Sultan recaptures Jerusalem, leading to the Seventh Crusade.
1251	Mangu Khan becomes the Great Khan and his brother, Kublai Khan, becomes governor of China.
1270	Eighth Crusade.
1271	Marco Polo sets off on his travels.
1280	Kublai Khan founds the Yuan dynasty in China.
1309	Papal court set up in Avignon, France.
1338	Hundred Years War between France and England begins.
1348	The Black Death sweeps Europe.
1368	Yuan dynasty falls in China and is succeeded by the Ming dynasty which lasts until 1644.
1369	Timurlane becomes the Great Khan and causes great devastation in Asia.
1378	The Great Schism; Europe divides into two camps – Urban VI is Pope in Rome and Clement VII is Pope at Avignon.
1446	First printed books in Europe.
1452	Leonardo da Vinci is born.
1453	Constantinople falls to the Ottoman Turks.
1473	Copernicus is born.
1483	Martin Luther is born.
1492	Columbus discovers America. The Moors are driven from Spain.
1509	Henry VIII becomes King of England.
1534	Reformation in England.
1546	Death of Martin Luther.
1547	Ivan IV (the Terrible) takes the title of Tsar of Russia.
1565	Shakespeare is born.
1603	James I becomes King of England and Scotland.
1618	The Thirty Years' War in Europe begins.
1620	*Mayflower* colonists land in New England.
1649	Execution of Charles I in England.
1660	Charles II is restored to the English throne.
1665	Great Plague of London.
1666	Great Fire of London.
1745	Jacobite rebellion in England and Scotland led by Prince Charles Edward Stuart.
1746	Final defeat of Jacobites at Culloden Moor.
1756–63	Seven Years' War in Europe, involving Britain, France, Prussia, Saxony, Austria, Russia, Sweden, Spain and Portugal.
1759	General Wolfe captures Quebec from the French.

1775	Beginning of American War of Independence.
1776	American Declaration of Independence.
1783	Peace treaty between Britain and the new United States of America.
1789	French Revolution begins; Bastille is stormed.
1792	France declares war on Austria; Prussia declares war on France.
1793	Louis XVI of France is beheaded.
1794	Execution of Robespierre.
1796	Napoleonic Wars begin.
1804	Napoleon becomes Emperor of France.
1805	Battles of Ulm and Austerlitz; Battle of Trafalgar.
1812	Napoleon retreats from Moscow.
1815	Battle of Waterloo. Treaty of Vienna.
1825	First railway (Stockton to Darlington).
1833	Britain abolishes slavery.
1837	Queen Victoria comes to the throne.
1840	Penny post introduced in Britain.
1854–56	Crimean War.
1859	Franco-Austrian War; Battles of Magenta and Solferino.
1861	Victor Emmanuel becomes first King of Italy. Abraham Lincoln becomes President of the USA. American Civil War begins (ends in 1865).
1863	USA abolishes slavery.
1867	Dominion of Canada established.
1869	Suez Canal opened.
1870–71	Franco-Prussian War.
1877	Russo-Turkish War; Turkish power in Europe is broken. Queen Victoria becomes Empress of India.
1883	Death of Karl Marx.
1894–5	Japanese War with China.
1899	Boer War begins in South Africa.
1901	Death of Queen Victoria.
1903	First airplane flights by Wright brothers.
1904–5	Russo-Japanese War.
1909	Blériot makes first cross-channel flight.
1912	China becomes a republic. Ocean liner *Titanic* sinks on its maiden voyage.
1914	World War I begins.
1917	Russian revolution; Bolshevik regime established in Russia. USA enters World War.
1918	World War I ends.
1919	Treaty of Versailles between Allies and Germany. First trans-Atlantic flight made by Alcock and Brown.
1920	First meeting of the League of Nations.
1922	Separation of Southern Ireland from Great Britain. Mussolini marches on Rome.
1924	Death of Lenin.
1926	General strike in Great Britain.
1933	Hitler comes to power in Germany.
1935	Italy invades Ethiopia.
1936–39	Spanish Civil War.
1937	War breaks out between China and Japan.
1938	Hitler annexes Austria.
1939	Germany invades Czechoslovakia, and later Poland. France, Britain and

	the Commonwealth declare war on Germany (World War II).
1940	Germany invades Denmark, Norway, the Netherlands, Belgium and Luxembourg. Fall of France. Evacuation of Dunkirk by British. Battle of Britain.
1941	Japanese attack Pearl Harbor. USA enters the War.
1943	Italy surrenders to the Allies.
1944	Allies liberate France.
1945	All German forces surrender. Atomic bombs dropped on Hiroshima and Nagasaki. End of World War II. United Nations established.
1947–70	Many European colonies gain independence.
1948	State of Israel proclaimed. Conflict starts between Israel and Arab neighbours.
1949	People's Republic of China founded under leadership of Mao Tse-tung. Foundation of NATO.
1950–3	Korean War.
1955	Civil war in Vietnam. Warsaw Pact formed.
1957	EEC created. USSR launches first man-made satellite.
1961	First manned space flight (USSR).
1969	First men on the Moon (USA).
1975	Vietnam War ends.
1979	Islamic revolution in Iran.

Great Explorers

Amundsen, Roald ((1872-1928)
The first explorer to sail through
the Northwest Passage, and also to
reach the South Pole. Aboard the
Gjoa, this famous Norwegian
navigated the Northwest Passage
during the years 1903–6 and then,
in 1911, beat his great rival, Scott,
to the South Pole, arriving there on
14 December.
Baffin, William (1584-1622)
English discoverer, in 1616, of the
bay which bears his name. It lies
between the northeast coast of
Canada and Greenland.
Bering, Vitus (1680-1741) A Dane
who entered into the service of
Russia, Bering gave his name to the
strait between the USSR and the
USA's state of Alaska, which he
navigated in 1728.
Blashford-Snell, John Nicholas

(1936-   ) A British Army officer in
the Royal Engineers, and author of
books on exploration, Blashford-
Snell led the following expeditions:
Great Abbai (Blue Nile) in 1968;
Dahlak Quest in 1969–70; British
Trans-Americas in 1971–2; and the
Zaire River in 1974–5.
**Burton, Sir Richard Francis
(1821-90)** Principally known for his
exploration of Central Africa, this
English linguist (he mastered 35
languages) discovered Lake
Tanganyika in 1858. He also
travelled from Afghanistan to
Mecca in 1853, disguised as a
pilgrim.
Cabot, John (1450-c. 1500) Born
in Genoa, John Cabot went to live
in Bristol, England. In 1497 he
received letters-patent from King
Henry VII to voyage westwards.

Columbus

Cook

He discovered Newfoundland and Nova Scotia, and possibly the American mainland ahead of Columbus – lands which he believed were part of eastern Asia.

Cabot, Sebastian (1474-1557) The son of John Cabot, Sebastian was born in Venice. He sailed as far as Hudson Bay, in search of a north-west passage to Asia, and then, in 1512, explored the Plate and Paraná rivers in South America for Spain. In the service of England, Sebastian Cabot sought a means of reaching India by way of a northeast passage, which opened up trade with Russia.

Cameron, Verney Lovett (1844-1894) An English explorer, Cameron was the first man to cross the continent of Africa from east to west. He also surveyed Lake Tanganyika and set out to look for Livingstone in 1872.

Cartier, Jacques (1494-1557) Born in St Malo, this French navigator was responsible for considerable exploration of Canada, particularly the St Lawrence gulf and river.

Columbus, Christopher (c.1451-1506) Christopher Columbus was born in Genoa. He set off on his famous voyage from Spain with the financial backing of King Ferdinand and Queen Isabella. He reached the Bahamas and Cuba in 1492, and the mainland of America in 1498.

Cook, James (1728-79) An English sailor and officer in the British Royal Navy, Cook commanded the *Endeavour, Resolution* and *Adventure* on Pacific Ocean voyages which led to the charting of a great deal of the coastlines of Australia and New Zealand. On his first expedition, in 1770, he found so many interesting plants in one area of Australia that he named it Botany Bay. Cook also surveyed the coast of Newfoundland and reached the Hawaiian Islands, where he met his death at the hands of the inhabitants.

Cortés, Hernando (1488-1547) Responsible for opening up the land of Mexico for his native Spain, Cortés conquered a vast region with a handful of men and destroyed the ancient Aztec civilization which existed there.

Dampier, William (1652-1715) This English seaman succeeded in sailing right round the world. He explored Australian waters and rescued Alexander Selkirk, the castaway who became the model for Defoe's character Robinson Crusoe.

Davis, John (*c*. 1550-1605) Discoverer of Davis Strait, between Canada's Baffin Island and Greenland. This Elizabethan sailor from Devonshire, in England, invented the backstaff, or Davis's quadrant, a nautical instrument for measuring the height of the Sun.

Diaz, Bartholomew (*c*. 1445-1500) A Portuguese navigator who explored the West African coast and then, during a storm, rounded the Cape of Good Hope.

Diemen, Anthony Van (1593-1645) As Dutch governor-general in the Far East, Van Diemen promoted exploration which led to Tasman's discovery of New Zealand and the naming of Van Diemen's Land, now known as Tasmania.

Drake, Sir Francis (*c*. 1540-96) The English seaman who, in 1577–1580, sailed round the world aboard the *Golden Hind*. Renowned for his exploits against the Spaniards, this Devon-born sailor died at sea off Panama.

Eric the Red (10th century) A leading Viking explorer, who is believed to have discovered and named Greenland, possibly in the year 982.

Ericsson, Leif (10th century) Credited with finding North America and landing on its coast, Leif Ericsson was another of the great sailor-explorers of this period from Scandinavia.

Flinders, Matthew (1774-1814) A navigator from England who made a number of discoveries in and around the continent of Australia. Bass Strait, through which Flinders sailed, was named in honour of his surgeon. His own name was given to the largest island in the Furneaux Group off Tasmania, and also to a chain of mountains in South Australia.

Frobisher, Sir Martin (1535-94) An English seaman from Yorkshire, Frobisher made three voyages in search of the Northwest Passage, via Arctic waters, from the Atlantic Ocean to the Pacific. His great exploratory ventures are commemorated at Frobisher Bay, on Canada's Baffin Island.

Fuchs, Sir Vivian Ernest (1908-) Leader of the British Commonwealth Trans-Antarctic Expedition, 1957–8, Fuchs was the first explorer who succeeded in crossing the continent of Antarctica.

Gama, Vasco da (*c*. 1460-1524) A great Portuguese navigator who, by rounding the Cape of Good Hope in 1498, discovered and opened up the sea route to India.

Henry the Navigator (1394-1460) This famous prince was the son of King John I of Portugal. He organized important voyages of exploration, a result of which was the discovery of Madeira and the Azores, both of which remain Portuguese possessions to this day.

Hudson, Henry (died 1611) This English sailor, of whom nothing is known prior to 1607, discovered the Hudson River, Strait and Bay which are named after him. On his last voyage, Hudson's crew mutinied and set him adrift to die in the cold waters of northeast Canada.

Humboldt, Friedrich Heinrich Alexander, Baron Von (1769-1859) This German naturalist explored South America. He recorded his experiences in *Voyage de Humboldt* (1805–34) and *Kosmos* (1845).

Drake

Livingstone

Jansz, Willem (17th century) A
Dutch Pacific explorer, Jansz
unwittingly discovered Australia in
1606 while searching for New
Guinea. He reached Torres Strait a
few weeks before Torres himself.

Livingstone, David (1813-73) A
renowned Scottish explorer and
missionary who travelled widely in
southern Africa. He discovered the
course of the Zambezi River, the
Victoria Falls and Lake Malawi
(then named Lake Nyasa).
Livingstone fought very hard
against the slave trade. Believed
lost on one of his expeditions, he
was found by Stanley (q.v.) on 10
November 1871.

**Magellan, Ferdinand (*c*. 1480-
1521)** In 1519, Magellan, a
Portuguese sailor, became the first
expedition commander to sail round
the world. He successfully navigated
the winding passage, 787 km
(365 miles) in length and named
after him, separating the tip of
mainland South America and the
island of Tierra del Fuego.

Mawson, Sir Douglas (1882-1958)
A notable explorer of the Antarctic,
Mawson took part in the Shackleton
expedition, before leading the
Australian Antarctic Expedition of
1911–14 and the British-Australian
and New Zealand Expedition of
1929–31. In 1912, he was the only
survivor of his party, which
endured dreadful conditions and
suffering.

Nansen, Fridijof (1861-1930) A
Nobel peace-prize winner in 1922,
this Norwegian explorer wrote an
account of his north-polar expedition of 1893 in *Farthest North*. On
that occasion, Nansen's party
reached 86° 14' – at that time the
highest latitude achieved.

**Oates, Lawrence Edward (1880-
1912)** The English Antarctic
explorer who reached the South
Pole with Scott (q.v.) and three
others. On the return journey he
deliberately left his companions in
camp, to go out into a blizzard and
meet his death, because his severe
frost-bite was holding up the party's
progress.

Park, Mungo (1771-1806) Author
of *Travels in the Interior of Africa*
(1799), Mungo Park was a Scottish
explorer in the area of West Africa.
He explored the course of the River
Niger, in which he was drowned.

**Parry, Sir William Edward (1790-
1855)** Rear-Admiral Parry, R.N.,
was an English commander of

Marco Polo

Raleigh

expeditions in the Arctic, where he made a number of important discoveries and attempted to reach the North Pole.

Peary, Robert Edwin (1856-1920) An American Rear-Admiral and Arctic explorer, Peary first conducted a sledging expedition towards the North Pole in 1891–2. Further expeditions took place in the Arctic in 1893, 1895, 1898, 1900–2 and 1906. Finally, on 6 April 1909, Peary succeeded in reaching the Pole.

Polo, Marco (1256-1323) Setting out from his native Venice, Marco Polo carried out amazing journeys – considered incredible in his day and age – through China, India and other eastern lands. He visited Kublai Khan, and wrote the story of his wonderful travels, experiences and discoveries.

Raleigh, Sir Walter (1552-1618) In 1584, this prominent English seaman started the colonization of Virginia, and he was responsible for the introduction of potatoes and tobacco to Europe. After a spell of 12 years as a prisoner in the Tower of London, Raleigh was released in 1615 by King James I to head an expedition to the region of the

Orinoco River, in northern South America, to search for gold. The failure of Raleigh's mission led to his execution.

Ross, Sir James Clark (1800-62) Accompanying his uncle, Sir John Ross (q.v.) on expeditions to the Arctic, Sir James Ross achieved distinction. He later commanded his own expedition (1839–43) to the Antarctic, during which he discovered the Ross ice barrier. Earlier, in 1831, he was responsible for discovering the North Magnetic Pole.

Ross, Sir John (1777-1856) A Rear-Admiral and eminent Scottish Polar explorer (the uncle of Sir James Ross), Sir John Ross searched for the Northwest Passage and found Boothia Peninsula, on the Arctic coast of Canada.

Scott, Robert Falcon (1868-1912) This English Antarctic explorer was the leader of two expeditions. The first, in 1901–4, resulted in the discovery of King Edward VII Land. The second expedition left in 1910 aboard the *Terra Nova* and reached the South Pole on 18 January 1912, only to find that Amundsen had already reached it on 14 December 1911. The party of five all perished

Scott

Vespucci

on their journey back to base.

Shackleton, Sir Henry Ernest (1874-1922) Commander of the Nimrod Farthest South expedition of 1907–9, Shackleton reached a point within 160 km (100 miles) of the South Pole. On his fourth expedition, a scientific voyage to the Antarctic, the explorer died.

Smith, John (1580-1631) This noted English seafarer and adventurer carried out a colonizing and pioneering expedition to Virginia in 1605. During an expedition among the Red Indians his life is said to have been saved by Pocahontas, the daughter of the Indian chief who had captured him.

Soto, Hernando De (*c.* 1500-42) A Spaniard, De Soto discovered what is now Florida and Georgia in southern USA, and also the Mississippi River.

Speke, John Hanning (1827-64) A British explorer, Captain Speke first discovered Lake Victoria in 1858. Accompanied by Lt.-Col. J. A. Grant, he then went on in 1860 to locate the River Nile flowing out of the great lake.

Stanley, Sir Henry Morton (1841-1904) Born at Denbigh, Wales, Stanley went to the USA where he fought on the Confederate side in the American Civil War and then became a *New York Herald* correspondent. His newspaper appointed Stanley to find the lost explorer Livingstone (q.v.). He was successful at Ujiji in 1871, and the two men then explored Lake Tanganyika. Stanley founded the Congo Free State for Belgium in 1879.

Stefansson, Vilhjalmur (1879-1962) Of Icelandic parentage, this Canadian explorer carried out a lot of valuable work in the Arctic region, and recorded his findings in *Unsolved Mysteries of the Arctic*.

Tasman, Abel Janszoon (1603-1659) Sent on a voyage of discovery by Van Diemen (q.v.), Tasman, a Dutch navigator, reached the Australian island of Tasmania (formerly Van Diemen's Land) and New Zealand in 1642.

Vespucci, Amerigo (1454-1512) A Florentine merchant and explorer-navigator, Vespucci went on voyages across the Atlantic Ocean. He travelled along the coast of South America and discovered the Rio de la Plata. The continent was later called after his first name.

HOBBIES AND PASTIMES

Guide to Outdoor Activities

The following guide to outdoor pursuits does not cover the various activities in full detail but it will give you some idea of what is involved in each sport. You may then wish to find out more and take an active part in one or more of them.

Backpacking

This is a type of hiking in which people carry food, clothing, tent or shelter, and other equipment on their backs. Sometimes it is the only possible way to explore wild and remote areas where supplies cannot be obtained.

To hold all that you need on an expedition lasting several days you must have a carrier which will remain comfortable during long hikes. There are two basic types of carrier. First, there is the rucksack. It is mounted on a metal frame which fits around the contours of your back and has a curved waist support. The adjustable straps, made of leather or webbing, take the load. Modern rucksack designs are fairly narrow at the bottom, widening out at the top. Some old types are too wide at the base, allowing the load to hang too low and causing the wearer to stoop forwards. The second type of carrier is the packframe and sack. The frame is made of a light alloy to which is attached two well-padded, adjustable shoulder straps and the sack. The sack is generally made of nylon and has several large pockets.

Whether you choose a rucksack or a packframe and sack, the principles of packing them are the same.

1 The heaviest articles are packed at the top; it is easier to carry them high on your back.

2 Articles you may need in an emergency should be readily available.

3 Light items, particularly those you will want last, should be packed at the bottom or wrapped in a waterproof cover and strapped to the bottom of the frame below the sack.

4 Pack hard objects carefully so that they don't dig into your back.

5 Don't make yourself a pack-horse. Carry only essentials. Too heavy a load will spoil your trip.

When you can be certain of fine weather, it is fun to improvise a bivouac shelter for the night using sheets of polythene, string and local materials such as fallen logs and tree branches. A rubber mattress adds to your comfort but is very heavy to carry. A soft mattress may be made from dry bracken or hay. Instead of carrying a tent, some hikers pass the night in a water-proof sleeping bag with an improvised head shelter constructed with polythene and sturdy sticks. Inexpensive ready-made polythene shelters may also be purchased.

Most backpackers use tents. There are several lightweight tents on the market specially designed

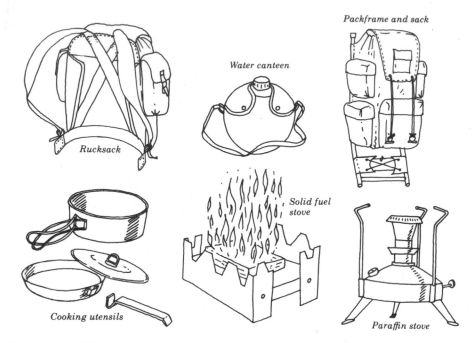

Rucksack

Water canteen

Packframe and sack

Solid fuel stove

Cooking utensils

Paraffin stove

for backpacking. Some are for a single person, others for two. The latter type may weigh a little more than a tent for one, but when you are camping with another person it is obviously more practical for one of you to carry a two-man tent than for each of you to have your own tent. The backpacker's tent is generally made of waterproof nylon which is light in weight, does not shrink and is rot-proof. Because there is only sufficient room in it for sleeping, this tent is not suitable for ordinary, leisurely camping.

Sleeping bags must be as light and warm as possible and should fold up compactly. The lightest sleeping bag is the type filled with down, and this can be folded up into a very small bundle. Some polyester-filled sleeping bags are almost as warm as down and they do have the advantage that when

they become damp they are easily dried out, unlike the down-filled type.

Cooking equipment should also be light and compact. There is a number of suitable camping stoves, each using a different kind of fuel: methylated spirit (meths), solid fuel, paraffin, petrol or camping gas.

One of the simplest, lightest and inexpensive stoves is a little picnic stove which runs on methylated spirit. The cup-like fuel container stands inside the combined pot-stand and windshield. Methylated spirit is poured into the centre of the container, which has hollow walls, to a set level. When a lighted match is applied to the surface a ring of fire is produced. Although the stove is comparatively safe you must take care not to pour in more fuel while a flame is still burning. The fuel may flare up and cause a

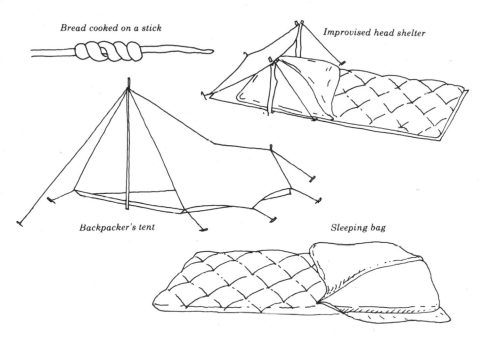

Bread cooked on a stick

Improvised head shelter

Backpacker's tent

Sleeping bag

serious accident. Always be careful when using methylated spirit because it burns with an almost invisible flame.

The lightest of all camp stoves is the type that burns solid fuel. When folded up, this stove is not much larger than a pack of playing cards. It opens out to form a pot-stand and a burner plate on supporting legs. When closed, it doubles as a container for a solid fuel, such as Meta. This stove is not a very speedy cooker and the best results are obtained using lightweight aluminium cooking utensils.

The primus stove, which uses paraffin, is a powerful cooker that burns for a considerable time on one filling. A disadvantage is that it is not easy to use, requiring some practice to operate. It also needs 'priming' to get it going and for this you need a second fuel such as

meths or Meta. A petrol stove is also powerful, but the fuel is expensive and it can be risky to operate.

Several makes of lightweight camping gas stoves are obtainable. They are extremely simple to use. You light them by turning on a valve and applying a match to the gas ring. The gas is either propane or butane. In cold conditions, below 1°C, butane gas liquefies and will not light but there is no such problem with propane. The disadvantage of camping gas stoves is that the fuel is expensive.

Camping stoves are generally efficient and reliable. Carry a stove rather than an axe to chop wood for a camp fire. Fires take time to build up, but a fire can be lit when you need to conserve your stove fuel. When you feel cold, a camp fire is very cheering as well as warming. For ways to build camp fires, see the section on camping.

Cooking pots and pans can take up a lot of room in your rucksack. A nest of lightweight cooking utensils, obtainable at camping stores, is therefore worth consideration. The utensils shown on page 140 pack neatly together; they are fastened down with the hinged handle of the frying pan. To lift the water pot you need a special gripping device. Another useful item is a set of cutlery consisting of a knife, fork and dessert spoon which clip together for packing purposes.

These days, finding food for backpacking that is both light in weight and nutritious is no problem at all. There are plenty of packet soups to choose from and dehydrated vegetables such as mashed potato, peas, beans, onion, mushrooms and mixed vegetables. Among the dried fruits are apricots, prunes and apple-rings. Bread is bulky and can be replaced by crispbread. Alternatively, you can make your own bread out of self-raising flour and water. Mix four parts of flour to one of water and add a little salt. The dough can be made into flat cakes and baked in a frying pan, or twisted around a hot stick and cooked over a fire.

Camping

The popular recreation of camping can include everything from bivouacking in the backwoods to spending a leisurely family holiday in a frame tent large enough to sleep six. Camping is a means of escaping the pressures of town life and is not necessarily a rough back-to-nature pastime for hardy open-air types. People with cars can carry enough equipment to ensure a comfortable holiday, including such items as gas stoves, charcoal grills, folding beds and chairs, foam mattresses and a multitude of gadgets. Organized camping grounds provide every facility: a pure-water supply, washhouse, toilets, and sometimes even shops. Many people, on the other hand, find camping more enjoyable when the equipment is simple and basic. When the camper has to carry his tent, equipment and all supplies on his back, only lightweight essentials can be taken. (See the section on backpacking.)

Tents vary in design, but perhaps the most common type of small tent is the ridge tent. This has two vertical poles, normally made up of three sections of either wood or aluminium. Sometimes there is a third, horizontal, pole which fits along the top of the tent, holding the other poles apart and tightening the canvas between them to give maximum height inside. Guy ropes are attached to pegs in the ground. They hold the tent down in windy conditions and ensure that it stands symmetrically.

Many tents have a sewn-in groundsheet which helps to keep out wind and rainwater. Also adding protection is the flysheet. The flysheet is an extra roof that keeps the inner tent waterproof in heavy rain. Because there is a layer of air between it and the tent walls, the flysheet also serves to insulate the inner tent against the cold. In hot, stifling weather the flysheet may be used on its own.

Many tents are made from nylon and terylene. They are light and wear well, however, condensation does tend to form inside. Cotton fabric (treated against rain and rot), on the other hand, allows moisture to pass through the fine weave while still being waterproof. A cotton fabric tent with a nylon flysheet makes a good compromise.

When looking for a suitable site to pitch your tent there are many things to consider. A site near a clear stream is a good one as you can use the water for washing purposes and, if necessary, for drinking. Sterilize stream water by boiling it for at least five minutes, or by using soluble water-purifying tablets. Avoid places where there are too many insects, and where there is long grass because it holds dew and will remain damp for a long time. Do not camp under trees. The leaves will drip heavily long after a rain shower has passed, and in a strong wind branches may fall on your tent. It is dangerous to be at the foot of a tall, isolated tree in a thunderstorm, for the tree may attract lightning.

Pick a spot that is dry and level, and not likely to be flooded in a rainstorm. The ground should not be stony, lumpy or sprouting with thistles. If the ground is too hard to drive in the tent pegs, you may be able to anchor the guy ropes with rocks.

Before you pitch your tent, remember to ask the landowner's permission first. If you promise to leave the site as you found it consent is likely to be granted. Many landowners do not let campers build fires, so you should

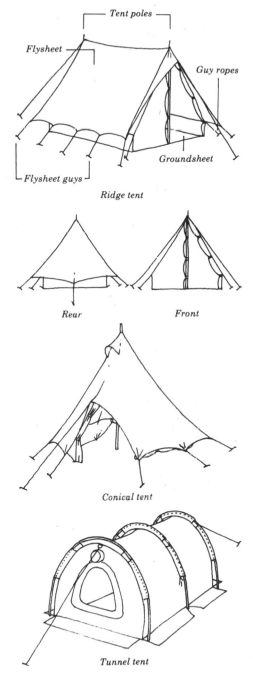

Ridge tent

Rear   Front

Conical tent

Tunnel tent

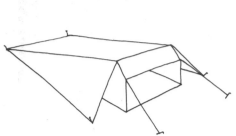

Polythene bivouac tent

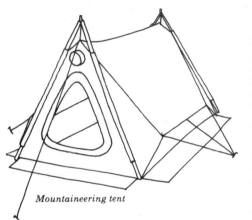

Mountaineering tent

Correct angle for tent peg

obtain permission if you wish to make one. Do be careful where you build your fire, especially in dry, hot conditions. Heath and forest fires are easily started. To build a camp fire you need to collect:

1 kindling wood (small sticks and pieces of wood),

2 tinder (material that will catch fire easily and burn long enough to enable the fire to catch the kindling wood, such as feathers, bundles of dry grass and tree bark),

3 small logs.

Make stockpiles of the kindling material so that there is no chance of the fire going out for lack of fuel. You need only a small fire for cooking purposes.

There are many ways of making a fire. A basic type of fire-lay is a triangle of sticks enclosing the tinder at the centre. The uppermost stick lies on the windward side so that the draught can blow through to the tinder. Light a match and push it under the windward stick into the tinder. As the tinder catches, quickly add more kindling so that it forms a cone over the blaze. Take care not to stifle the fire by adding too much.

In windy conditions, build your fire in a hole about 30 cm (1 ft) across and 15 cm (6 in) deep. Place your cooking pot over the hole, supported by green sticks. The sticks may have to be replaced as they dry out, otherwise they may ignite. Here is an easy way to keep a fire going. When you have the fire ablaze, place the ends of several long pieces of wood into the centre.

Ignite them one by one and place them so that they radiate like the spokes of a wheel, burning only where the ends meet at the centre of the fire. As the inner ends burn away you simply push the logs inwards. This star-shaped fire is slow-burning, economical and needs very little attention.

Basic fire-lay

Canoeing

Canoes vary in size, shape and construction according to their purpose. Most measure from about 3.5 to 6 m (11 to 20 ft) long and 90 to 100 cm (35 to 40 in) in beam (the width at the widest part). Their depth varies from 30 to 36 cm (12 to 14 in). The most common types of canoe are:

1 folding, with sectional framework and flexible skin,
2 rigid construction in plywood,
3 rigid construction in glass fibre,
4 rigid, with plasticized canvas skin,
5 Canadian, a wooden canoe modelled on Red Indian lines, sometimes with a plasticized skin.

Star-shaped fire-lay

Some canoes are open boats without a deck. Others have an enclosed deck and a small cockpit where the canoeist sits. A spray-cover is usually used to cover the cockpit except in calm waters. Decked canoes, resembling Eskimo kayaks, are used in rough water where an open canoe would quickly fill up with water. Most canoes are either single seaters or double seaters.

Paddles, which are usually of wood, vary greatly in length and

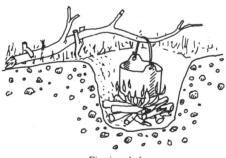

Fire in a hole

width. A wide blade provides a powerful stroke but needs someone with both strength and skill to operate it. A narrow blade requires less strength but gives less power. Decked canoes are propelled by double-bladed paddles, open canoes by single-bladed paddles.

Some canoes have a keel which consists of a flat piece of wood or metal extending into the water from the bottom of the hull. A canoe with a keel can be steered easily on a straight course in still water (a lake, for example). On a fast-moving river, however, it is difficult to manoeuvre.

The size and shape of a canoe also affect its characteristics. A short hull gives manoeuvrability, a long one gives speed. A narrow hull is fast, but it has less stowage space than a wide one and is not sea-

A kayak is decked except for the centre cockpit. It has a sharp bow and stern and is propelled with a double-bladed paddle.

worthy. The shape of the cross-section is another factor influencing a canoe's speed and stability.

Because a canoe has a draught of only 5 cm (2 in), it can be used to explore shallow waters inaccessible to most other craft. On some expeditions the craft may have to be carried overland, to take a short cut for example, or to avoid waterfalls or rapids. The canoeist may then use a padded yoke which enables him to carry the canoe upside down on his shoulders.

While many canoeists like to explore placid lakes and rivers, many enthusiasts prefer the open sea or fast-running mountain rivers where they can shoot the rapids.

An essential accessory for each person on a canoe trip is a life-jacket. Another important item is a bailer to empty out water from the bottom of the craft.

There is plenty of space in a canoe for stowing camping gear. Furthermore, considerable extra weight can be carried without a great difference in the power needed to propel the canoe. Anything that must be kept dry should be wrapped in waterproof bags. Goods stored in the canoe should be tied to cross-members or fittings so that in the event of a capsize they will not be washed out.

Caving (Potholing)
Caving is a pursuit devoted to the exploration of underground caverns and potholes. A pothole (or pitch) is a cylindrical shaft which descends from the surface of the ground or from levels inside caves. The shaft is climbed by using ladders and ropes. Ordinary mountaineering techniques usually cannot be employed in climbing a deep shaft because in most cases the smooth, water-polished vertical walls offer no holds at all.

The basic equipment for caving consists of a lamp and a wire ladder about 9 m (30 ft) long. A series of ladders can be clipped together for descending a long shaft. Security is provided by a nylon life-line.

Sometimes caving involves squeezing through damp, narrow holes – not many people's idea of having a good time. It can also involve swimming in cold underground rivers. But caving also has its rewards: there are beautiful underground caverns ornamented with stalactites, stalagmites and mineral encrustations of many colours. Total silence and total darkness are further experiences to be had by the caving enthusiast. Some people go caving for the team spirit to be found in the sport. Above all, there is the thrill of exploration, adventure and physical challenge.

Cycling
Touring by bicycle has long been a popular recreation. Some medical experts say that cycling is the healthiest of all sports. The touring bicycle, once heavy and fitted with balloon tyres, today looks more like a racing bike. When selecting a bicycle for touring, you should think more of distance and comfort than speed. Dropped handlebars or high handlebars are not suitable for touring.

Adjust the saddle so that your knees are very slightly bent when the pedals are at their lowest point. You should just be able to reach the ground with the tips of your toes when seated on the bike. Set the height of the handlebar grips at no more than 7.5 cm (3 in) above the saddle.

A variable gear is recommended. One or two low gears are more useful than high ones when you want to get up hills. If you want to go faster on a level stretch you can always pedal faster.

Fit your bike with a pump, lamps and a repair kit. If you are going to travel in isolated country take a spare inner tube with you. To travel in groups you need to be fit enough to keep up with the others. When you travel alone or

Parts of a bicycle

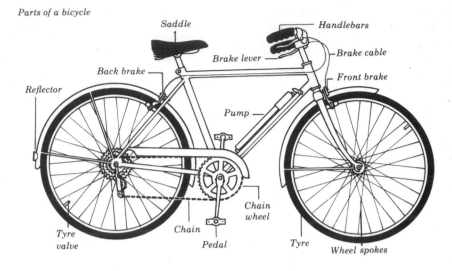

Saddle

Handlebars

Brake lever

Brake cable

Back brake

Front brake

Reflector

Pump

Chain
wheel

Tyre
valve

Chain

Pedal

Tyre

Wheel spokes

A bicycle loaded for camping

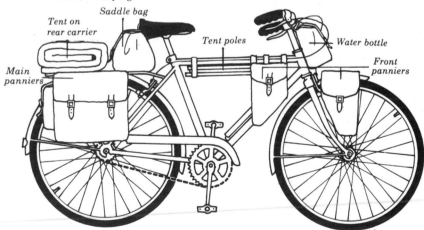

Saddle bag

Tent on
rear carrier

Tent poles

Water bottle

Main
panniers

Front
panniers

in pairs you can set your own pace.

A cyclist who is a keen camper can use his bicycle to carry camping gear. The load should be distributed as evenly as possible in panniers and the saddle-bag. The load should be kept low, otherwise the bike will be difficult to handle. Waterproof clothing should be strapped on top of the saddle-bag where it is easily accessible in bad weather.

Hiking

Hiking is a popular recreational activity for all ages. It is one of the most economical pastimes because it requires no special equipment. Furthermore, hiking is an excellent way of keeping fit.

A hike may last a few hours or be spread over several days. Some people walk alone, or in pairs. Others join hiking or rambling expeditions arranged by youth clubs and other groups, generally following a planned route. Skill in reading a map and using a compass is an asset in unfamiliar territory. Youth hostels provide cheap accommodation for walkers. Backpackers (q.v.) take their shelter with them in the form of a lightweight tent.

The ability to walk considerable distances without becoming overtired is basic to many other outdoor pursuits and is acquired with practice. For example, mountain climbers often have to walk steadily hour after hour up the lower mountain slopes before making the final steep ascent, and birdwatchers may do a considerable amount of walking on field trips.

In fine weather no special

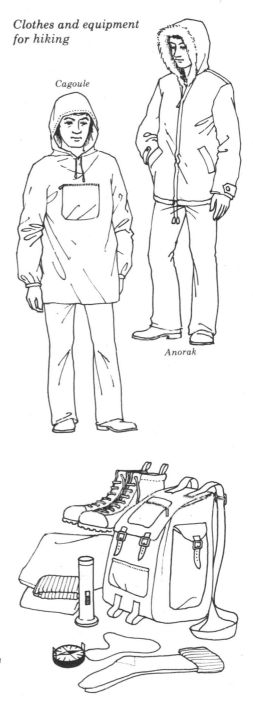

Clothes and equipment for hiking

Cagoule

Anorak

clothing is required for walking. A stout pair of shoes and garments suitable for the weather will suffice. Always be prepared, however, for a change in weather. In winter and on hill walks you need adequate protection against the cold. Wear two or three woollen shirts or thin sweaters rather than one very thick one. To keep out the wind and rain you should wear a garment such as a waterproof cagoule or a hooded anorak. The anorak should be large enough to cover your sweaters and long enough to come well down over your hips. As with a cagoule, the hood and hem of your anorak should be fitted with drawstrings and the sleeves should be elasticated. In bad weather, therefore, all the openings can be sealed up.

Using an ice-axe for braking

You should carry a change of clothes, maps, compass and your packed lunch in a small, frameless rucksack. Make sure that the straps, when adjusted, allow the load to be carried high on your back. Don't have it resting on your hips. For information about larger rucksacks used on extended hikes, see the section on backpacking. For hill walking you need special walking boots which are thick-soled and flexible. These will cushion your feet on stony ground and also support your ankles.

Mountain climbing (Mountaineering)

Why does anyone climb a mountain? One famous answer is 'because it's there'. For many people the pleasure of mountaineering lies mainly in the challenge of physical effort. For others, the impressive solitude and beauty of mountain peaks more than make up for the arduous labour of the ascent. Human comradeship is another important factor. In no other sport is so much co-operation necessary. Consideration for the other team members is essential for their safety, especially when climbing with ropes.

Accidents are usually caused by ignorance or inexperience. Nevertheless, mountain climbing always involves an element of risk from such hazards as falling stones or ice. Even very skilled climbers have lost their lives attempting challenging peaks.

Hill walking and rock scrambling are excellent ways to gain experience for the young person who wants to take up mountaineering. Some mountaineers may later branch into rock climbing (q.v.) and snow and ice climbing. It is advisable to have at least one companion with you when hill walking and scrambling, especially when there is snow and ice about. Never climb alone at any time.

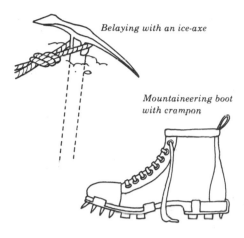

Belaying with an ice-axe

Mountaineering boot with crampon

Equipment essential for climbing on snow and ice includes:

1 vibram-soled footwear and crampons (spiked metal frames for walking on ice),
2 suitable clothing for the conditions,
3 a knapsack loaded with first-aid supplies, food and extra clothing,
4 an ice-axe,
5 slings (a sling is a loop of rope, usually 122–350 cm (4–10 ft) long, tied by a double fisherman's knot),
6 a nylon rope,
7 pitons, a piton hammer, nuts and karabiners.

A piton is a metal spike, with an eye or ring at one end, that can be driven into a crack in rock or ice. A karabiner, or snap-link, is a metal loop that can be snapped into a piton and through which a rope may be passed. Mountaineers' nuts are threaded on to ropes to wedge them in rock crevices. Climbers usually have a range of nuts to fit different types of fissure.

Perhaps the most versatile item in the mountaineer's array of equipment is his ice-axe. It is used as a firm point of support, for probing crevasses, to cut steps in the snow, for stopping a fall and emergency braking. Another important use is for belaying. 'Belaying' means securing the rope that is tied round a climber. When used for this purpose the ice-axe is plunged vertically in the snow up to its head. A figure of eight knot is tied in the main rope and placed over the head of the axe. A team of climbers, when roped up, should be belayed so that the fall of one person will not pull the others off as well. Normally every member is belayed while he is not moving.

If you wish to learn mountain climbing it is best to accompany older friends who are already experienced. Alternatively, you could join a local mountaineering club.

Orienteering
Orienteering is a competitive sport originating from Sweden. It combines cross-country running over rough and wooded terrain with map reading and direction-finding skills.

Participants use a compass and a map which they are given just before the race. They leave at timed intervals and must check in at control points shown on the map. The route between the control points is for them to choose, but the fastest to complete the course wins.

Orienteering does not depend on

Orienteering

Punting

athletic ability alone. The fleet-footed are often left far behind by others whose map reading and selection of routes have been more shrewd. The shortest time-distance between two control points is not always a straight line. Considerations to be borne in mind when choosing a route include:

1 how severe are the obstacles (hills, cliffs, fences, etc.)?
2 what is the nature of the ground (thickly wooded, boggy, etc.)?
3 what useful landmarks are there (saving many time-consuming references to the map)?

Individual capacities must also be taken into account. A fast runner may prefer a long detour through open country or along paths. A slower one may gamble on a shorter but more complicated route, such as through a thick wood.

Punting

A punt is a narrow, flat-bottomed boat which is propelled by pushing a long pole against the river-bed. The punter must let the pole drop vertically to the bottom. Then he pushes against the river-bed, drawing the pole up again as the punt moves away. If the river has a muddy bottom the pole sometimes gets stuck in the mud. The punter then has the choice of letting the pole go, or to stay clinging to it as the punt moves away. Punting is easier on rivers with shingle beds.

Riding

Children and young people often learn to ride at a riding school. The most suitable mount for youngsters is a pony (a small kind of horse). There are several breeds of pony, including the hardy Shetland, the Dartmoor, the Exmoor, the grey Highland pony and the Welsh Cob. If you are lucky enough to have your own pony, you will be responsible for all its needs and a friendship will quickly grow between you. Even at a riding school you may ride the same pony at each lesson and so build up a relationship with it.

A relatively inexpensive way of enjoying riding is pony trekking. Sure-footed ponies carry their riders over rough moorlands, forests and mountainsides. Pony-trekking holidays are arranged by a number of organizations. Groups of riders may spend up to six hours a day trekking. A different route is generally taken each day, and a break is taken for a picnic lunch. Trekking ponies rarely move faster than a walk and are therefore ideal for nervous and inexperienced riders. Experienced riders may in fact find the pace too slow. Pony-trekking holidays are not suitable for children under 12 even when accompanied by an adult.

Rock climbing
The techniques of rock climbing were originally developed by mountaineers in order to scale rock faces on the ascent to mountain peaks. They practised the techniques on crags and cliffs nearer home. Eventually, by the end of the 19th century, rock climbing had become a sport in its own right. Hill walking and rock scrambling are sound ways for a beginner to gain some experience. The difference between scrambling and rock climbing is only in the degree of difficulty.

Correct footwear is the most important equipment in rock climbing. The majority of rock climbers wear special boots for the purpose. These are less heavy and much more supple than stiff-soled mountaineering boots. Plimsolls, which are much cheaper, may be worn as long as they fit well and have smooth rubber or neoprene soles. Some climbers wear helmets to protect their heads from falling stones and to lessen injury should they happen to fall.

Ropes are crucial for safety. Most beginners use a single 11mm rope which is 36–45 m (118–147 ft) long. More experienced climbers use two ropes that are 45 m (147 ft) or

Before climbing starts, leader and second are tied to each end of the rope. The second anchors himself so that he is held in position if the leader falls. The leader fixes running belays, clipping them to his climbing rope with a karabiner. On reaching a ledge the leader then finds two or three anchors and belays himself so that the second can follow.

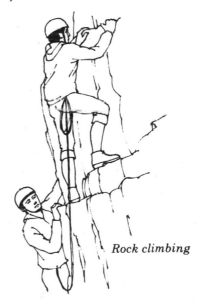

Rock climbing

50 m (164 ft) long. Normally, about six slings are carried, as well as pitons, nuts, karabiners, etc. (see Mountaineering).

When using ropes, rock climbers look first for safe natural anchor (belay) points such as a spike on a rock crag. If there is no good natural anchor then a piton or a nut must be used. The piton is hammered into a suitably sized crack in the rock and then the rope is attached to it. Nuts threaded on to a rope are used to firmly wedge the rope in rock fissures.

The rowing stroke

Lift

Drop

Pull

Rowing and Sculling

Rowing as a general term means propelling a boat by means of oars. In racing terms 'rowing' is the use of a single oar grasped in both hands, while the use of two oars, one in each hand, is called 'sculling'.

To row a dinghy, sit facing the stern (the back end) and place the oars in the rowlocks. To proceed on a straight course, pull evenly on the oars. At the beginning of the stroke, push the ends of the oars away from your chest, lifting the blades out of the water behind you. Then lower the blades into the water and pull. At the end of the stroke, raise the blades again and repeat the process. The rhythm is therefore: lift, drop, pull, raise. To row astern (backwards), lower the blades in the water and push on the oars instead of pulling.

To turn right, pull more steadily on the left oar. Similarly, to turn left, pull more strongly on the right oar. For extra leverage, push on the opposite oar while pulling on the turning oar.

Sailing

Sailing boats are classified according to their size and the way their masts and sails are arranged. There are many combinations of sails and masts, including the catboat, sloop, yawl, ketch and schooner.

Most small sailing boats are catboats or sloops. A type of catboat that children and beginners often learn to sail is called a sailing dinghy. It is small enough to handle and takes little looking after. You learn to sail quickly in a dinghy because it is very responsive to

Catboat

Sloop

Yawl

Ketch

Schooner

Direction
of wind

Sailing into the wind

Sailing across the wind

Sailing with the wind

every movement of the wind, crew weight and sail adjustment. All movements are quicker than in a larger boat, so you have to make quick decisions.

A boat is designed to sail in all directions – across the wind, into the wind and with the wind. The sail has a deep curve down the leading edge, or *luff*, which gradually flattens at the after part, or *leach* edge. When the wind blows across the curved surface of the sail a difference in air pressure is set up between one side of the sail and the other. This tends to force the boat along. If there were no means of controlling the boat it would be driven downwind no matter in which direction its bow happened to be pointing.

Direction is partly controlled by the rudder. Also, to prevent the boat moving sideways when sailing across the wind, there must be something which offers a large area of lateral resistance to redirect the force into a forward movement. This is the function of the keel or centreboard under the hull. The same effect is achieved by the deep underwater shape of some boats.

Sailing with the wind is called *running before the wind*. The sail, almost at right angles to the direction of the wind, is simply pushed along by it. Because of the great wind resistance, running is the slowest of manoeuvres. Racing boats sometimes use a special triangular sail called a spinnaker when running before the wind. The spinnaker is rigged out on its own boom called a spinnaker pole.

Sailing into the wind is called *beating to windward* or sailing

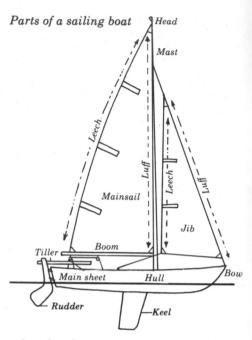

Parts of a sailing boat

Head
Mast
Leech
Luff
Leech
Luff
Mainsail
Jib
Tiller
Boom
Main sheet
Hull
Bow
Rudder
Keel

close hauled. A boat cannot sail directly into the wind (the sail would just flap and be useless) but it can head to within 45 degrees of the direction from which the wind is blowing before the sail starts to luff (flap). Progress is made by following a zig-zag course at a 45-degree angle to the wind. This is known as *tacking*. When tacking, the sails should be trimmed as parallel as possible to the boat's direction.

Sailing across the wind, i.e. with the wind *abeam*, is called *reaching*. This is the fastest of manoeuvres. When the wind is brought abaft the beam the boat is said to be *broad reaching*. A good helmsman becomes finely attuned to his boat. He can anticipate a change in wind direction and trims the sails accordingly.

Small sailing boats can easily

BOATING TERMS

abaft Towards the aft of a boat

abeam On a line at right angles to a ship's length

aft Towards the stern of a boat

athwartships Anything that runs across a boat from side to side is athwartships

beam A boat's breadth

booms and gaffs The spars that extend at right angles to the masts and hold the sails straight out. Booms are fastened to the bottom of the sail, gaffs are fastened at the top

bow The front part of a boat

even keel A boat is on an even keel when it is level in the fore and aft line

halyards The ropes that hoist and lower the sails

heeled If a boat leans to the wind it is heeled

leeward Away from the wind

listing A boat which has a permanent lean through a leak or a shift in weight is listing

mainmast The mast that holds the largest sail. Some large sailing boats have a shorter mast towards the stern (the mizzenmast) or a shorter mast towards the bow (foremast)

making way A boat is making way when it is moving through the water

masts Upright poles that hold the sails

midships The middle of a boat

port The side of a boat that is on the left when you face forwards

rig The way a ship's masts, sails etc. are arranged

running rigging A collective term for the sheets and halyards

sheets The ropes that trim the sails

spars The poles that support the sails. They include masts, booms and gaffs

standing rigging The wires that hold the mast upright. They consist of a fore stay, a back stay and shrouds on either side

starboard The side of a boat that is on the right when you face forwards

stern The hind part of a boat

trimming Adjusting the sails to take full advantage of the wind

under way A boat is under way when it is not made fast to the shore, not at anchor, or not secured to a buoy

windward Into the wind

---

capsize if not handled correctly. Experienced sailors, however, know how to place their weight and will let the sails out (slacken off) when the pressure on them is so great that the boat tips too far. All crew members of sailing boats should wear a life-jacket. If the boat capsizes they should cling on to it until they are rescued. A small sailing boat that has gone over on its side in the water can usually be pulled upright again by its crew.

Scuba diving

Scuba diving is the sport of diving with the use of self-contained underwater breathing apparatus, from which it gets its name. One or more tanks of compressed air are strapped to the diver's back and are connected to an air hose. The flow of air is controlled by a device called a demand regulator which ensures that the air pressure in the diver's lungs is equal to that in the water. A diver using one tank can remain at a depth of 12 m (40 ft) for about an hour providing he does not exert himself too strenuously. An increase in depth would result in his oxygen supply being used more rapidly.

The diver's other equipment includes a face mask, a weighted belt, swim-fins and a snorkel (for conserving the air supply in the tanks when he swims near the surface). A flotation vest is worn so that he may return quickly to the surface in the event of an emergency – the vest is simply inflated with air.

Even in warm seas the temperature is low below 9.5 m (30 ft) because the Sun's rays cannot penetrate to that depth. To overcome the problem of having to spend prolonged periods in the cold, the diver wears a wet suit. The suit is made of a spongy rubber called neoprene which has a smooth outer surface. It is lined with nylon inside. A wet suit must be very close-fitting. When the diver is immersed, a thin layer of cold water creeps in between the suit and his skin. This layer is quickly warmed up to body temperature, but it would not be if there were large pools of water between his body and an ill-fitting suit.

Experienced divers may go to depths of about 40 m (130 ft). Those with less experience should not go deeper than 18 m (60 ft).

Skiing

There are two principal types of skiing: Alpine (downhill) and Nordic (cross-country and jumping). Skis are long, narrow runners curved up at the front ends (tips)

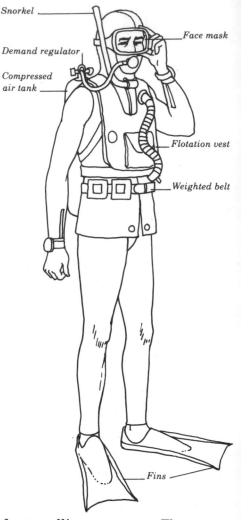

Snorkel

Face mask

Demand regulator

Compressed air tank

Flotation vest

Weighted belt

Fins

for travelling over snow. They are made of fibreglass, plastic, metal or wood. Alpine skis have bindings which clamp the ski-boot at the toe and heel. The bindings release the boot from the ski in the event of a fall, to help avoid injury. A safety strap prevents the released ski from hurtling down the slope where it might endanger other skiers.

Alpine ski-poles are usually

Downhill ski and boot

Cross-country ski and boot

metal. They are pointed at the bottom and have a ring called a *basket* about 8 cm (3 in) from the point. The baskets prevent the poles from sinking too deeply into the snow. The pole handle is usually rubber or plastic. It has a strap loop which fits around the skier's hand to prevent it slipping down the pole. Skiers carry a pole in each hand. These help them to maintain balance during manoeuvres.

Downhill skiing is both a popular recreation and a competitive sport. There are three basic manoeuvres to be learned. *Schussing* is skiing in a straight line without turning. *Traversing* is skiing across the slope at an angle. This manoeuvre can help skiers to control their speed. *Turning* is changing direction in a curving line when skiing downhill.

To slow down or stop without changing direction, skiers may use the *snowplough* method. The legs are spread open with the skis in a V form from the tips. In a *snowplough turn*, skiers make the V and then complete the manoeuvre by putting their weight on one ski only. Parallel turns, with the skis close together, are much more difficult, although more elegant in appearance.

Cross-country skiing is ski-touring across undulating terrain. The skis are narrower and lighter than Alpine skis. The boots are lighter, flexible and usually cut below the ankle. They are clamped to the ski only at the toe, leaving the heel free so that the skier can lift it when moving forward. The most basic movement is a diagonal

Downhill skiing

Schussing   Snow-plough   Traversing

Snow-plough turn   Parallel turn

Cross-country skiing: diagonal stride

stride, rather like skating. To travel faster the skier pushes on his ski-poles.

Ski-jumping is from hills up to 90 m (294 ft) in height. After sliding down a track called an inrun, jumpers try to leap as high as possible, keeping a straight, forward-leaning position.

At ski resorts there is usually a variety of ski trails, from low, smooth 'nursery' slopes to steeper, more challenging ones for the experts. Ski lifts and ski tows bring skiers back to the top of a slope after their run.

Skin diving

Skin diving is an underwater sport in which the participant holds his breath. Diving with the aid of self-contained breathing apparatus, on the other hand, is known as scuba diving (q.v.).

Most skin divers wear a face mask and flippers, and a short J-shaped breathing tube called a snorkel. A wet suit is often worn in cold waters. One of the main interests in the sport is the exploration of marine life. The mask permits clear vision for this. It consists of a glass plate in a rubber frame that fits over the face. The rubber flippers or swim-fins help even a mediocre swimmer to swim effortlessly through the water. Skin divers cannot descend very deeply because they must continuously return to the surface to breathe.

Surfing

Surfing is a thrilling water sport requiring good balance and split-second timing. It originated in Hawaii but is now enjoyed on open coastlines throughout the world.

The surfer stands on a long, narrow board which is borne towards the shore on the crest of a wave. Surfers sometimes train for surfboard riding by body surfing. A body surfer is swept along by the wave without using a board. He keeps his head down, his back arched and his hands at his sides. This sport helps a person to get used to the surf and to develop balance.

For a surfboard ride, the surfer lies on his board and paddles out beyond the breaking crests of waves to where the rollers rise up. As a wave approaches him, he paddles his board ahead of it. Then, as he coasts down the face of the wave, he rises to a standing position. The surfer rides the wave until it dies out near the beach. To increase

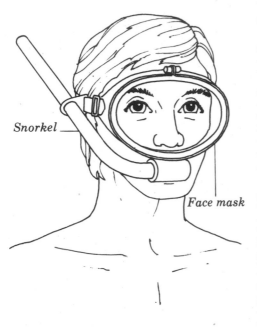

Snorkel

Face mask

speed and distance, skilled surfers usually ride diagonally towards the shore.

The size of surfboards varies according to the size of the waves they are to ride. For light surf, flat boards 120–180 cm (4–6 ft) long and 30 cm (1 ft) wide are used. Where the waves are up to 6 m (20 ft) in height, surfers use a tapered, hollow board 3–3.7 m (10–12 ft) long and 60 cm (2 ft) wide with a stabilizing fin near the back.

Another kind of surfing, which can be performed on long, gentle beaches, is bellyboarding, using a kind of miniature surfboard. You must stand in the water waist-deep and wait for the biggest waves. Face the shore and, as the wave is almost on top of you, with a forward movement of your arms leap on to the board. You do not stand on it but simply lie on it prone. If your

Skin diving with the aid of a face mask and snorkel

Surfing

1. Paddling the board

2. Rising to the standing position

3. Riding the wave

timing is right you will be carried forwards on the wave towards the shore.

Tobogganing

A toboggan is a sled without runners used for sliding down snow-covered slopes and artificial ice-covered chutes. It is usually built of straight-grained boards fastened together by cross-pieces. The front end is curved back. The sled is usually about 1.8–2.4 m (6–8 ft) long and 46 cm (1½ ft) wide. Several people can ride on it at a time, either sitting or in the prone position. Sitting on a toboggan is called lugeing; lying on it is called cresta tobogganing. A toboggan team usually consists of four people. The one at the back does the steering. Steering is achieved by either twisting the front or by dragging a foot in the snow.

An offshoot of tobogganing is bobsledding, which is a sport included in the Winter Olympics. Made of steel, bobsleds may weigh as much as 230 kg (500 lb). Speeds of 145 km/h (90 mph) can be reached. The bobsled run has sharp turns, but banked walls prevent the sleds from hurtling off course.

Water skiing

Water skiing originated in France in the 1920s. The water skier planes on the surface of the water, using one or two skis. (In trick riding, one ski may be used.) He is towed by a motor-boat which usually travels at speeds from 24 to 56 km/h (15 to 35 mph). There is a wooden handle attached to the towline for the skier to grip. The towline, which is often made of

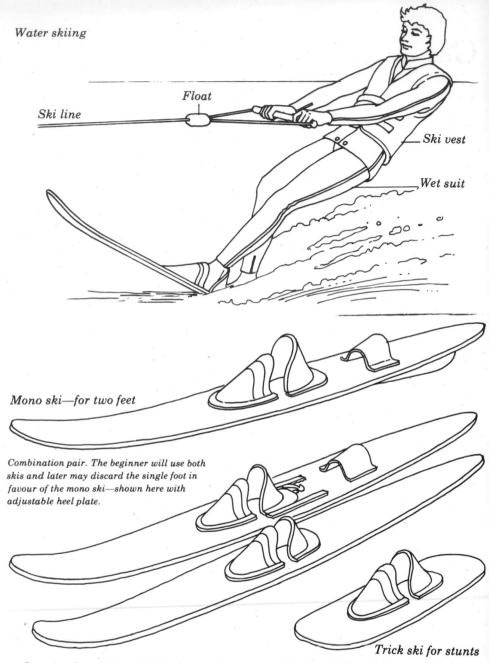

Water skiing

Ski line

Float

Ski vest

Wet suit

Mono ski—for two feet

Combination pair. The beginner will use both skis and later may discard the single foot in favour of the mono ski—shown here with adjustable heel plate.

Trick ski for stunts

nylon, is about 23 m (75 ft) long. A typical water ski is of wood, 16.5 cm (6½ in) wide and 175 cm (5 ft 9 in) long, with a stabilizing fin near the heel. The skier uses tight-fitting rubber foot bindings which stretch, if he falls, and release his feet without injury.

Car and Plane Spotting

Car spotting

Cars travelling outside their countries of registration carry special identification letters as well as their normal number plates. In the following list of national markings, countries bearing an asterisk (*) are those where the rule of the road is to drive on the left, while for the others it is to drive on the right. Among the most frequently seen are:

MARKING	COUNTRY
A	Austria
ADN	Yemen People's Democratic Republic*
AL	Albania
AND	Andorra
AUS	Australia,* Norfolk Islands*
B	Belgium
BDS	Barbados*
BG	Bulgaria
BH	Belize*
BL	Lesotho*
BP	Botswana*
BR	Brazil
BRG	Guyana*
BRN	Bahrain*
BRU	Brunei*
BS	Bahamas*
BUR	Burma*
C	Cuba
CDN	Canada
CGO	Congo
CH	Switzerland
CI	Ivory Coast
CL	Sri Lanka
CNB	Malaysia*
CO	Colombia
CR	Costa Rica
CS	Czechoslovakia
CY	Cyprus*
D	Germany (Federal Republic)
DK	Denmark, Faroe Islands
DOM	Dominican Republic

MARKING	COUNTRY
DY	Dahomey
DZ	Algeria
E	Spain, Balearic Islands, Canary Islands, Spanish Guinea
EAK	Kenya*
EAU	Uganda*
EAZ	Tanzania*
EC	Ecuador
EIR	Republic of Ireland*
ET	Egypt
F	France, and French overseas departments
FL	Liechtenstein
GB	Great Britain and Northern Ireland*
GBA	Alderney*
GBG	Guernsey*
GBJ	Jersey*
GBM	Isle of Man*
GBY	Malta, Gozo*
GBZ	Gibraltar
GCA	Guatemala
GH	Ghana*
GR	Greece, Crete, Dodecanese Islands
H	Hungary
HK	Hong Kong*
I	Italy, Sardinia, Sicily
IL	Israel
IND	India*
IR	Iran

MARKING	COUNTRY	MARKING	COUNTRY
IRQ	Iraq	RL	Lebanon
IS	Iceland*	RM	Madagascar
		RMM	Mali
J	Japan*	RNR	Zambia*
JA	Jamaica*, Cayman	RNY	Malawi*
	Islands*, Turks and	RSM	San Marino
	Caicos Islands*	RSR	Zimbabwe*
JOR	Jordan		
		S	Sweden
K	Kampuchea	SD	Swaziland*
KWT	Kuwait	SF	Finland
		SGP	Singapore*
L	Luxembourg	SK	Sarawak*
LAO	Laos	SME	Surinam
LT	Libya	SN	Senegal
		SU	USSR
MA	Morocco	SUD	Sudan
MC	Monaco	SWA	South West Africa*
MEX	Mexico	SY	Seychelles*
MS	Mauritius*	SYR	Syria
N	Norway	T	Thailand*
NA	Netherlands Antilles	TG	Togo
NGN	West Irian	TN	Tunisia
NIC	Nicaragua	TR	Turkey
NIG	Niger*	TT	Trinidad and Tobago*
NL	Netherlands	TZ	Tanzania*
NZ	New Zealand*		
		U	Uruguay
P	Portugal, the Azores,	USA	United States of
	Cape Verde Islands,		America
	Madeira, São João		
	Baptista de Ajuda	V	Vatican City
PA	Panama	VN	Vietnam
PAK	Pakistan*		
PE	Peru	WAG	Gambia*
PI	Philippine Islands	WAL	Sierra Leone*
PL	Poland	WAN	Nigeria*
PTM	Malaysia*	WD	Dominica*
PY	Paraguay	WG	Grenada
		WL	St Lucia
R	Romania	WS	Western Samoa*
RA	Argentina	WV	St Vincent*
RCB	Zaire		
RCH	Chile	YU	Yugoslavia
RH	Haiti	YV	Venezuela
RI	Indonesia		
RIM	Mauritania	ZA	South Africa*

IDENTIFYING CAR MAKES BY THEIR BADGES

Car badges are the manufacturers' means of making their products readily recognizable. Originally all that seemed necessary was a brass nameplate fixed to the front of the vehicle or on the dashboard. Later, trade marks were introduced. Once a trade mark was familiar there was no need for a passer-by to read the name plate because the car was instantly identifiable.

The trade mark was either in a special style of lettering or pictorial. Both types of car badge are used today.

BMW

Mercedes-Benz

Volvo

British Leyland

Jaguar

Volkswagen

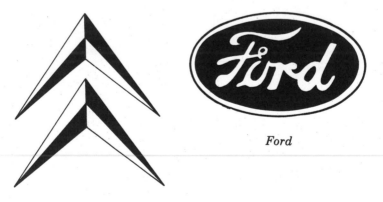

Ford

Citroën

Aston Martin

Renault

Fiat

MG   *Datsun*

Plane spotting

As a means of transport, the aircraft offers many advantages over surface vehicles. The main one is that it has the freedom of the skies; it is able to use the extra dimension of height, unfettered by the limitations of over-populated land. Today, however, even this advantage is diminishing as more and more aircraft join the airways and crowd-holding patterns above their destinations, awaiting their turn to land.

Away from these crowded areas aircraft give us a wide choice of destination and direction. They can travel over land and sea, mountain and city, connecting countries, continents and islands. Some people fly their own aircraft on business, for pleasure or as farm machines, but most air travellers are chauffeured by airline pilots. A great deal of freight is also transported by air.

The many demands we make on flying machines have made it necessary to build a vast range of different aircraft: civil airliners, helicopters, military aircraft and so on. Each type is either specially designed for its purpose or adapted for use with special equipment. Many of these aircraft are common sights and are easily recognized. Others, although just as common, are less easily identified. In these pages you will be able to look at pictures of aircraft in use today, learn their names and some of the details of their specifications. Few people would not recognize Concorde, but do you know its wing span? On the other hand, can you name an aircraft made specially

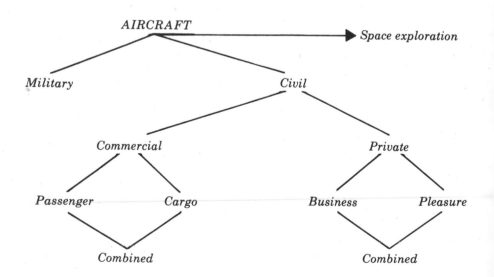

for long-range maritime patrol?

The two main categories are military and civil, which can be subdivided as shown in the diagram on page 170.

Many countries in the world have aircraft industries producing aircraft of their own, while some countries have joined together to produce combined efforts. Concorde, the Airbus and the Jaguar fighter are products of such co-operation. America probably has the greatest number of constructors but the USSR, Germany, the Netherlands, France, Britain, Poland, Italy, Switzerland, Brazil, India, New Zealand, Spain, Japan, Australia and many others add their contributions to what is a huge list of varied types of aircraft. You are unlikely to see many of these unless you make a special study of aircraft. Plane spotting can become a fascinating hobby.

PRIVATE, EXECUTIVE AND AGRICULTURAL AIRCRAFT

BAe HS 125

United Kingdom
Accommodation: crew 2; normal seating for 8; alternative arrangements for up to 14
Power: two 3,700 lb (1,678 kg) thrust Garrett AiResearch TFE 731–3 turbofans
Performance: 495 mph (796 km/h)
Range: 2,705 miles (4,353 km)
Span: 47 ft (14.32 m)
Length: 50 ft 8½ in (15.4 m)

The HS 125 is a popular executive jet, the current series (the 700)

having the specification listed above. The 700 first flew on 28 June 1976 and production started on 8 November that year. The prototype was built by De Havilland and was designated the DH 125. It first flew on 13 August 1962. Hawker Siddeley continued the model as the HS 125 and produced civil, military and hybrid versions. The series 1 through to the series 600 were powered by turbojets. The 700, in the interests of fuel economy, is fitted with turbofans. Further developments are planned.

BEECHCRAFT SKIPPER 77

USA
Accommodation: two-seat primary trainer
Power: one 115 hp Avco Lycoming four-cylinder horizontally opposed engine
Performance: approx. 130 mph (209 km/h)
Span: 30 ft (9.14 m)
Length: 23 ft 10¾ in (7.2 m)

Designed as a two-seater, side-by-side trainer, the Skipper 77 is intended to be economical in initial cost and in running and maintenance. The prototype flew in 1975. The first production prototype flew in September 1978.

PIPER PA-44 SEMINOLE

USA
Accommodation: pilot and 3 passengers
Power: two 180 hp Avco Lycoming 0–360–EIAD four-cylinder horizontally opposed engines
Performance: max. speed 192 mph (309 km/h)

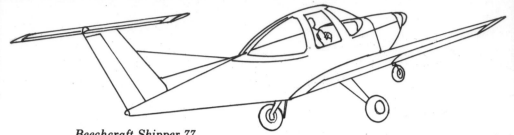

Beechcraft Skipper 77

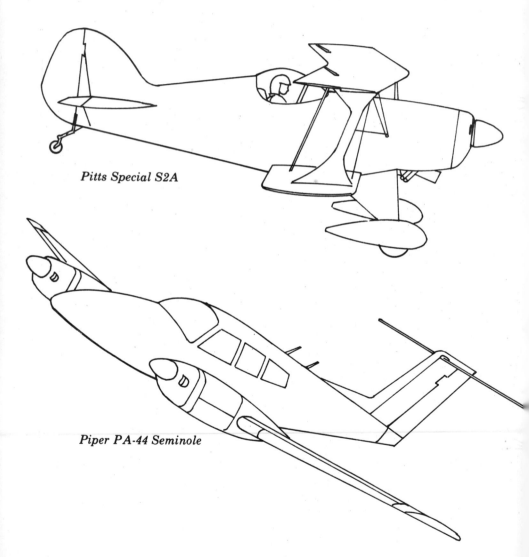

Pitts Special S2A

Piper PA-44 Seminole

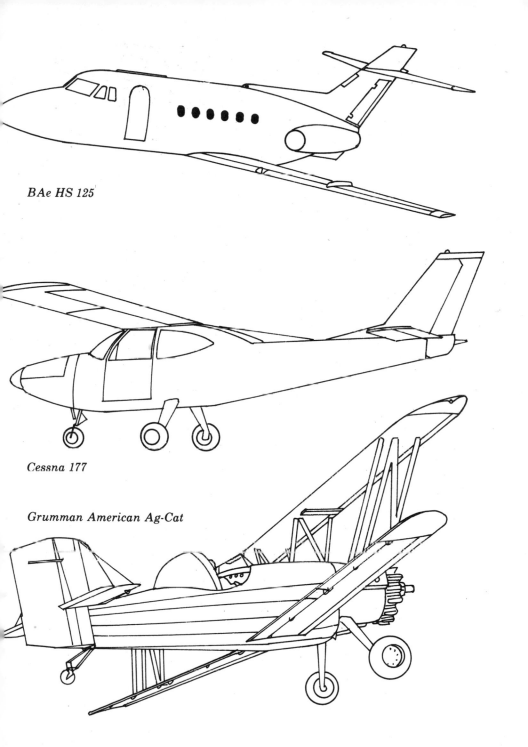

BAe HS 125

Cessna 177

Grumman American Ag-Cat

Range: max. 960 miles (1,544 km)
Span: 38 ft 6½ in (11.7 m)
Length: 27 ft 7 in (8.4 m)

The Seminole is a light cabin monoplane, one of the many manufactured by Piper. The prototype flew in May 1976 and production commenced in May 1978.

PITTS SPECIAL S2A

USA
Accommodation: pilot plus one
Power: 200 hp Lycoming
Performance: max. speed 140 mph (225 km/h)
Range: 450 miles (724 km)
Span: 20 ft (6 m)
Length: 18 ft 3 in (5.5 m)

Although the original Pitts Special flew as long ago as September 1944, these aircraft are still often seen in air displays performing aerobatics, the purpose for which they were built. Single- and two-seat models were produced. Power was increased from the original 90 hp to the present 200 hp. Its achievements include the 1972 US national team successes. The British Rothmans Aerobatics team uses S2As.

CESSNA MODEL 177

USA
Accommodation: 4 plus 2 children
Power: 180 hp Lycoming
Performance: 140–170 mph (225–273 km/h)
Range: 785–1,005 miles (1,263–1,617 km)
Span: 35 ft 6 in (10.8 m)
Length: 27 ft 3 in (8.3 m)

The Cessna model 177 was introduced in 1971 and by the beginning of 1977 nearly 5,000 had been delivered. The 177 has a tricycle undercarriage and a cantilever wing, the latest model having a gull-wing shape to the leading edge. An extremely popular aircraft for private fliers, the 177 is part of the company's range of light planes.

GRUMMAN AMERICAN AG-CAT

USA
Crew: 1
Power: latest power units used are Pratt and Witney 450 or 600 hp
Performance: 80–100 mph (128–160 km/h)
Span: 35 ft 11 in (10.9 m)
Length: 24 ft 3 in (7.4 m)

The Ag-cat is a single-seat agricultural crop-spraying biplane which was introduced in May 1967. It has an outstanding safety record.

COMMERCIAL AIRCRAFT

CONCORDE

United Kingdom and France
Accommodation: crew 3 or 4; passengers 128 or 144
Power: four 38,050 lb (17,259 kg) thrust reheat Rolls-Royce/SNECMA Olympus 593 Mk 602 turbojets
Performance: max. cruising speed Mach 2.02 (1,354 mph, 2,179 km/h) at 50,000 ft (15,240 m)
Range: 3,870 miles (6,228 km)
Span: 83 ft 10 in (25.6 m)
Length: 203 ft 9 in (62 m)

Concorde, first planned in 1955, is

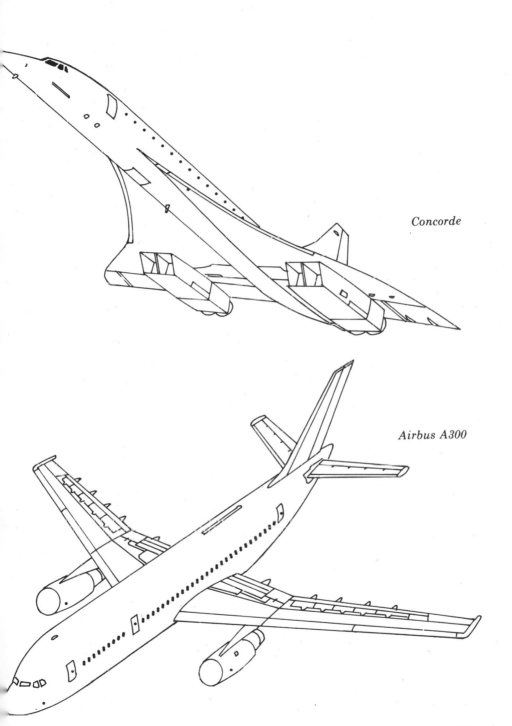

Concorde

Airbus A300

the world's first supersonic airliner to be used in regular passenger-carrying service. The combined resources of France's Aerospatiale and the British Aircraft Corporation achieved a first flight, with Concorde 001, on 2 March 1969 from Toulouse. Supersonic speed was achieved on 1 October 1969, and Mach 2 on 4 November 1970. The British Concorde, 002, flew from Filton on 9 April 1969. Production models, modified with a longer fuselage and revised wing leading-edge, made their maiden flights on 6 December 1973 and 13 February 1974. The first fare-paying passengers were carried on 21 January 1976. Accommodation is for 128 passengers in one-class luxury, or 144 in high-density loading.

Concorde has been received with mixed feelings. Some people are so enthusiastic that they have formed Concorde fan clubs and arrange outings to fly in it. Opposition is mainly on the grounds of noise. Because of this, Concorde is denied access to some airports and is not allowed to fly over some countries. The soaring cost of fuel has also caused problems. The result is that many orders have not been taken up and at the beginning of 1979 five aircraft remained unsold.

AIRBUS A300

United Kingdom, France, Germany, the Netherlands, Spain
Accommodation: flight crew 3; passengers 220–336
Power: two 51,000 lb (23,133 kg) thrust General Electric CF6-50C turbofans

Performance: max. cruising speed 578 mph (930 km/h) at 28,000 ft (8,534 m)
Range: 2,618 miles (4,212 km)
Span: 147 ft (44.84 m)
Length: 175 ft 9 in (53.75 m)

The Airbus is built by a French/German/British/Dutch/Spanish consortium, with the final assembly being carried out at Aerospatiale in Toulouse. The plane is a wide-bodied, twin-engined 'jumbo' jet, built for short or medium distances. It is the quietest of the big jets because of the special design of the engines.

The project was started in 1965 and the first A300 Airbus entered service with Air France on 23 May 1974. There are several variations offering alternatives in seating and range. Further development work will produce the A310, a short-bodied variant, due to fly in 1981.

BAC ONE-ELEVEN

United Kingdom
Accommodation: minimum crew 2; passengers 119 max.
Power: two 12,550 lb (5,692 kg) thrust Rolls-Royce Spey turbofans
Performance: max. cruising speed 550 mph (885 km/h) at 21,000 ft (7,308 m)
Range: 1,440 miles (2,316 km)
Span: 93 ft 6 in (28.5 m)
Length: 93 ft 6 in (28.5 m)

From a project initiated in 1956 by Hunting Aircraft Ltd., the BAC One-Eleven first flew on 20 August 1963. Original plans had gone through several changes and the resulting aircraft seated 79 people.

The standard version was the 200; for the American market it was the 400; and an uprated engine specification was given to the 300. Certification was given on 6 April 1965 and BUA flew the first One-Eleven service on 9 April. Later variations have been the 500 (longer fuselage) and the 475 with hotted-up engines and low-pressure tyres. The details above refer to the 670 which started testing in April 1979.

BOEING 747

USA
Accommodation: flight crew 3; first-class passengers 66; economy class passengers 308; alternative: 447 or 490 (all economy)
Power: four 47,000 lb (21,319 kg) thrust Pratt and Whitney JT 9D 7W turbofans
Performance: max. speed 608 mph (978 km/h)
Range: max. with special equipment 7,180 miles (11,552 km)
Span: 195 ft 8 in (59.64 m)
Length: 231 ft 4 in (70.51 m)

The details above refer to the 747-200B. This is one of the many variations of the 747 which, under different series numbers, offers alternatives in seating arrangements and capacities, cargo-carrying facilities, and a choice of engines. Some have an extended flight range with reduced carrying capacity, and there are smaller, economy versions.

The 747 was developed from the 707; it is the world's largest airliner and the first 'jumbo'. First flown on 9 February 1967, it entered service with Pan Am on 22 January 1970.

By the beginning of 1979 over 400 had been ordered. The 747 is now in service with airlines all over the world. One interesting variation has been used by NASA to carry the space shuttle Orbiter on its air launch.

FOKKER F28 FELLOWSHIP Mk 4000

Netherlands
Accommodation: flight crew 2; passengers 85 single-class
Power: two 9,850 lb (4,468 kg) thrust Rolls-Royce RB183-2 Spey Mk 555-15 turbofans
Performance: max. cruising speed 523 mph (841 km/h) at 23,000 ft (7,010 m)
Range: 2,566 miles (4,128 km)
Span: 82 ft 3 in (25.07 m)
Length: 97 ft 1¾ in (29.61 m)

The Fokker F28 Fellowship was planned in early 1962 as a short-haul jet airliner to complement the F27 Friendship, which was later to become the world's best-selling turboprop airliner. The Fellowship was originally designed as a 65-seat one-class aircraft – the Mk 1000. A version was made with a forward, side cargo loading door for combined cargo/passenger work. The Mk 2000 was longer and carried 79 passengers over shorter distances.

Currently in production are the Mks 3000 and 4000, also the 6000 and the 6600 which is 87 in (221 cm) longer. These later models have a greater wing span than the originals and better noise reduction. Plans are in hand for the F29 series which will seat 115.

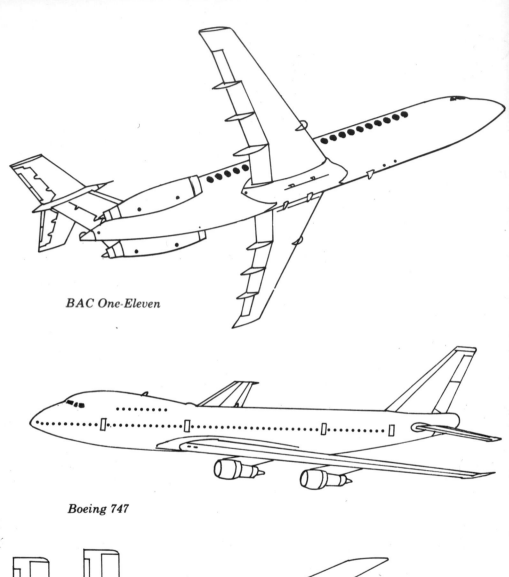

BAC One-Eleven

Boeing 747

Shorts 330

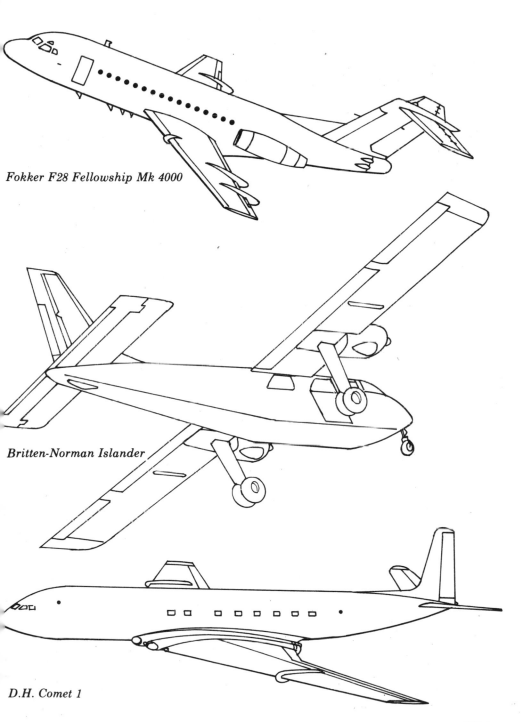

Fokker F28 Fellowship Mk 4000

Britten-Norman Islander

D.H. Comet 1

MCDONNELL DOUGLAS DC-10 SERIES 30

USA
Accommodation: flight crew 3+2; passengers 225–70 (max: 380+11 crew)
Power: three 52,500 lb (23,814 kg) thrust General Electric CF6-50CI turbofans
Performance: 594 mph (955 km/h) at 31,000 ft (9,449 m)
Range: 7,400 miles (11,906 km) at 540 mph (869 km/h)
Span: 165 ft 4 in (50 m)
Length: 181 ft 4 in (55 m)

Design work started in 1966 on an American Airlines specification for a 'jumbo' twin jet. The three-engine formula was later adopted. First flight of the series 10 was on 29 August 1970 and the first service flight was a year later. Alternative specifications of power, size and range have been provided by the series 30 and 40 variants. Initial orders from American and United airlines helped to give the three-jet jumbo market to the DC-10 over the Lockheed Tri-Star. Many airlines the world over have DC-10s in their fleets.

DE HAVILLAND COMET 1

United Kingdom
Accommodation: 36 passengers
Power: four 5,000 lb (2,268 kg) thrust D. H. Ghost turbojets
Performance: max. speed 480 mph (772 km/h) at 40,000 ft (12,192 m)
Range: 2,000 miles (3,218 km)

The Comet is not now in production in any form although some Comet 4s are still flying with Dan Air of London. The importance of the Comet 1 is that it was the world's first passenger airliner powered by jet engines. In 1952 it introduced a new standard of speed and passenger comfort previously unknown in commercial aircraft. In a pressurized cabin, passengers enjoyed smooth, almost silent travel at 40,000 ft, moving at 480 mph. Britain had made a very significant 'first', leaving the rest of the flying world behind – and below. Unfortunately, structural weakness, arising from the pressurization of the cabin, led to two disastrous crashes. All Comets were grounded except for testing. The development programme was held up for a time. Comet 2 was used by the RAF. Then came the Comet 3, built as a development airframe prototype for the Comet 4. The Comet 4 entered service in 1958 at the same time as the Boeing 707. As a transatlantic competitor the Comet 4 was outclassed.

LOCKHEED TRI-STAR

USA
Accommodation: flight crew 3; passengers 222 (economy) 24 (first-class)
Power: three 48,000 lb (21,772 kg) thrust Rolls-Royce RB211-524 turbofans
Performance: max. cruise speed 608 mph (978 km/h) at 31,000 ft (9,449 m)
Range: 4,855 miles (7,811 km)
Span: 155 ft 4 in (47.24 m)
Length: 164 ft 2 in (50 m)

In 1966, following a four-year lull

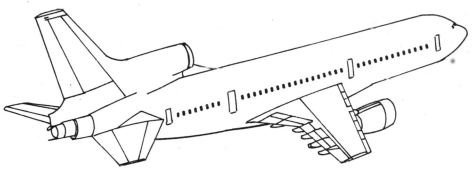

Lockheed Tri-Star

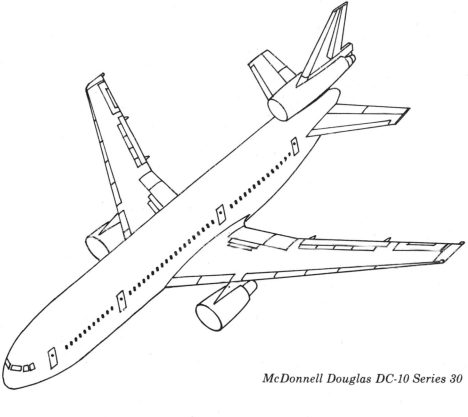

McDonnell Douglas DC-10 Series 30

after the ending of the production of the Electra, Lockheed took up the American Airlines specification enquiry and designed the model 385 Tri-Star. Using the three-engine format (one under each wing and one in the rear fuselage), the Tri-Star competed with the DC-10 for the American order – and lost. Other internal airlines in America placed orders and production started in 1968. The first flight was made on 16 November 1970 and deliveries began in April 1972. Various models have been built, a current one being the L-1011-500 whose specification is listed above. Powered by Rolls-Royce RB211 engines, the Tri-Star project was in financial trouble when Rolls-Royce went bankrupt in 1971. Financial recovery has been slow.

SHORTS 330

United Kingdom
Accommodation: crew 2; up to 30 passengers and 1,000 lb (454 kg) baggage
Power: two 1,173 shp Pratt and Whitney PT6A-45A turboprops
Performance: max. cruise speed 221 mph (355 km/h) at 10,000 ft (3,048 m)
Range: 1,013 miles (1,630 km)
Span: 74 ft 9 in (22.78 m)
Length: 58 ft 0½ in (17.69 m)

The Shorts 330 is a third-level airliner and utility transport designed for commuter travel and local transportation. Directly developed from the Shorts Skyvan, the 330 is very boxlike in shape. It has the ability to take off and land on restricted airfields, and is used

worldwide by various operators. There is also a maritime surveillance version equipped with special radar equipment.

BRITTEN-NORMAN ISLANDER

United Kingdom
Accommodation: flight crew 1 or 2; up to 9 passengers
Power: two 260 hp Avco Lycoming six-cylinder engines
Performance: max. speed 180 mph (290 km/h) at sea level
Range: 700 miles (1,126 km)
Span: 49 ft (14.94 m)
Length: 35 ft 7¾ in (10.86 m)

The Islander is a light, twin-engined, passenger-carrying aircraft designed for short-haul work. It is able to take off and land in restricted space. Economy in cost and maintenance has added to its attraction and made it the best-selling multi-engined light commercial aircraft. By early 1978 sales had reached 750. It was first flown on 24 April 1967 and deliveries began on 13 August. It is now made under licence in Romania. Variations include crop sprayers, fire fighters and a turboprop version called the Turbo Islander.

MILITARY AIRCRAFT

GENERAL DYNAMICS F.16

USA
Crew: 1 pilot (F.16A); two-seat trainer (F.16B)
Power: one 25,000 lb (11,340 kg) thrust reheat Pratt and Witney turbofan
Performance: 1,255 mph

(2,019 km/h) at 36,000 ft (10,973 m)
Range: max. 340 miles (547 km)
tactical radius with 6 Mk-82 bombs
Armament: one 20mm cannon
plus 15,200 lb (6,795 kg) of bombs
and rockets
Span: 31 ft (9.45 m)
Length: 47 ft 7¼ in (14.5 m)

The F.16 is a lightweight fighter of
advanced aerodynamic design. It
attains stable flight only at supersonic speeds, when it is highly
manoeuvrable. The first prototypes
flew on 29 January 1974. It is now
operational in many countries.

BAe HARRIER G.R. Mk 3

United Kingdom
Crew: 1 pilot
Power: one 21,500 lb (9,752 kg)
thrust Rolls-Royce Bristol Pegasus
Mk 103 vectored-thrust turbofan
Performance: 720 mph (1,158 km/h)
Range: tactical radius 260 miles
(418 km)
Armament: two 30mm cannon
plus three 1,000-lb (454-kg) bombs
and 36 38mm rockets
Span: 25 ft 3 in (7.69 m)
Length: 45 ft 7¼ in (13.86 m)

The Harrier is the world's first
V/STOL strike and reconnaissance
fighter. The first pre-production
prototype flew on 31 August 1966.
It entered service with the RAF on
28 December 1967. Its vertical take-
off is achieved by deflecting the
engine thrust downwards through
rotating nozzles which turn to give
forward thrust for normal flight.
Naval and trainer versions have
also been built.

BAe NIMROD

United Kingdom
Crew: operating crew of 12 (2
pilots, 1 flight engineer, 9 navigators
and sensor operators)
Power: four 12,160 lb (5,516 kg)
thrust Rolls-Royce RB168–20 Spey
Mk 250 turbofans
Performance: max. speed 575 mph
(925 km/h)
Range: up to 5,755 miles (9,259 km),
12 hours endurance
Armament: homing torpedoes,
mines, depth charges, four AS 12
air/sea missiles
Span: 114 ft (35 m)
Length: 126 ft 9 in (38.4 m)

The Nimrod is a long-range
maritime patrol aircraft fully
equipped for sea search and attack
operations. In peacetime it is used
in air/sea search and rescue; its
extensive electronics and radar
equipment enable it to carry out
communications links and rescue
direction. The first Nimrods were
built on Comet 4C airframes and
the first one flew on 23 May 1967.
Development and improvement
work still continues.

DASSAULT-BREGUET MIRAGE F1

France
Crew: 1 pilot
Power: one 15,873 lb (7,200 kg)
thrust SNECMA Atar 9K-50
turbojet
Performance: Mach 2.2 at 39,370 ft
(12,000 m)
Range: 560 miles (901 km) with
max. combat load
Armament: two 30mm cannon

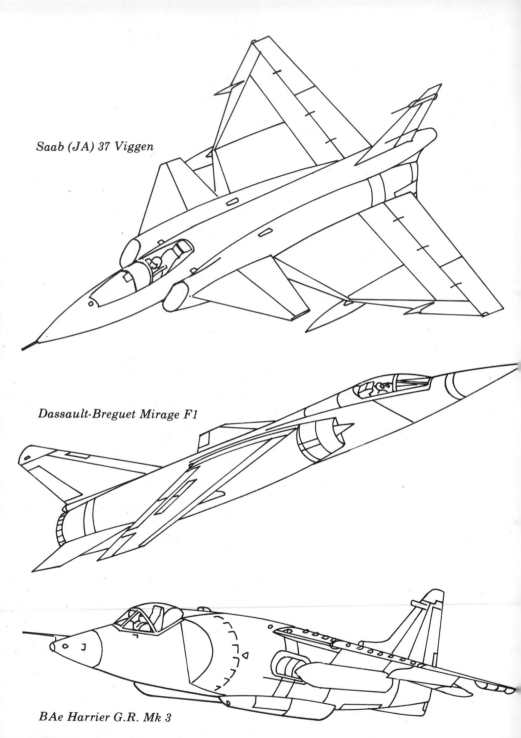

Saab (JA) 37 Viggen

Dassault-Breguet Mirage F1

BAe Harrier G.R. Mk 3

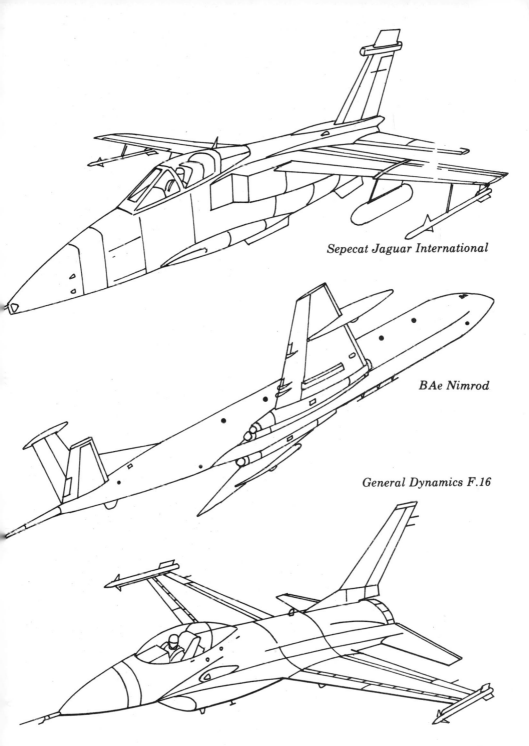

Sepecat Jaguar International

BAe Nimrod

General Dynamics F.16

185

plus up to 8,820 lb (4,000 kg) bombs
and rockets
Span: 27 ft 6¾ in (8.38 m)
Length: 49 ft 2½ in (15 m)

The Mirage F1 single-seat multipurpose fighter prototype flew on
23 December 1966. The first
production plane flew on 15
February 1973. Currently about five
are produced each month. Its
primary use is for all-weather
interception at any altitude but it
is also suitable for ground attack.
The two-seat version is used as a
trainer.

MIG 25 FOXBAT

USSR
Crew: 1 pilot
Power: two 24,250 lb (11,000 kg)
thrust afterburning turbofans
Performance: max. speed Mach 3.2
Range: 700 miles (1,126 km)
Armament: four AA6 Acrid air-to-
air missiles
Span: 45 ft 11 in (14 m)
Length: 73 ft 2 in (22 m)

The MiG 25 entered service in
1970–1 and was recognized as the
best interceptor aircraft in the
world. It is used for interception
and reconnaissance work and can
operate at 80,000 ft (24,384 m). In
1975 the MiG 25 set a world record
by climbing to 114,829 ft (35,000 m)
in 251 seconds.

SEPECAT JAGUAR
INTERNATIONAL

France and United Kingdom
Crew: 1 pilot
Power: two 5,368 lb (2,435 kg) thrust

Rolls-Royce/Turbomeca Adour
Mk 102 turbofans
Performance: max. speed
1,057 mph (1,700 km/h) at 32,810 ft
(10,000 m)
Range: tactical range 710 miles
(1,142 km) max.
Armament: two 30mm cannon
plus up to 10,000 lb (4,536 kg)
bombs and rockets
Span: 28 ft 6 in (8.68 m)
Length: 50 ft 11 in (15 m)

The Jaguar was first flown as a
prototype on 8 September 1968, and
the first production flight took
place on 2 November 1971. Jointly
produced by Britain and France,
the Jaguar is in service with their
air forces and with other countries.
The Jaguar is a single-seat strike
aircraft. It is highly versatile and
able to operate from forward,
semi-prepared bases.

GRUMMAN TOMCAT F-14A

USA
Crew: 2
Power: two 20,900 lb (9,480 kg)
thrust reheat Pratt and Witney
TF30-P-412A turbofans
Performance: max. speed
1,545 mph (2,486 km/h) at 40,000 ft
(12,192 m)
Range: tactical radius 450 miles
(724 km)
Armament: one 20mm cannon
plus air-to-air missiles or bombs
Span: 64 ft 1½ in (19.5 m) max.
37 ft 7 in (11.5 m) min.
Length: 61 ft 11¾ in (18.8 m)

The Tomcat is a swing-wing
carrier-based fighter. Its multipurpose role includes carrier task

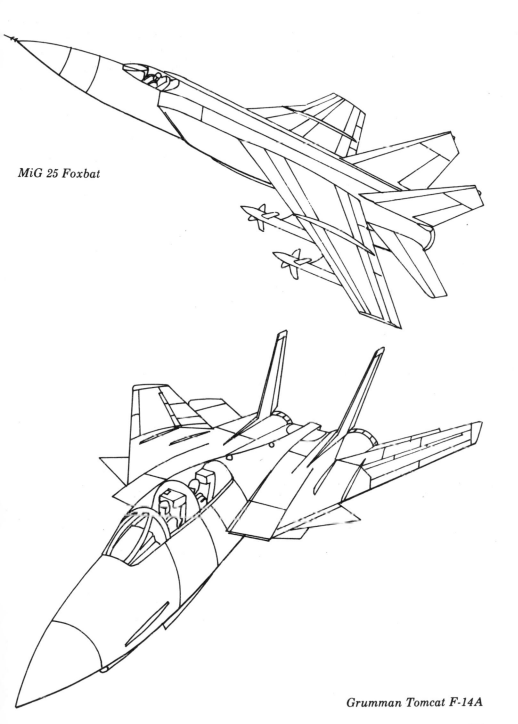

MiG 25 Foxbat

Grumman Tomcat F-14A

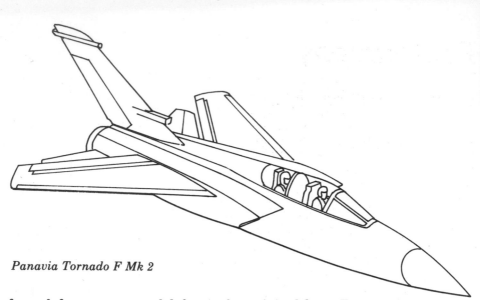

Panavia Tornado F Mk 2

force defence, escort and defence of attack aircraft, and ground target tactical attack. The first prototype flew on 21 December 1970.

PANAVIA TORNADO F Mk 2

United Kingdom
Crew: 2
Power: two 16,000 lb (7,257 kg) thrust reheat Turbo-union RB199 Mk 107 turbofans
Performance: max. speed 1,385 mph (2,229 km/h) at 36,000 ft (10,973 m)
Range: 450 miles (724 km) from base
Armament: one 27mm cannon plus rockets and bombs
Span: 45 ft 8 in (14 m)
Length: 58 ft 9 in (18 m)

The F Mk 2 is the United Kingdom's version of the original British/German/Italian project. It differs in engine power, radar equipment, length and fuel capacity. The Mk 2 has an air-to-air refuelling facility. This multipurpose fighter entered service in 1974 in its original form. From 1979 it became the Mk 2.

SAAB (JA) 37 VIGGEN

Sweden
Crew: 1 pilot
Power: one 28,108 lb (12,747 kg) thrust afterburning Volvo Flygmotor RM8B turbofan
Performance: max. speed 1,320 mph (2,124 km/h) above 36,000 ft (10, 973 m)
Range: 250 miles (402 km) tactical radius
Armament: one 30mm cannon plus two air-to-air missiles
Span: 34 ft 9¼ in (10.6 m)
Length: 50 ft 8¼ in (15.5 m)

The Viggen is a multipurpose combat aircraft used for ground attack, interception and reconnaissance, and training. Its unusual wing arrangement gives it extremely good take-off and landing characteristics. It was first flown in June 1974. Its predecessor, the AJ 37, originated in 1967.

Photography

Photography allows as much scope for creativity as any other art form. The word itself, from the Greek *photos* (light) and *graphos* (writing), literally means 'writing with light'. Light, with its infinite gradations, is the medium of the camera-artist.

When you press the shutter of a camera, light passes through the aperture and lens to strike a film, or a plate, at the back of the camera. The surface of the film or the plate is coated with light-sensitive chemicals. When the light strikes the surface, chemical changes occur so that when the film is developed and fixed, an image is clearly visible on the print or transparency. This, basically, is the way all cameras work.

The simplest model is the box camera. Provided that you make the best of its limitations, it is capable of producing good pictures. In more elaborate models, the size of the aperture (denoted by an f-number) can be controlled by a diaphragm.

The shutter, too, can be adjusted, to regulate the length of time the diaphragm will admit light through the lens. The lens itself will be bigger and of better quality than the lens in a simple box camera.

By manipulating the size of the aperture and the speed of the shutter, you can extend your range of subjects considerably. If you are photographing outdoors on a sunny day, for instance, when there is plenty of light, a small aperture and fast shutter speed will suffice. In the evening, when the daylight is fading, you will need to use a larger aperture and a slower shutter speed to admit more of the available light to activate the chemicals on the film. Some cameras have automatic exposure meters but it is great fun and good experience to work out your own exposure times and speeds until you can afford to buy an exposure meter of your own. When making exposures longer than 1/25 of a second, it is advisable to use a

How a box camera works

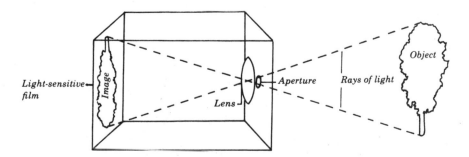

Light-sensitive film · Image · Lens · Aperture · Rays of light · Object

tripod, or to rest the camera on a stable object, since it is difficult to hold a camera steady for longer periods.

Whether you use black and white or colour, roll or cassette film, you will have to take into account the film speed (the light-sensitivity of the chemical emulsion on the film) when calculating your exposures. A fast film needs less light to activate the chemicals than a slow film. The speed is indicated on the packet; two gradings commonly used are DIN and ASA. Colour film is not generally available in the faster gradings. Ask the advice of your local photographic dealer (and tell him the type of camera you use) when you buy film. Remember to go indoors or into shadow when you load the camera. Otherwise, light may get into the edges of the film and ruin it by causing the chemical reactions to take place too soon.

There are many different kinds of camera available. The best advice is to buy as good a camera as you can afford – preferably under the guidance of a knowledgeable friend. A secondhand camera from a reputable dealer may be the ideal solution if your financial means are limited. The older-type folding cameras, for instance, often contain excellent lenses and give first-rate results.

Perhaps the best all-purpose model is the so-called miniature camera, which takes standard 35mm film with perforated edges. This camera has many advantages for the beginner. Being light, it is easily portable; the lenses are often interchangeable; and the film is comparatively inexpensive. It is an ideal camera, especially for 'human interest' and sports photography.

Other models include the single-lens reflex camera. The main advantage of this type is that you can view through the lens the exact scene you are about to photograph. The twin-lens reflex model has a viewing lens just above the 'taking' lens. The viewing lens enables you to see your subject as you take the picture. However, if a near object is being photographed, the image you see won't coincide exactly with the image on the film because of the different position of the two lenses. For all normal purposes, however, the twin-lens reflex model is perfectly satisfactory.

Let's assume you are about to take your first pictures. Why not start with a portrait of a member of the family? If using a box camera, do not move in close to the subject, or the resulting picture will be out of focus. Consider the background carefully – choose a setting that is pleasing to the eye but not obtrusive. The beginner's most common mistake is failing to notice in the background a tree or telegraph pole that appears to be growing out of the subject's head when the picture is developed!

Hazy sunlight generally gives better results in portraiture than brilliant sunlight, unless you wish particularly to emphasize the wrinkles on the face of an elderly sitter. Hands can be expressive; but if you pose your subject caressing a kitten or reading a book, for example, try to make the whole position of the sitter look natural. Take at least two or three photo-

The parts of a single-lens reflex camera

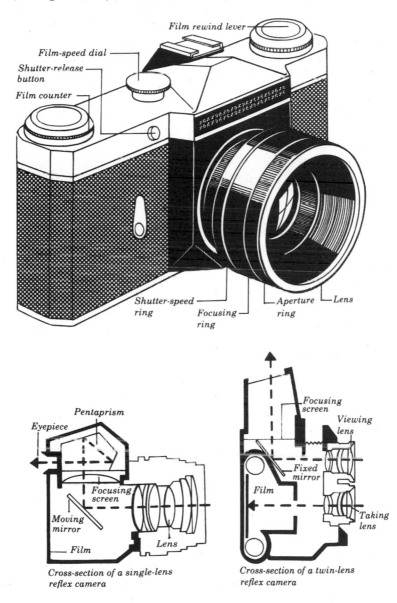

Film rewind lever

Film-speed dial

Shutter-release button

Film counter

Shutter-speed ring

Focusing ring

Aperture ring

Lens

Eyepiece

Pentaprism

Focusing screen

Moving mirror

Film

Lens

Cross-section of a single-lens reflex camera

Focusing screen

Viewing lens

Fixed mirror

Film

Taking lens

Cross-section of a twin-lens reflex camera

Compose the elements of your pictures carefully. This composition would have been improved by placing the chair and bottle in slightly different positions.

graphs of the same pose, all slightly different, and choose the best for enlargement.

While landscapes present no real technical problems for the beginner, first attempts are often disappointing. Having checked from different angles to find the best vantage point, compose your picture very carefully. Different times of the day produce different lighting effects; for instance, shadows are longer in the late afternoon. You may need to introduce a sense of scale by including a near object, such as a cottage – or a gate, perhaps, with a friend leaning on it and looking away from you towards the view.

Action pictures with sharp images can be obtained only by giving very short exposures on fast film. If the minimum exposure possible on your camera has failed to produce a sharp image, try moving further back next time. The risk of movement visible on the photograph is lessened as the distance between camera and subject is increased. Alternatively, you can 'pan' the camera (move it round in the direction of, and at a speed relative to, the moving object) as you take the shot. This will produce a blurred background, which will add to the impression of speed in the photograph. Successful results have been secured with box cameras using this approach.

It is a good idea to keep your camera loaded and near to hand at all times, ready for the unexpected event or the chance of a candid shot. Try setting your focusing distance at one metre and keeping it at that setting when the camera is not in use. When shooting the unexpected, it is quicker to move to the set distance of one metre than to reset the camera. Pausing to reset every time will considerably lessen your chances of catching a good shot.

Collecting as a Hobby

Philately

Of all the collecting hobbies, stamp-collecting, or philately, is probably the greatest, measured by numbers of enthusiasts and worldwide coverage. The scope for stamp-collectors is enormous, and continues to grow every day as countries issue new sets in vast numbers. One big advantage for the beginner is that no great outlay is required when starting a stamp collection. You need basically only an album, some stamp hinges and tweezers, plus a suitable catalogue.

First you should decide what form your collection is going to take. You may wish to collect stamps of every kind from all over the world, or concentrate on specimens from a single country. You may also collect stamps from a group of nations such as the British Commonwealth, or stamps devoted to a particular subject e.g. sport, anniversaries, transport.

When you have obtained your first stamps, possibly by buying some at a local shop, you should place them in the album, as described in the catalogue, using the tweezers at all times. The stamp hinges, for mounting the stamps in the album, should be folded over 6 mm ($\frac{1}{4}$ inch) with the gummed side outwards. Moisten this fold slightly and fix it to the top of the stamp. Then moisten the other part of the hinge and stick it, together with the stamp, in place on your album leaf.

As your collection grows you will acquire duplicates of stamps. These can be set aside in a separate book or album for use as swaps. You may also need additional equipment such as a magnifying glass, watermark tray and perforation gauge.

Many collectors form groups or join stamp clubs to add to the hobby's interest and for the speedier development of their collections. In this way, catalogues and other books of reference can be shared, and the door is opened to the endless fascination and interest of philately. Stamps have historical associations and provide exciting background information on a range of subjects. Your collection will increase in value, particularly as you acquire rare specimens and complete older sets.

Over the years collecting hobbies have increased in number and range, and some of the leading ones are mentioned in the following summary.

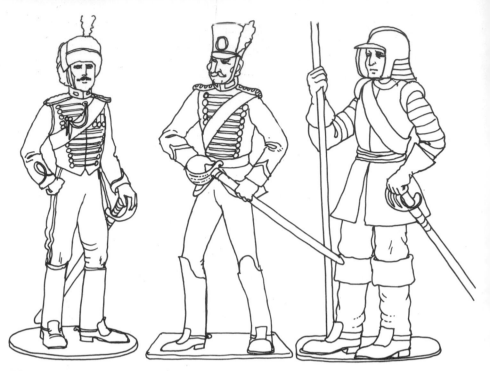

Phillumeny

Phillumeny is the collecting of matchbox labels. Like stamp-collecting, it offers worldwide scope. Some phillumenists gather all specimens, while others prefer to confine themselves to either box labels or book-matches. There are a great many varieties of both kinds. An interesting example of matchbox labels is provided by a modern Dutch series depicting veteran and vintage cars, and book-matches are issued by countless hotels and restaurants everywhere in order to advertise themselves.

There are worldwide collectors of cheese labels, beer mats (also issued by the producers of other drinks), tickets (covering transport by land, sea and air in every part of the world, and many other services and performances) and sports and theatre programmes.

Cigarette cards were widely collected in pre-World War II days but tobacco companies have now ceased to issue them. Opportunities for collecting these cards are restricted unless prospective collectors are prepared to pay considerable sums of money to acquire them. Similar series were distributed more recently by producers of tea and other commodities.

Models

The collection of models – particularly soldiers, but also many other metal miniatures – has become very popular indeed. Lead models produced from about 1890 until the time of World War II are avidly sought by keen collectors. There is a broad range of model soldiers representing the armies and

regiments of many nations, at different periods in history. They appear in both action and ceremonial dress and those in perfect condition can command high prices. Much prized are special items such as models of the celebrated British coronation coach, complete with horses and riders, and the military band of the Guards in their full-dress uniforms.

Some collectors prefer to concentrate on civilians and lead models of farm and zoo animals, or gardens complete with beds and a variety of flowers to slot into them. Rare figures, such as the village curate, can be valued highly. The range of Dinky Toy vehicles presents another interesting opportunity for collectors of models. Their value is also rising. Other popular collectors' items are model aircraft which are built from kits.

Numismatology

The collecting of coins, numismatology, is another hobby which provides great scope. Nations have minted coins since the earliest historically-recorded times. Designs are changed frequently, particularly when a new monarch or ruler takes office.

In recent years many countries have converted their currencies to a decimal system, offering collectors the opportunity to acquire the old, outgoing coins. Inflation, too, often causes a change of coinage, one example being the introduction of the new franc in France not long after World War II. At that time many comparatively short-lived coins were minted as a result of military actions and the political changes that arose from them.

Closely associated with numismatology is the collection of paper money, which circulated in China as far back as AD 650. Collectors sometimes specialize by concentrating on notes from only one country, on artistic design, on associations with historical events, or on a particular theme. There is a great variety of notes from World War II, including military notes, occupation notes, and paper money issued by partisan forces or for prisoners of war.

Ordinary stamp albums can be used for a paper money collection if you use photo-corners for mounting, but banknote albums are also available. These are designed so that you can see both sides of the notes. The historical and geographical interest to be derived from collecting paper money is enormous, besides which there is every probability that the value of notes will increase as years go by.

Playing cards
Playing cards appeal to a growing number of people as collectors' items. Before the 16th century, playing cards were hand-made on a small scale and were often works of art in their own right. After that time they were printed in large quantities. Early examples are rare and valuable but in those manufactured nearer our own time the range and variety are enormous.

Specialization often takes place in this hobby, like so many others. Some enthusiasts are interested in only the back or front designs of cards; some adopt a particular theme or concentrate on jokers only. There are packs devoted to specific themes: artistic, comical, educational or political. Fashion also plays a part as, for instance, during the French Revolution, when court cards were designed without crowns and sceptre-heads, in deference to republicanism. Christian religious symbolism is to be seen on tarot cards, first issued in medieval times in Italy.

Postcards
Postcard-collecting is, perhaps, one of the simplest hobbies to take up because there are so many types of card available everywhere, generally at low cost. Ordinary view-cards, sent by people on holiday, may provide the foundation of a collection which can later be expanded or directed into special subjects. Old cards showing places, buildings, streets, vehicles and people of bygone days are interesting in themselves and can often be compared with modern cards depicting the same scenes as they appear today. Stamp shops, antique or bric-a-brac dealers and some market stalls are likely places to pick up such cards for a collection.

If and when you decide to start specializing in postcard-collecting, the following categories are suggested: art reproduction, art nouveau, aviation, railways, religious or romantic themes, royalty, shipping, sport, theatre, military, heraldic, political, novelty and fantasy.

Prints and maps
Purchasing original prints and maps, or copies of them, can be a rather expensive hobby but a great

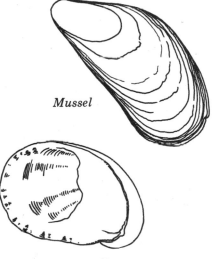

Mussel

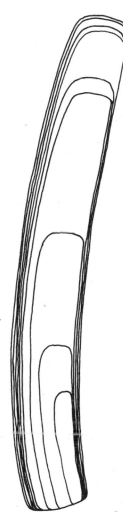

Slipper limpet

Winkle

Topshell

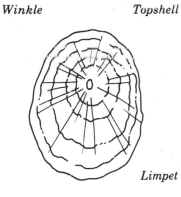

Razor shell

Limpet

deal can be achieved without too great an outlay. Searching for prints and maps can provide pleasure and interest for a lifetime, and the results of the collector's efforts can be framed and displayed. There is great scope for specialization. You may wish, for example, to concentrate on the work of a particular artist or collect maps of a certain region showing changes that have taken place throughout two or three hundred years.

Natural history

A natural history collection offers special interest to ramblers and lovers of the outdoors. There are plenty of botanical and geological specimens awaiting the collector everywhere, but no collector should pick any protected flowers or plants. The seashore offers considerable scope, too, with a large variety of seashells and seaweeds obtainable in many places.

Frequently, however, natural history enthusiasts prefer to observe wildlife in its natural environment. Instead of collecting specimens at random, they compile a large album of drawings, photographs, maps and notes of what they have seen, recording exactly when and where discoveries were made. All manner of relevant items can be included so that the collector builds up a comprehensive survey of a particular area, complete with all the necessary pictorial and textual information of what can be found there throughout the year. Sometimes items from the past come to light as well, adding a little archaeological and historical interest to the collection.

Nowadays, people are interested in making collections of almost anything, but particularly items which become increasingly rare as time goes on. Old bottles of every shape and size, tins of bygone days, wooden boxes, old-fashioned toys, utensils and ornaments, and gramophone records of past times are a few examples of objects which offer a great deal of interest to collectors.

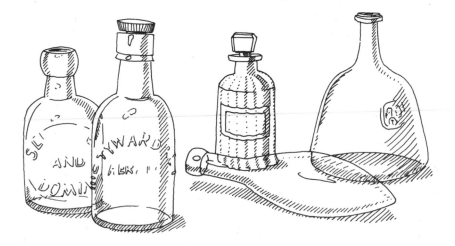

LOOKING
AFTER YOURSELF

How to Survive

Should you ever find yourself in a dangerous situation, you may need to use all your resourcefulness in order to cope. However, it is wise to be prepared in advance and to know what kinds of action you may have to take.

How to tackle a fire

If the fire is indoors, shut all doors and windows to prevent air currents fanning the flames. Throw water over the fire *except*:

1 When the water could hit live electric wires. A shock could flash back and electrocute you. Switch off the electricity at the mains. If the television set is on fire, pull out the plug first before dowsing with water.

2 When a pan of fat is burning. Burning oil floats on water, so you will merely succeed in scattering the flames round the room. Stifle the fire by covering it with a large lid.

If you need to extinguish a bonfire, throw water on to the centre of the blaze, or shovel sand or earth on the flames.

If a fire shows any sign of getting out of hand, call the fire brigade.

Escape from a building on fire

You may wake in the night smelling burning. If you then find that the door handle is too hot to turn, you know that the fire is right outside. If there is no alternative route to escape the fire, do *not* try to open the door by padding the handle with a cloth. Smoke and fumes would instantly pour into the room. With luck, the fire would take some time to burn the door down and reach you. Until help comes, seal the bottom of the door with a carpet or rug to help keep out the fumes. If there is thick smoke, it is best to keep your head near the floor where the smoke is less dense. But first call for help at a window so that rescuers will know where you are.

It is always dangerous to jump from a height. However, if you are on the first floor you may have to do it. If necessary, break the window by throwing a chair through it. Then hang by your hands from the window-sill, thereby reducing the distance you have to jump by the length of your body. Let go and bend your knees when you hit the ground to take the shock. Another method of getting out of a burning building is to make a rope. Tear curtains, sheets or blankets and join the strips with reef knots. Tie one end securely to a heavy piece of furniture and lower the other end out of the window. Climb down the rope hand over hand – it won't be easy.

Safety on the water

The best safety precaution against drowning is to learn to swim. A non-swimmer will be lucky to survive a crisis in the water. Whether you swim or not, it is sensible to wear a life-jacket when out boating.

When a boat capsizes, even

Drownproofing

though you may be a swimmer, the rule is to *stay with the boat*. Not only will you be able to cling to it, you will be seen more easily by rescuers. If you try swimming towards the shore against a strong current you may never make it. If possible, make yourself more conspicuous by holding up a piece of brightly coloured clothing. In rough weather, when it is difficult to cling to the side of a rowing dinghy, swim underneath the hull and cling to the seats inside. There will be plenty of air to breathe underneath the boat.

When there is nothing to cling to, such as a boat or a lifebelt, the natural buoyancy of your body will keep you floating as long as you don't panic and throw your arms up in the air (the weight of your arms out of the water will make

you sink). If the water is calm, you can float on your back. If it is choppy, treading water is a good way of staying afloat for long periods. This uses very little energy. With your nose and mouth clear of the water, take up a vertical position and slowly pedal with your feet as if on a bicycle. Your hands should make circling movements just under the water.

When you tread water, you have to hold your head – which is quite heavy – out of the water. An even less tiring method of staying afloat is 'drownproofing'. After taking a deep breath, you float vertically, being completely submerged apart from the back of your head, with your arms spread out. Hold your breath for several seconds, then breathe out through the nostrils. To take a fresh breath, lift your head upwards and backwards, and at the same time sweep your arms downwards. Your mouth should then clear the surface.

Avoid swimming where there are strong currents or tides. However, if you ever do have to battle against a current, swim across it diagonally. Swimming directly against it is more exhausting.

High winds in the mountains

A sudden upcurrent of air in a gale-force wind could fill your cagoule, or anorak, like a balloon and lift you bodily, perhaps over a precipice. So tuck your cagoule into your trousers. When the wind gusts fiercely, flatten yourself against a rock if you happen to be climbing. If walking, fling yourself to the ground.

Danger from lightning

One of the worst places to be in a thunderstorm is under a tall, isolated tree. But in the midst of a dense wood where all the trees are about the same height you are comparatively safe. Avoid any high, isolated object such as a tower or a pylon, and do not think you will be safe in the middle of an open plain. You will be standing higher than anything else around and therefore likely to attract lightning. When caught in a wide-open space by a thunderstorm, make yourself as low as possible by lying on your stomach.

Other places to avoid are mountain crests, steep rock faces and the mouths of caves (ionization at a cave entrance can draw lightning). A good spot to choose would be a hollow in the ground, or a few yards away from a solitary tree. You can also safely shelter in a car.

Danger from animals

Avoid the centres of fields where there are horses or cattle. Although such animals are usually harmless they can be unpredictable. Should you be unfortunate enough to be charged at by a cow or a bull, throw down whatever you happen to be carrying, or any clothing you can get off quickly as you run. The animal will be temporarily distracted by them while you make your getaway.

When confronted by an angry dog, the best thing to do is to freeze. Talk to it gently but on no account run. If the dog does not then leave you but starts to attack, try hitting it on the nose and, as soon as possible, grab it by the scruff of the neck. If a dog grips your arm or leg in its teeth do not try to tug the limb away; you will cause a nasty tear instead of a clean wound. Try pushing your limb towards the attacker's throat and he may then let go. Afterwards, wash the wound in cold water and immediately go to a doctor for an anti-rabies injection.

Cold can be a killer

It is important to be well prepared for cold weather and to know what to do in a crisis where it is essential to stay warm until help comes. Even on a hot summer's day temperatures can be freezing on a high peak. If you are hungry, wet, exhausted and perhaps lost or injured, you can easily succumb to cold even when temperatures are not much below

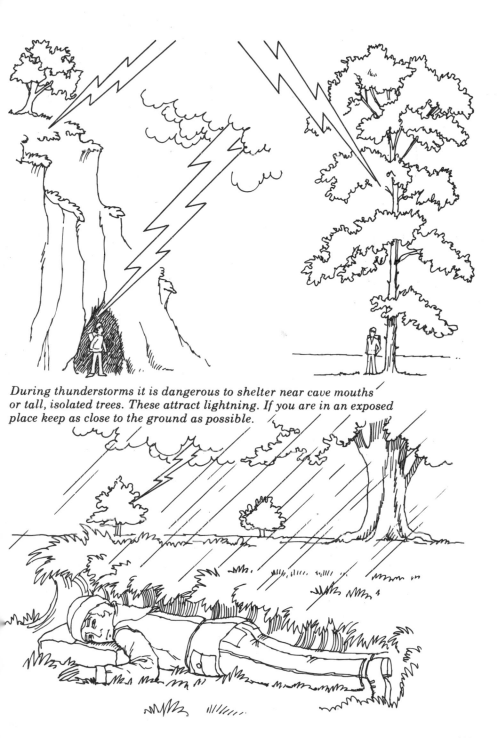

During thunderstorms it is dangerous to shelter near cave mouths or tall, isolated trees. These attract lightning. If you are in an exposed place keep as close to the ground as possible.

Improvise a shelter if you are stranded in remote places.

Tin lid signalling. Hold the lid up to the sun. With your other arm outstretched, hold your hand up in front of your face so that it blots out whoever you are signalling to. Tilt the lid this way and that until you hit your hand with a reflection of the sun. Sight the person through the slits between your fingers while keeping the lid flashing on that hand. A mirror or a broken piece of glass can also be used for flashing by this method.

freezing point. Your body heat can leak away so that you are chilled to the very core. You will then be suffering from a dangerous condition known as 'exposure', more correctly termed 'hypothermia'.

To beat the cold it is wise to wear several loose-fitting layers of warm clothing rather than just one thick sweater. When hiking, carry some extra pullovers in your rucksack as a safety precaution. You must take care not to get wet, so have a waterproof jacket and trousers with you as well. To keep you going, take some quick-energy foods that you can eat as you walk along, such as barley sugar, nuts, raisins or chocolate.

Should you become stranded in remote places, you will need to improvise a shelter from whatever materials are available at the time. One of the simplest is a sloping roof standing against a solid support such as a stone wall or rock face, or even a large fallen tree trunk. It could be made of logs or branches, or it might be a sheet of plastic anchored by small rocks and secured by string. Make sure that the entrance faces away from the wind.

Snow, surprisingly, can help you keep warm in an emergency. It is a good insulator against cold and can be used to make a shelter. In a deep snow drift, for example, you could dig a tunnel. For a shovel, use an ice axe, a chunk of tree bark, a rock, or whatever you happen to have with you that will suffice. Don't make the tunnel too big or it will be less warm. When the tunnel is finished, block the entrance with snowballs, but not completely. It is essential to have adequate ventilation in a snow shelter. An alternative is to dig a fairly deep trench in the snow with hollowed-out chambers to sit in. The top can be covered with large snowballs pressed together. Leave one free so that it can be rolled away when you come in or out. Cover the place where you sleep or sit with ever-green branches. Do not sit on or lean directly on the snow.

Shortage of water

It is possible to go without food for several weeks, but one cannot go completely without water for many days, especially in hot weather. On a long trek it is essential to take some water with you.

When water is scarce, you can conserve what you already have in your body by reducing perspiration. Button up your clothing. Uncomfortable though this may be in the heat, it will prevent you sweating so much. If you have a fair distance to cover, rest in the shade while the sun is at its hottest and resume your journey later when it is cooler.

Signalling for help

You will have to act according to circumstances and improvise a means of attracting attention. For example, you may have a mirror or a tin lid which you could use to flash reflected sunlight as a signal. This is one way of signalling to an airplane or helicopter pilot who is trying to locate you from the air. Another way is to light fires. Three fires set several metres apart, making an equilateral triangle, are recognized by pilots the world over as a distress signal. If you have no

SOS bonfire signal

means of lighting a fire, a large SOS spelt out in white stones or snow will also serve the same purpose.

If you are in trouble in mountain country, remember that six blasts of a whistle blown during one minute, followed by a minute's silence, is the international mountain distress signal. Anyone hearing your signal for help should reply with three whistle blasts in a minute, followed by a minute's silence. If you have no whistle, or can't whistle yourself, use a flash-light. Flash the on/off switch in the same sequence.

The international Morse code distress signal is different. You make three short flashes (or whistle blasts), then three long ones, and end with three short ones again. In Morse code this spells out 'SOS'. Another signal for help that is recognized everywhere is a white flag flying.

First Aid and Home Remedies

It is important to stress that the following instructions provide only a brief introduction to the important subject of first aid. Readers should contact their local voluntary first aid centre if they wish to study first aid thoroughly.

A vital point to be borne in mind is that if you are presented with a serious accident the first essential is to contact medical aid. Then attend to the casualty, remembering that an injured person, such as somebody knocked down in the street, should *not* be moved (steps should be taken to guard the casualty from any traffic) and should not be given anything to drink. Keep the person's head low, warm the body with any suitable covering, and wait for help to arrive. Severe bleeding or halted breathing call for immediate action (see appropriate entries).

Bleeding

When bleeding is severe, the following five steps should be taken at once:

1 Ensure that whatever caused the cut or cuts cannot inflict any further damage, by separating the casualty from the cause.

2 Using a clean cloth or towel (or just your fingers if these are unavailable), press the wound's edges together, and continue doing this until the bleeding ceases. This may take up to 15 minutes.

3 As soon as possible, get the patient to lie down, raising the feet higher than the head. If the wound is on an arm or leg, raise the injured limb while you are compressing the wound.

4 Use any handy material, such as a sock or stocking, to bind the wound as soon as you are sure that the bleeding has stopped.

5 Telephone for an ambulance or doctor.

In less serious cases, when bleeding is slight, expose the wound and remove any foreign matter from it, being careful not to disturb any blood-clots. Gently wash away any dirt by pouring water (sterilized if possible) freely over the wound. Apply an antiseptic and cover the wound with a dry dressing, followed by cotton-wool or lint, and a bandage. Support the injured part and treat the patient for shock.

Nose-bleeding should be treated by sitting the patient in an air current from an open window, with the head thrown slightly back and hands raised above the head. Tight clothing around the neck and chest should be undone. The patient must keep the mouth open for breathing, and must on no account blow his nose. Something cold, applied to the nose and the spine at collar level, generally helps to stop the bleeding.

Shock

Various accidents can cause a wide range of injuries, external or internal, sometimes breaking bones or damaging organs of the body. In all such cases, first aid must include treatment for shock. Shock always occurs when there is injury, severe blood loss or pain. It arises from an insufficient supply of blood to the brain, resulting in oxygen deficiency. The patient may feel faint, or feel cold and clammy and possibly sick. Treatment should be carried out as follows:

1 Ensure that the casualty is not in danger of further injury, but never move the person unless it is *absolutely essential*. Just provide as much comfort as you can, using cushions for example.

2 Raise the patient's legs higher than the head if this can be done without affecting the injured part of the body.

3 Make sure that warmth is maintained by covering the casualty with a light blanket – but *never* use hot water bottles or fires to provide artificial heat.

If the injured person shows sign of the shock becoming worse, an ambulance should be called at once. This should be done anyway whenever a patient has been seriously injured. In cases of heart attack the casualty should be propped up, in order to aid breathing, before you call an ambulance.

Burns, scalds and bruises

Dry heat (a fire or hot metal) causes burns, and moist heat (boiling water or steam) causes scalds. Treatment is the same, except for the first step:

1 *Burns:* If the person's clothing is on fire, approach the casualty, holding a rug, blanket, coat or tablecover in front of you. Wrap it round the patient to smother the flames and lay the person on the floor as fast as possible. *Scalds:* Remove soaked clothing and anything tight such as bracelets, belts or boots.

2 Cool the burnt or scalded parts with cold water for at least ten minutes.

3 Do not move the patient if the burn or scald is serious, but do all you can to make the person comfortable.

4 Cover the burn or scald lightly with a pillowcase or sheet to prevent infection, but *never* touch the affected areas or prick any blisters.

5 If the burn or scald is serious, call an ambulance.

The treatment for sunburn is the same as that for other burns. Bruising can be eased by rubbing the affected area gently with olive oil or by applying something cold to it, such as ice or a cold compress.

Choking

When somebody has something stuck in the throat, bend the person's head and shoulders forward and thump the back hard between the shoulderblades. If this is unsuccessful, try to make the person vomit by passing two fingers right to the back of their throat. Should the choking continue, call a doctor.

Foreign matter in the eye
Usually, grit or an eyelash can be removed simply by rolling the eyelid back from the eye and carefully applying a soft cloth or handkerchief. If, however, a quantity of sand, grit or some chemical such as ammonia is in the patient's eye, persuade the person to put his head into a basin of cool water and blink several times. Repeat the process, after a change of water, and generally you will find the eye clear of the foreign matter.

Poisoning
More often than not, drinking a poison is something done by small children. It is vital to telephone for an ambulance immediately, as only a hospital can cope properly with poisoning. While waiting for the ambulance, keep the child as quiet as possible and do not give it anything to drink or eat – although if the patient complains of a burning mouth or throat, you can give water, as the casualty has almost certainly swallowed an acid. It is equally important to get adults to hospital as quickly as possible. Try to avoid making the patient sick, as vomit may be inhaled thereby causing choking.

Squeezed fingers, stings and removal of splinters
If you have accidentally squeezed the top of a finger, hold it in warm water for a few minutes. This causes the nail to expand and soften, and the blood beneath it has more room to flow, thus lessening the pain and throbbing sensation.

When a sting is still present, it should be extracted, if possible, with the point of a sterilized needle. For bee stings, apply spirit, toilet water, sal volatile, or a solution of baking soda to relieve the pain. For wasp or hornet stings, use a weak acid such as vinegar or lemon juice. Finally, put on a dry dressing and treat for shock.

Splinters can be removed by nearly filling a bottle with hot water, and then holding the injured part over this and pressing it down tightly. The suction acts as a poultice and draws the flesh down, whereupon the splinter will normally come out quite easily.

Sprains
Place the affected limb in a comfortable position and prevent movement of it. Next, uncover the sprained joint and apply a firm bandage, which should be wetted with cold water and kept wet. When in doubt, treat the injury as a break (fracture).

Sunstroke
In cases of sunstroke, get the patient to a cool and shady place. Then strip the person to the waist, laying the casualty down with head and shoulders well raised. Fan the patient rigorously and sponge the body with cold water. Apply cold water or ice-bags to the head, neck and spine. When the person is conscious, give him plenty of cold water to drink.

Convulsions
Convulsions (fits), often occurring as a result of epilepsy, should be

If a victim of electric shock is conscious, he should be laid on his back with his legs raised.

An unconscious victim should be laid in the recovery position as shown here.

treated as follows. Remove any objects nearby which can cause injury. Protect the patient but do not restrain him in any way. If choking occurs, put a piece of cloth or anything soft into the mouth, but never use force. Stay with the patient after the convulsions have stopped as he may suffer from a temporary loss of memory and a headache.

Electric shock
Before any assistance can be given to a victim of electric shock, the electric contact must be broken. Do this by switching off the appliance or by turning off the current at the mains. Failing this, push the person away from the electricity with a piece of dry wood. Next, see if the casualty is breathing. If he is not, give him mouth-to-mouth respiration (see below). A badly shocked but conscious person should be laid on his back with the legs raised. If

he is unconscious, he should be laid in the recovery position (see diagram).

MOUTH-TO-MOUTH BREATHING
It is very important that as many people as possible know how to apply mouth-to-mouth breathing, as it is the surest method of saving the life of a person who has ceased to breathe as the result of a heart attack or an accident such as drowning or electric shock.

Practice, after studying this form of first aid in the following description, is a very good idea but *never* practise on another person. Try to attend a proper class where mouth-to-mouth breathing can be practised on dummies.

As soon as you are certain that a casualty is not breathing, start the mouth-to-mouth process at once. Delay can cause damage to the brain in as little as three minutes!

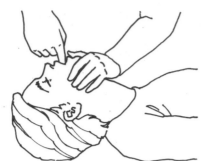

MOUTH-TO-MOUTH BREATHING

Your first step is to clear the person's airway because, once it is cleared, the casualty may start breathing again without further help. Anything that you find in the mouth (blood, vomit, false teeth, etc.) must be instantly cleared out.

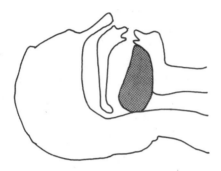

It is also vital to tilt the casualty's head well back to prevent the unconscious person's tongue falling back and obstructing the airway.
By tilting the head back you will extend the neck and so bring the tongue clear of the airway.

If you then breathe into the casualty's mouth and the person's chest rises and falls, you will know that the airway is clear. Otherwise, you must immediately repeat the first step by again clearing the mouth of any obstruction and making sure that the head is tilted back far enough.

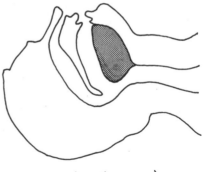

When applying mouth-to-mouth breathing, remember to pinch the casualty's nostrils to close them, as this will stop any of the air you are breathing in escaping by way of the person's nose.

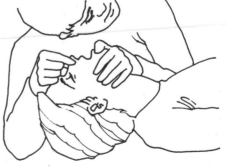

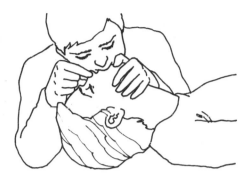

At this point, you immediately commence the life-saving breathing, beginning with four quick breaths in order to give the casualty's blood a good and speedy supply of oxygen. Enough oxygen for the person's needs remains in your breath when exhaled.

Now settle down to steady breathing at the normal rate of 10–15 breaths per minute, remembering to keep the casualty's nostrils pinched at the same time. This must be kept up until medical help arrives, somebody takes over from you or the person starts breathing again properly without your help.

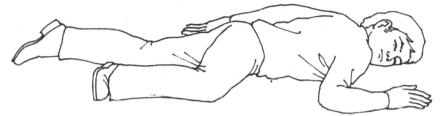

When a casualty starts breathing, place him carefully in the recovery position shown in the illustration. This makes it possible for the casualty to breathe easily without the tongue falling back across the airway or any further vomit being inhaled.

Should you have to deal with a heavy person, turning him into the recovery position is best done by kneeling alongside the casualty, placing the arms at the sides of the body, crossing the far leg over the near one, and then pulling the person over by the clothes at the hip. After that, put the casualty's arms and legs into the proper recovery position, as illustrated.

There are a few additional points to keep in mind for special cases. Gentle breathing is essential for young children and babies, and you may have to apply your breathing to them by sealing your lips right over both the nose and the mouth of the casualty. When injury to the casualty's mouth makes it impossible to give breathing aid by this method use mouth-to-nose breathing instead.

PETS AND THEIR CARE

A pet of your own can be a source of great pleasure. If it is to be a happy, well-cared-for pet, however, you must bear in mind the responsibilities as well as the joys of owning an animal. Your pet's welfare should always be of prime importance – the occasional personal inconvenience is a small penalty to pay for your pet's well-being.

The golden rules of pet-care

1 Your pet must be fed at regular times with the correct type and quantity of food.

2 Its living quarters must be of adequate size and kept thoroughly clean.

3 Your pet must always have access to fresh drinking-water.

4 At first, handle your pet only when necessary. If treated initially with gentleness, it will soon gain enough confidence to invite more lively play.

5 If your pet seems unwell, or acts strangely, consult your local vet.

6 Cats and dogs require injections to protect them from disease. Your vet will advise you on when such protection is needed; and also on when a female pet should be spayed if you don't want her to have a lot of babies.

7 As far as possible, let your pet enjoy its natural surroundings.

8 Respect its rights and individuality.

The choice of pet must depend on several factors. If you live in a flat on the twentieth floor, for instance, it would be neither sensible nor kind to keep a very large dog. Large dogs require a lot of room indoors and many need lengthy exercise outdoors. Equally important, many cats and dogs pine if they are shut out or cooped up on their own throughout the day. If everyone in your household is at school or work all day long, you should consider keeping a pet which is less dependent on human companionship. Expense is another factor; the larger the animal, the more it will cost to feed.

Dogs

If you live in the country or have a large garden and plenty of suitable walks nearby, you may decide to acquire what will eventually be a very big dog indeed! Remember, though, that the larger breeds of dog need 1.4–2.7 kg (3–6 lb) of food daily when fully grown. At all stages of their development most large dogs require regular vigorous exercise. City-dwellers would be better advised to choose from one of the many medium-sized and smaller breeds.

Whether your final choice rests on a pedigree puppy (a puppy bred at a registered breeding kennel from pure-bred parents) or on a mongrel pup (in whom no single breed is usually recognizable), you will be acquiring a delightful and devoted companion for the years ahead. Having taken delivery of your puppy, do remember that,

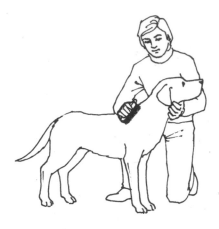

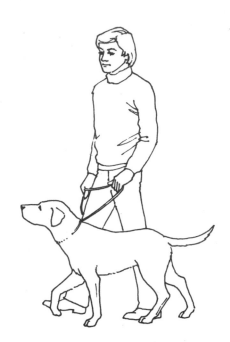

whatever his eventual size, he is at first only a baby and therefore needs to be given small, frequent meals. Pedigree pups usually come to you with a diet sheet; but in any case, your local vet can supply appropriate diet sheets. From the moment of his arrival in your house, your dog should always have access to a bowl of fresh drinking-water.

An expensive dog-basket is not a necessity; a sturdy box, placed in a draught-free area, is quite adequate. A large piece of old blanket material, folded at least twice, makes a soft mattress and another piece can provide a snug top cover. In case your puppy is missing the warmth of his mother and brothers and sisters, fill a stone or metal bedwarmer with warm water, wrap the bedwarmer in an old towel and

tie it at both ends. This will ensure that he settles down happily at night.

Every dog is born with a number of roundworms in its intestines but no puppy can thrive when worm-ridden. Reputable breeders worm their puppies before letting them go to new homes. If your puppy came from any other source, it is almost certain that he has not had a worming treatment. Modern treatments are available in liquid, pill and powder form, but do ask your vet's advice on the best way to go about the process. Remember also to ask him about the vaccinations required to protect your dog from disease.

To house-train your puppy, put him outside first thing every morning when his first instinct is to relieve himself. Be lavish with your praise when he has finished.

Dogs soon learn to recognize and respond to key words, such as 'good', if they are uttered with sufficient emphasis.

All dogs should be brushed daily. Make a game of it from the beginning and the puppy will very soon look forward to his daily grooming session. It is not necessary to bath him often, unless he is very muddy or has been rolling in some-thing particularly unpleasant. Frequent bathing removes the natural oils of a dog's skin. If your dog becomes ill you should take him to see the vet. You may also wish to take advantage of the services offered by animal welfare organizations and clubs. Many of these give advice on how to look after your pet.

Cats

The cat is an extremely independent animal in many ways. He comes and goes at will, and appears to take very much for granted the affection and admiration of all who behold him! Nevertheless, he makes a rewarding pet. An invariably graceful animal, he possesses a captivating charm and personality that quickly establish his place in the family circle.

Pedigree kittens, which belong to recognized breeds in one of the two official classifications, Longhair (including Persian) and Shorthair (including Siamese and British Blue), are best obtained from a registered breeder. Mongrel kittens, however, are often just as beautiful as the feline aristocrats! Non-pedigree kittens may often be obtained from a friend or neighbour whose own cat has recently produced a litter of kittens. When choosing a kitten, you should preferably see the whole litter. Pick the one that seems the most playful and the least nervous – he is probably the healthiest of the litter. He should be at least ten weeks old before you take him into your home. Before that age, he needs the continued care of his mother.

While cats, generally, will sleep almost anywhere, your new kitten will appreciate a little cosseting. A large shoe-box, cushioned with soft rags and positioned well away from draughts, should prove irresistibly attractive for the many naps he will take in the early months of his life. As he grows, of course, he will need larger sleeping quarters, but since comfort is the priority of every cat, he will be quite as happy with a large, padded cardboard box as with an expensive wicker cat-basket.

Being naturally fastidious animals, cats require very little encouragement in the matter of toilet-training. While your kitten is very small, however, it is kinder to provide him with a litter tray indoors and to introduce him to the garden over a number of days. Don't worry if he seems timid outside at first. He will explore a little further each day and become steadily bolder. In fact, in a very short time he will be demonstrating his ownership of the garden by chasing out intruders! The litter tray for those first few days can be any shallow, watertight box or tray filled with earth, sand or wood-shavings. The contents should be changed frequently and the tray washed with a non-toxic disinfectant. If the tray remains dirty, your cat will not use it and 'accidents' elsewhere in the house will be inevitable.

Other essential items of equipment are his own food and water bowls (which should be washed and stored separately from the family's dishes), a diet sheet from the vet (your kitten will need very small, frequent meals at first) and a brush and fine-toothed comb. Daily grooming with the comb removes dirt, parasites and loose hair, while brushing gives a final polish to his elegant appearance. Start the grooming routine when he is very small and he will soon come to look forward to it.

All cats and kittens need to scratch, to keep their claws sharp. The risk of damage to furniture can be avoided by providing your kitten with his own scratching-post: a firm, upright wooden base, covered with a piece of old carpet or other tough material.

Contrary to popular opinion, cats cannot see in the dark. The structure of a cat's eyes enables him to make more efficient use than humans of any available light, however dim, but in total darkness he can see no more than you can. Another myth is the cat's preference for being put out to roam all night. Nothing could be further from the truth; like us, cats prefer their warm, comfortable beds at night! By all means let your cat out each evening for a short period but make sure he is safely indoors before the house is locked up for the night. Treat your cat with respect for his character and concern for his needs, and he will reward you with true affection and companionship.

Rabbits

Rabbits are vegetarians, that is, they do not eat meat. They like cereals such as hay, oats and bran, green foods such as cabbage, grass and clover, and root vegetables, especially carrots.

Your rabbit's house, or hutch, should be at least 92 cm (3 ft) long and at least 46 cm (1½ ft) in both width and height. Partition off one end as a sleeping compartment and put down bedding of clean, fresh straw. The rest of the hutch will serve as your rabbit's livingroom and should be furnished with sawdust. The floor of the hutch must be above ground level and the hutch-ends draughtproofed. Keep the hutch in an open-fronted shed or on a platform in the garden.

Guinea pigs

This most attractive rodent cannot endure cold, so keep his little home inside your house or in a dry shed. He lives most happily in a nest, which you can make out of an inverted box about 30 cm (1 ft) square. Cut a 15 cm (6 in) diameter hole in one side of the box and fill it with straw or hay.

Feed your guinea pig with fresh grass, lettuce and celery leaves, dandelions, parsley and the

occasional apple. Also give him a regular supplement of carrots, which help to keep him healthy.

Tortoises

The tortoise is another vegetarian. His favourite foods include dandelions, lettuce and sowthistles. He does not eat insects.

The tortoise is not a year-round companion because he hibernates (sleeps throughout the winter) but during the rest of the year he proves an engaging pet who is at his happiest exploring the garden.

Canaries

The cage for a canary should be at least 46 cm (1½ ft) long, and as high as possible. His perch should be rounded and placed so as not to interfere with his exercise. Hang the cage indoors in a place where there is plenty of light but no draught.

Supplement his diet of packaged food from the pet shop with chick-weed and lettuce in the summer and apple in the winter. A cuttlefish bone, renewed every three months, will aid his digestion.

These are just a few of the many kinds of animal that, in return for a little tender care and attention, make excellent pets. Sentiment alone is not enough. Consistent care and kindness on your part will build a satisfying relationship of complete trust between you and your pet.

SPORTS
AND GAMES

Outstanding Sportsmen

ALEXEEV, Vasili Born USSR, 1942. Weightlifter, super-heavyweight class. Broke his 80th world record on 1 November 1977 by lifting 256 kg. He has broken more world records than any other sportsman.

ALI, Muhammad (Cassius Clay) Born USA, 1942. Boxer, heavyweight class. Won the World Heavyweight Championship three times, first by beating Sonny Liston (1964), secondly by beating George Foreman (1974) and thirdly in 1978 by beating Leon Spinks. He is the most highly paid of all boxers, having earned probably as much as 60 million dollars between 1960 and 1979.

ASHE, Arthur Born USA, 1943. Tennis player. Wimbledon champion 1975, US Open champion 1968, World champion 1975.

'BABE' RUTH (Full name George Herman Ruth.) Born USA 1895, died 1948. Baseball player. Held world record for home runs (60 in a 164-game season). Left-handed pitcher and batter. Played with the Boston Red Sox, the New York Yankees and the Boston Braves. Became coach to the Brooklyn Dodgers in 1938.

BANNISTER, Sir Roger Gilbert Born UK, 1929. Doctor and athlete. He was the first man in the history of sport to run a mile in under 4 minutes. On 6 May 1954, at Oxford, he ran 1 mile in 3 mins 59.4 secs.

BARRY, Rick Born USA, 1944. Basketball player. He led the Golden State Warriors to victory in the National Basketball Championship in 1975. Considered to be the most accurate free-throw shooter in the world.

BIKILA, Abebe Born in Ethiopia. Marathon runner. Won the gold at the 1960 Olympics with a time of 2 hrs 15 mins 16.2 secs, running barefooted. The marathon is run over a distance of 26 miles 385 yards (42.105 km).

BORG, Bjorn Born Sweden, 1956. Tennis player. The only man ever to have won five consecutive Wimbledon championships (1976–80).

BROOME, David Born UK, 1940. Horseman. Winner of George V Gold Cup and Queen Elizabeth II Cup four times.

CAMPBELL, Sir Malcolm Born UK 1885, died 1948. Racing driver. Holder of the water speed record from 1937 until his death. His hydroplane *Bluebird* reached 141.75 mph on Coniston Water, England. Also held land speed record from 1924 to 1935, reaching 301.13 mph in his car *Bluebird*.

CAMPBELL, Donald Malcolm Born UK 1921, died 1967. Engineer and designer son of Sir Malcolm Campbell. Following in his father's footsteps, he set the world water speed record of 276.33 mph in 1959 and the world land speed record, in 1964, of 403.1 mph. He was killed in 1967 attempting to beat his own record in the jet powered boat *Bluebird*.

CHARLTON, Bobby, OBE Born UK, 1937. Soccer player. His long career as a member of the England team spanned the years 1958–70, during which he scored 49 goals.

CHICHESTER, Sir Francis Born UK 1901, died 1972. Yachtsman and aviator. The first to cross the Tasman Sea in an East/West direction flying solo. In 1966–7 he sailed single-handed round the world in *Gypsy Moth IV*.

CLARKE, Bobby Born USA, 1949. Ice hockey player. Captain of the Philadelphia Flyers (winners of the 1974–5 Stanley Cup). Although diabetic, he has consistently led his team to victory. One of the youngest captains in the National Hockey League.

CONNORS, Jimmy Born USA, 1954. Left-handed tennis player. Won the US Open, Australian and Wimbledon championships in 1974 but was barred from the French Open by the Association of Tennis Professionals. Considered to be one of the most powerful players on the international circuit.

COOPER, Henry William, OBE Born UK, 1934. Boxer. British heavyweight champion 1959–69 and 1970–1. Winner of three Lonsdale Belts. He voluntarily relinquished his title in 1969 but fought again in 1970 and regained it.

CURRY, John Antony, OBE Born 1949, in the UK. Ice skater. Probably the world's most graceful male performer on ice. The only skater to have won all three major titles (World, Olympic and European) in a single year. His style is greatly influenced by his training in ballet.

FAIRFAX, John Born UK. Soldier and adventurer. In 1969 he made the first solo East/West crossing of the Atlantic Ocean by rowing boat. He left Las Palmas in the Canary Islands on 20 January and took 180 days to reach Fort Lauderdale in Florida. His boat, the *Britannia*, was only 6.7 m (22 ft) long. He also made the first rowboat crossing of the Pacific Ocean from San Francisco to the Hayman Islands (Australia). This took 362 days from 26 April 1970 to 22 April 1971. He was accompanied by Sylvia Cook in the 10.6 m (35 ft) *Britannia II*.

FANGIO, Juan Manuel Fangio y Cia Born Argentina, 1911. Racing driver. The only man to win the World Racing Drivers' Championship five times (between 1951 and 1957). He retired in 1958, having won 24 Grand Prix races.

FISCHER, Robert (Bobby) James Born USA, 1943. Chess Grand Master. Considered to be the greatest chess player alive. He won 20 grand master games in succession from 1970 to 1971.

FOSBURY, Richard Born USA. Athlete. The 'Fosbury flop', a new innovation in high jumping, was developed by this remarkable man. Before Fosbury's time, the high jump was made forwards but Dick Fosbury attained a height of 7 ft 4¼ in (2.2 m) with a backward flop over the bar.

GRACE, William Gilbert Born UK 1848, died 1915. Cricketer. Known as 'the father of modern batting'. He scored over 54,000 runs during his long career and took 2,876 wickets in first-class cricket.

HILL, Graham Born 1929 in the UK, died 1975. Engineer and racing driver. He won 14 Grand Prix races and competed in a total of 176 Grand Prix events. He raced for the Lotus team, 1950–9 and 1967–9, and for the British Racing Motors 1960–6. He won the Indianapolis 500 in 1966, driving a Lola 90 Ford. He was killed near Elstree, England, while trying to land a light aircraft in fog.

HILLARY, Sir Edmund Percival Born 1919, in Australia. He was initially a beekeeper but was always fascinated by exploration and mountaineering. In 1953 he and Tensing Norgay, a Sherpa, were the first men to reach the summit of Mount Everest, the highest mountain in the world. Hillary was also the first man after Captain R. F. Scott to reach the South Pole overland (1958).

KNIEVEL, (Evel) Robert Craig Born USA, 1938. Stunt rider. One-time petty thief and Hell's Angel, he boasts that he has broken every bone in his body, except his neck, while attempting to beat self-imposed records. He leaps his motorbike over rows of parked cars and buses, and even attempted to vault the Grand Canyon in 1974. This was a fiasco; his safety parachute opened too soon and he glided to the canyon floor.

LOUIS, Joseph Louis Barrow Born USA, 1914. Boxer, heavyweight class. The longest reigning heavyweight ever. He held the title from June 1937 until May 1949 when he announced his retirement. He defended his title 25 times.

MARCIANO, Rocky Born 1923 in the USA, died 1969. Boxer, heavyweight class. His career lasted from 1947 to 1956 and he was undefeated world champion from 1952 to 1956.

MERCKX, Eddie Born in Belgium, 1945. Cyclist. He won the Tour de France five times.

MOORE, Robert (Bobby) Frederick Born in the UK, 1941. Footballer. Played for England 108 times. Between 1962 and 1977 he played in 1,000 games for West Ham United, Fulham and England.

NICKLAUS, Jack Born USA, 1940. Golfer. Winner of the USA Masters Championship five times (1963, 1965, 1966, 1972, 1975). He also played on six winning teams in the World Cup (1963, 1964, 1966, 1967, 1971, 1973) and took the individual title three times. He has earned more than three million dollars and is the only man to have won the five major titles twice.

OWENS, Jesse Born USA, 1913. Athlete. Probably the finest all-round athlete in Olympic history. On 25 May 1935, at the Intervarsity Athletics Meeting in Michigan, within one hour he set four world records (100 yards dash in 9.4 secs, 26 ft 8¼ in in the long jump, 220 yards low hurdles in 22.6 secs, 220 yards in 20.3 secs). In 1936 at the Berlin Olympics he won four gold medals.

PELE, Edson Arantes Do Nascimento Born in Brazil, 1940. Soccer player known as 'the king of soccer'. Played for Brazil and the Santos Football Club, and then the North American soccer league. When in Brazil, over his eighteen-year career, he scored 1,216 goals in 1,253 games. His estimated earnings at the height of his career were two million dollars.

RED RUM Born UK, 1965. The most famous racehorse of all time. Trained by Ginger MacCaine, he won the Grand National three times (1973, 1974, 1977). Holder of the fastest time for the course, and winner of the most prize money of any British horse. Now retired owing to a tragic injury.

RICHARDS, Sir Gordon Born UK, 1904. Jockey. He has won 4,870 races. He was champion jockey 26 times, and was knighted in 1963.

SCHOCKEMOHLE, Alwin Born West Germany, 1937. Show jumper. In 1975, riding *Rex the Robber*, *Warwick Rex* and *Santa Monica*, he won the European Championship. He won a gold medal at the 1976 Olympics with no faults.

SIMPSON, Orenthal James (O.J.) Born USA 1947. Professional American football player. Plays running back position. Winner of the Superstars Competition held on US television.

SOBERS, Sir Garfield St Aubrun Born Barbados 1936. Cricketer. One-time captain of the Barbados team, Gary Sobers played for the West Indian team and Nottinghamshire. He has scored 8,032 runs in test cricket and has appeared in 85 consecutive tests between 1955 and 1972.

SPITZ, Mark Born USA, 1950. Swimmer. Most outstanding athlete of the 1972 Olympics. He won seven gold medals (100 and 200 m freestyle, 100 and 200 m butterfly, 4 × 100 m freestyle relay, 4 × 200 m freestyle relay, 4 × 100 m medley relay).

SULLIVAN, John Lawrence Born USA 1858, died 1918. Boxer. World heavyweight champion from 1882 to 1892, when he was beaten by James ('Gentleman Jim') Corbett. A bare-knuckle fighter, he amassed a fortune of over a million dollars (an immense sum in those days) but lost it all. He became a teetotaller and lectured on prohibition until his death.

The Olympic Games

Traditionally, the first Olympic Games were held in 776 BC at Olympia in the western Peloponnese, Greece. They continued to be held at four-year intervals until AD 393, when the Roman emperor Theodosius abolished them.

At first the games lasted for one day and consisted of only one race run the length of the stadium. Some time later other events were added. These included the discus, the javelin, the broad jump, boxing, chariot racing, wrestling and the pentathlon. When competitors from all the Greek colonies were allowed to enter, a sacred truce was declared to allow the competitors to travel to the games freely. Women were not allowed to compete or watch, except for the priestesses of Demeter who observed the proceedings. The The greatest honour was to win a branch of wild olive, and the games attained such importance that an 'Olympiad' or the four-year span between the games became an official measure of time.

In 1894 Baron Pierre de Coubertin called an international conference at the Sorbonne in Paris. He proposed the creation of a modern cycle of Olympic Games. The representatives of 12 nations agreed to his proposal, and the first modern games took place in 1896 in Athens, in a marble stadium built specially for the occasion. Thirteen nations sent a total of 311 participants and there were 43 events covering nine sports.

The Olympic movement is controlled by the International Olympic Committee (IOC) based in Lausanne, Switzerland. According to article 26 of the IOC rules and regulations, contestants must be amateurs: they must always have participated in sport as an avocation, without material gain of any kind. An athlete is eligible for the Olympic Games:
1 If he has a basic occupation designed to ensure his present and future livelihood;
2 if he does not receive, or has never received, any remuneration for participation in sport;
3 if he complies with the rules of the International Federation concerned, and the official interpretations of this article (26).

A person who complies with these conditions is considered an amateur from the Olympic point of view.

The opening ceremony
The opening ceremony of the Olympic Games does not vary. The head of state of the host country is welcomed to the stadium by the president of the IOC, the national anthem of the host country is played and then there is a parade of all the competitors. Greece

always heads the parade and the host country comes last. Between these two the competing countries march past in alphabetical order, each contingent carrying a shield bearing the name of their country and their national flag. The competitors march round the stadium and then line up in the centre.

The president of the Olympic committee which has organized the games gives a speech of welcome and asks the head of state to open the games. A fanfare of trumpets sounds and the Olympic flag, bearing its linked rings, is raised. Hundreds of doves are released and there is a gun salute. At this moment a runner arrives carrying the Olympic flame. The flame is kindled at Olympia in Greece and is carried by teams of runners to the stadium, where it burns throughout the games. The games are then blessed and the Olympic hymn is sung. A contestant from the host country steps forward and takes the Olympic oath on behalf of all the contestants:
'In the name of all competitors I promise that we will take part in these Olympic Games, respecting and abiding by the rules which govern them, in the true spirit of sportsmanship, for the glory of sport and the honour of our teams.'

The choir then sings the national anthem of the host country and the competitors leave the stadium.

Throughout the games, as each event is completed, award ceremonies take place. The winner and the second- and third-place competitors step on to a rostrum and are presented with gold, silver and bronze medals respectively. The national flags of their countries are raised and the national anthem of the winning competitor is played.

At the completion of the games the president of the IOC draws the ceremonies to a close. He exhorts the youth of the world to gather again in four years for the next games:
'May they display cheerfulness and concord so that the Olympic torch may be carried on with ever greater eagerness, courage and honour for the good of humanity throughout the ages.'

With a last fanfare of trumpets, the Olympic flame dies down and the flag is lowered. There is a five-gun salute and the final anthem is sung. The games are over for another four years.

The events

From 1896 the main events in the Olympic Games consisted of track and field sports although from time to time other sports, from archery to yachting, were included. The 1896 Olympics covered nine sports with 43 events. By 1972, 23 sports with 205 events were covered.

Today, the Olympics contain some or all of the following events (but never less than 15 in any one games): Archery, Athletics, Badminton, Basketball, Boxing, Canoeing, Cycling, Diving, Equestrian sports, Fencing, Football (soccer), Gymnastics, Handball, Hockey, Judo, Tennis, Pentathlon (riding, fencing, shooting, swimming, running), Polo, Rowing, Shooting, Swimming, Track and Field Events (running, hurdling, relay, walking, high jump, long jump, shot put, pole vault, triple jump, discus, javelin, hammer, decathlon, steeplechase, marathon), Water polo, Weightlifting, Wrestling (Freestyle and Greco-Roman), Yachting.

The Winter Olympics contain these events: Figure skating, Speed skating, Ice hockey, Cross-country skiing, Ski relay, Ski jump, Biathlon, Slalom, Giant slalom, Bobsled, Luge.

LOCATIONS OF MODERN OLYMPIC GAMES

Year	Place	Country
1896	Athens	Greece
1900	Paris	France
1904	St Louis	USA
1908	London	UK
1912	Stockholm	Sweden
1916	No Games	
1920	Antwerp	Belgium
1924	Paris	France
1928	Amsterdam	The Netherlands
1932	Los Angeles	USA
1936	Berlin	Germany
1940	No Games	
1944	No Games	
1948	London	UK
1952	Helsinki	Finland
1956	Melbourne	Australia
1960	Rome	Italy
1964	Tokyo	Japan
1968	Mexico City	Mexico
1972	Munich	West Germany
1976	Montreal	Canada
1980	Moscow	USSR

LOCATIONS OF WINTER OLYMPIC GAMES

Year	Place	Country
1924	Chamonix	France
1928	St Moritz	Switzerland
1932	Lake Placid	USA
1936	Garmisch Parten-kirchen	Germany
1940	No Games	
1944	No Games	
1948	St Moritz	Switzerland
1952	Oslo	Norway
1956	Cortina d'Ampezzo	Italy
1960	Squaw Valley	USA
1964	Innsbruck	Austria
1968	Grenoble	France
1972	Sapporo	Japan
1976	Denver	USA
1980	Lake Placid	USA

THE OLYMPICS:
NUMBERS OF COMPETITORS AND SPORTS

Year	Where held	Number of sports	Number of competitors	Number of nations competing
1896	Athens	10	285	13
1900	Paris	13	1066	20
1904	St Louis	12	496	11
1908	London	20	2059	22
1912	Stockholm	14	2541	28
1920	Antwerp	19	2606	29
1924	Paris	19	3092	44
1928	Amsterdam	16	3015	46
1932	Los Angeles	16	1408	37
1936	Berlin	21	4069	49
1948	London	18	4468	59
1952	Helsinki	17	5867	69
1956	Melbourne	18	3183	67
1960	Rome	18	5396	84
1964	Tokyo	20	5558	94
1968	Mexico City	18	6059	112
1972	Munich	21	7147	122
1976	Montreal	21	6815	88

Besides the medals which are awarded during the games, the International Olympic Committee also makes the following awards:

The Olympic Diploma of Merit
This is awarded to an individual who has made an outstanding contribution to sport (amateur) or to the Olympic movement.

The Olympic Cup
Awarded to an organization which has contributed outstandingly to amateur or Olympic sport.

The Count Bonacossa Trophy
This is awarded annually to the national Olympic committee which has most furthered the Olympic movement.

The Mohammed Taher Trophy
Awarded to the most outstanding Olympic athlete.

The Fearnley Cup
Awarded to the most meritorious amateur sports club or local association.

The Tokyo Trophy
Awarded to the individual or group who have showed outstanding sportsmanship, whether or not medals have been won.

Olympic events

Long jump

Judo

Fencing

High jump

Boxing

Javelin

Discus

Running

Rowing

Diving

OLYMPIC MEDALS 1896–1932

(* not entered

COUNTRY	1896			1900			1904			1908			1912			1920			1924			1928			1932		
	G	S	B	G	S	B	G	S	B	G	S	B	G	S	B	G	S	B	G	S	B	G	S	B	G	S	B
United States	11	7	1	20	15	16	70	75	64	23	12	11	24	19	19	41	26	27	45	27	27	22	18	16	44	36	30
Soviet Union	*	*	*	–	–	–	*	*	*	–	2	–	–	2	3	*	*	*	*	*	*	*	*	*	*	*	*
Great Britain	3	3	1	17	8	12	1	1	–	56	48	37	10	15	16	15	16	12	9	14	2	4	11	7	5	7	5
France	5	4	2	26	36	33	*	*	*	5	5	9	8	5	3	9	20	13	14	15	12	7	12	6	11	5	4
Sweden	–	–	–	1	–	1	*	*	*	7	5	10	24	24	17	17	19	26	4	13	12	7	6	12	10	5	9
Italy	*	*	*	2	2	–	*	*	*	2	2	–	5	1	2	14	6	5	8	3	5	7	6	7	12	12	12
Germany	7	5	2	4	2	2	4	4	5	2	4	4	5	13	7	*	*	*	*	*	*	11	19	9	5	12	7
Hungary	2	1	2	1	2	2	2	1	1	3	4	2	3	2	3	*	*	*	2	4	4	5	5	–	6	5	5
Finland	*	*	*	*	*	*	*	*	*	1	1	3	9	8	9	14	10	8	14	13	10	8	8	9	5	8	12
Australia	2	–	–	2	–	4	–	–	–	1	2	1	2	2	2	–	2	1	3	1	2	1	2	1	3	1	1
Japan	*	*	*	*	*	*	*	*	*	*	*	*	–	–	–	–	2	–	–	–	1	2	2	1	7	7	4
Switzerland	1	2	–	5	3	1	1	–	1	–	–	–	1	–	–	2	2	7	7	8	–	7	6	4	–	1	–
Norway	*	*	*	–	2	3	–	–	–	2	3	3	4	1	5	13	8	8	5	2	3	1	2	1	–	–	–
Czechoslovakia	*	*	*	–	1	2	*	*	*	–	–	2	–	–	–	–	–	–	1	1	4	5	2	5	2	1	3
Belgium	*	*	*	5	6	3	*	*	*	1	5	2	2	1	3	16	12	13	3	7	3	–	1	2	–	–	–
Holland (see Netherlands)	*	*	*	1	1	3	*	*	*	–	1	–	–	3	4	2	5	4	1	6	8	10	5	2	5		
Denmark	1	2	4	2	3	2	*	*	*	–	2	3	1	6	5	3	9	1	2	6	3	3	2	4	–	5	
Canada	*	*	*	1	–	1	4	1	–	3	3	8	3	2	3	2	3	3	–	3	1	4	4	7	2	5	
Poland	*	*	*	*	*	*	*	*	*	*	*	*	*	*	*	*	*	*	–	1	1	2	1	4	3	2	
Turkey	*	*	*	*	*	*	*	*	*	*	*	*	–	–	–	*	*	*	*	*	*	–	–	–	–	–	–
Greece	10	19	7	–	–	–	1	–	1	–	3	1	1	–	1	–	1	–	1	–	–	–	–	–	–	–	–
Austria	2	–	3	–	3	3	1	1	–	1	–	1	–	2	2	*	*	*	–	3	1	3	–	1	1	1	
South Africa	*	*	*	*	*	*	*	–	–	–	1	1	–	4	2	–	3	4	3	1	1	1	1	–	2	2	–
Romania	*	*	*	*	*	*	*	*	*	*	*	*	*	*	*	*	*	*	–	–	1	–	–	–	*	*	
Argentina	*	*	*	*	*	*	*	*	*	*	*	*	*	*	*	–	–	–	1	3	2	3	3	1	3	1	
New Zealand	*	*	*	*	*	*	*	*	*	*	*	*	–	–	1	–	–	1	–	–	1	1	–	–	–	1	
Yugoslavia	*	*	*	*	*	*	*	*	*	*	*	*	–	–	–	–	–	–	2	–	–	1	1	3	–	–	
East Germany	*	*	*	*	*	*	*	*	*	*	*	*	*	*	*	*	*	*	*	*	*	*	*	*	*	*	*
Bulgaria	–	–	–	*	*	*	*	*	*	*	*	*	*	*	*	*	*	*	*	*	*	–	–	–	–	–	*
India	*	*	*	–	2	–	*	*	*	*	*	*	*	*	*	–	–	–	–	–	–	1	–	–	1	–	
Cuba	*	*	*	1	1	–	5	2	3	*	*	*	*	*	*	*	*	*	–	–	–	–	–	–	–	–	*
Mexico	*	*	*	*	*	*	*	*	*	*	*	*	*	*	*	*	*	*	–	–	–	–	–	–	–	–	2
Estonia	*	*	*	*	*	*	*	*	*	*	*	*	*	*	*	1	2	–	1	1	4	2	1	2	–	–	
Egypt	*	*	*	*	*	*	*	*	*	*	*	*	*	*	*	–	–	–	–	–	–	2	1	1	*	*	
Iran (Persia)	*	*	*	*	*	*	*	*	*	*	*	*	*	*	*	*	*	*	*	*	*	*	*	*	*	*	*
Ireland	*	*	*	*	*	*	*	*	*	*	*	*	*	*	*	*	*	*	–	1	1	1	–	–	2	–	

COUNTRY	1896			1900			1904			1908			1912			1920			1924			1928			1932		
	G	S	B	G	S	B	G	S	B	G	S	B	G	S	B	G	S	B	G	S	B	G	S	B	G	S	B
Jamaica	*	*	*	*	*	*	*	*	*	*	*	*	*	*	*	*	*	*	*	*	*	*	*	*	*	*	*
Kenya	*	*	*	*	*	*	*	*	*	*	*	*	*	*	*	*	*	*	*	*	*	*	*	*	*	*	*
Brazil	*	*	*	*	*	*	*	*	*	*	*	*	*	*	*	1	1	1	-	-	-	*	*	*	-	-	-
Ethiopia	*	*	*	*	*	*	*	*	*	*	*	*	*	*	*	*	*	*	*	*	*	*	*	*	*	*	*
Luxembourg	*	*	*	*	*	*	*	*	*	-	-	-	-	-	-	-	1	-	1	1	-	1	-	-	*	*	*
Pakistan	*	*	*	*	*	*	*	*	*	*	*	*	*	*	*	*	*	*	*	*	*	*	*	*	*	*	*
Uruguay	*	*	*	*	*	*	*	*	*	*	*	*	*	*	*	*	*	*	1	-	-	1	-	-	-	-	1
Spain	*	*	*	-	-	-	*	*	*	*	*	*	*	*	*	-	2	-	-	-	-	-	1	-	-	-	1
Tunisia	*	*	*	*	*	*	*	*	*	*	*	*	*	*	*	*	*	*	*	*	*	*	*	*	*	*	*
Venezuela	*	*	*	*	*	*	*	*	*	*	*	*	*	*	*	*	*	*	*	*	*	*	*	*	*	*	*
Bahamas	*	*	*	*	*	*	*	*	*	*	*	*	*	*	*	*	*	*	*	*	*	*	*	*	*	*	*
Peru	*	*	*	*	*	*	*	*	*	*	*	*	*	*	*	*	*	*	*	*	*	*	*	*	*	*	*
Chile	-	-	-	*	*	*	*	*	*	*	*	*	*	*	*	-	-	-	-	-	-	-	1	-	*	*	*
Korea	*	*	*	*	*	*	*	*	*	*	*	*	*	*	*	*	*	*	*	*	*	*	*	*	*	*	*
Portugal	*	*	*	*	*	*	*	*	*	*	*	*	*	*	-	-	-	-	-	-	1	-	-	1	*	*	*
Trinidad and Tobago	*	*	*	*	*	*	*	*	*	*	*	*	*	*	*	*	*	*	*	*	*	*	*	*	-	1	-
Latvia	*	*	*	*	*	*	*	*	*	*	*	*	*	*	*	*	*	*	-	-	-	-	-	-	-	-	3
Philippines	*	*	*	*	*	*	*	*	*	*	*	*	*	*	*	*	*	*	-	-	-	-	-	-	*	*	*
Mongolia	*	*	*	*	*	*	*	*	*	*	*	*	*	*	*	*	*	*	*	*	*	*	*	*	-	-	-
Haiti	*	*	*	-	-	-	*	*	*	*	*	*	*	*	*	*	*	*	-	-	1	-	1	-	*	*	*
Lebanon	*	*	*	*	*	*	*	*	*	*	*	*	*	*	*	*	*	*	*	*	*	*	*	*	*	*	*
Taiwan	*	*	*	*	*	*	*	*	*	*	*	*	*	*	*	*	*	*	*	*	*	*	*	*	*	*	*
Ghana	*	*	*	*	*	*	*	*	*	*	*	*	*	*	*	*	*	*	*	*	*	*	*	*	-	-	-
Uganda	*	*	*	*	*	*	*	*	*	*	*	*	*	*	*	*	*	*	*	*	*	*	*	*	*	*	*
Ceylon (Sri Lanka)	*	*	*	*	*	*	*	*	*	*	*	*	*	*	*	*	*	*	*	*	*	*	*	*	*	*	*
Iceland	*	*	*	*	*	*	*	*	*	-	-	-	-	-	-	*	*	*	*	*	*	*	*	*	*	*	*
Morocco	*	*	*	*	*	*	*	*	*	*	*	*	*	*	*	*	*	*	*	*	*	*	*	*	*	*	*
Singapore	*	*	*	*	*	*	*	*	*	*	*	*	*	*	*	*	*	*	*	*	*	*	*	*	*	*	*
Cameroon	*	*	*	*	*	*	*	*	*	*	*	*	*	*	*	*	*	*	*	*	*	*	*	*	*	*	*
Panama	*	*	*	*	*	*	*	*	*	*	*	*	*	*	*	*	*	*	*	*	*	-	-	-	*	*	*
Nigeria	*	*	*	*	*	*	*	*	*	*	*	*	*	*	*	*	*	*	*	*	*	*	*	*	*	*	*
Puerto Rico	*	*	*	*	*	*	*	*	*	*	*	*	*	*	*	*	*	*	*	*	*	*	*	*	*	*	*
Iraq	*	*	*	*	*	*	*	*	*	*	*	*	*	*	*	*	*	*	*	*	*	*	*	*	*	*	*
South Korea	*	*	*	*	*	*	*	*	*	*	*	*	*	*	*	*	*	*	*	*	*	*	*	*	*	*	*
North Korea	*	*	*	*	*	*	*	*	*	*	*	*	*	*	*	*	*	*	*	*	*	*	*	*	*	*	*
Netherlands	*	*	*	*	*	*	*	*	*	*	*	*	*	*	*	*	*	*	*	*	*	*	*	*	*	*	*

OLYMPIC MEDALS 1936–1976

(* not entered)

COUNTRY	1936			1948			1952			1956			1960			1964			1968			1972			1976		
	G	S	B	G	S	B	G	S	B	G	S	B	G	S	B	G	S	B	G	S	B	G	S	B	G	S	B
United States	24	21	12	38	27	19	40	19	17	32	25	17	34	21	16	36	26	28	48	28	34	33	31	30	34	35	25
Soviet Union	*	*	*	*	*	*	22	30	19	37	29	32	43	29	31	30	31	35	29	32	30	50	27	22	47	43	35
Great Britain	4	7	3	4	16	7	1	2	8	6	7	11	2	6	12	4	12	2	5	5	3	4	5	9	3	5	5
France	7	6	6	11	6	15	6	6	6	4	4	6	–	2	3	1	8	6	7	3	5	2	4	7	2	2	5
Sweden	6	5	10	17	11	18	12	12	10	8	5	6	1	2	3	2	2	4	2	1	1	4	6	6	4	1	–
Italy	9	13	5	9	13	11	8	9	4	8	8	9	13	10	13	10	10	7	3	4	9	5	3	10	2	7	4
Germany	38	31	32	*	*	*	–	7	17	6	13	7	12	19	11	10	22	18	5	11	10	13	11	16	10	12	17
Hungary	10	1	5	10	5	13	16	10	16	9	10	7	6	8	7	10	7	5	10	10	12	6	13	16	4	5	12
Finland	8	6	6	10	8	6	6	3	13	3	1	11	1	1	3	3	–	2	1	2	1	3	1	4	4	2	–
Australia	–	–	1	2	6	5	6	2	3	13	8	14	8	8	6	6	2	10	5	7	5	8	7	2	–	1	4
Japan	6	4	10	*	*	*	1	6	2	4	10	5	4	7	7	16	5	8	11	7	7	13	8	8	9	6	10
Switzerland	2	9	5	5	12	6	2	6	6	–	–	1	–	3	3	1	2	1	–	1	4	–	3	–	1	1	2
Norway	1	3	2	1	3	3	3	2	–	1	–	2	1	–	–	–	–	–	1	1	–	2	1	1	1	1	–
Czechoslovakia	3	5	1	6	2	3	7	3	3	1	4	1	3	2	3	5	6	3	7	2	4	2	4	2	2	2	4
Belgium	–	–	3	2	2	3	2	2	–	–	2	–	–	2	2	2	–	1	–	1	1	–	2	–	–	3	3
Holland (see Netherlands)	6	4	7	5	2	9	–	5	–	*	*	*	–	1	2	2	4	4	3	3	1	*	*	*	*	*	*
Denmark	–	2	3	5	8	9	2	1	3	1	2	1	2	3	1	2	1	3	1	4	3	1	–	–	1	–	2
Canada	1	3	5	–	2	2	1	2	–	2	1	3	–	1	–	1	2	1	1	3	1	–	2	3	–	5	6
Poland	–	4	5	1	–	1	1	2	1	1	4	4	4	6	11	7	6	10	5	2	11	7	5	9	8	6	13
Turkey	1	–	1	6	4	2	2	2	–	1	3	2	2	7	2	–	2	3	1	2	–	–	–	1	–	–	–
Greece	–	–	–	–	–	–	–	–	–	–	–	–	1	1	–	–	–	–	–	–	1	–	2	–	–	–	–
Austria	5	7	5	2	2	4	–	1	1	–	–	2	1	1	–	–	–	–	2	2	–	1	2	–	–	–	1
South Africa	–	1	–	2	2	2	2	4	4	–	–	4	–	1	2	*	*	*	*	*	*	*	*	*	*	*	*
Romania	–	1	–	*	*	*	1	1	2	5	3	5	3	1	6	2	4	6	4	6	5	3	6	7	4	9	14
Argentina	2	2	3	3	3	1	1	2	2	–	1	1	1	1	–	1	–	–	–	7	–	1	–	–	–	–	–
New Zealand	1	–	–	–	–	–	1	–	2	2	–	–	2	–	1	3	–	2	1	–	2	1	1	1	2	1	1
Yugoslavia	–	1	–	–	2	–	1	2	–	–	–	3	1	1	–	2	1	2	3	3	2	2	1	2	2	3	3
East Germany	*	*	*	*	*	*	*	*	*	*	*	*	*	*	*	*	*	*	9	9	7	20	23	23	40	25	28
Bulgaria	–	–	–	*	*	*	–	–	1	1	3	1	1	3	3	3	5	2	2	4	3	6	10	5	7	8	9
India	1	–	–	1	–	–	1	–	1	1	1	–	–	1	–	1	–	–	–	1	–	1	–	–	1	–	–
Cuba	*	*	*	–	1	–	–	–	–	–	–	–	–	–	–	1	–	–	–	4	–	3	1	4	6	4	3
Mexico	–	–	3	2	1	2	–	1	–	1	–	1	–	1	–	–	1	–	1	3	3	3	–	1	–	1	–
Estonia	2	2	3	*	*	*	*	*	*	*	*	*	*	*	*	*	*	*	*	*	*	*	*	*	*	*	*
Egypt	2	1	2	2	2	1	–	–	1	*	*	*	–	1	1	–	–	–	–	–	–	–	–	–	–	–	–
Iran (Persia)	*	*	*	–	–	1	–	3	4	2	2	1	–	1	3	–	–	–	2	2	1	2	1	–	2	1	–
Ireland	*	*	*	–	–	1	–	1	–	1	1	3	–	–	–	–	–	–	1	–	–	–	–	–	–	▼	

| | 1936 | | | 1948 | | | 1952 | | | 1956 | | | 1960 | | | 1964 | | | 1968 | | | 1972 | | | 1976 | | |
COUNTRY	G	S	B	G	S	B	G	S	B	G	S	B	G	S	B	G	S	B	G	S	B	G	S	B	G	S	B
Jamaica	*	*	*	1	2	-	2	3	-	-	-	-	-	-	2	-	-	-	-	1	-	-	-	1	1	1	-
Kenya	*	*	*	*	*	*	*	*	*	-	-	-	-	-	-	-	-	1	3	4	2	2	3	4	-	-	-
Brazil	-	-	-	-	-	1	1	-	2	1	-	-	-	-	2	-	-	1	-	1	2	-	-	2	-	-	2
Ethiopia	*	*	*	*	*	*	*	*	*	-	-	-	1	-	-	1	-	-	1	1	-	-	-	-	2	-	-
Luxembourg	-	-	-	-	-	-	1	-	-	-	-	-	-	-	-	-	-	-	-	-	-	-	-	-	-	-	-
Pakistan	*	*	*	-	-	-	-	-	-	1	-	1	-	1	-	1	-	1	-	-	-	1	-	-	-	-	1
Uruguay	-	-	-	-	1	1	-	-	2	-	-	1	-	-	-	-	-	-	1	-	-	-	-	-	-	-	-
Spain	*	*	*	-	1	-	-	1	-	*	*	*	-	-	1	-	-	-	-	-	-	2	-	-	-	-	-
Tunisia	*	*	*	*	*	*	*	*	*	*	*	*	-	-	-	-	-	1	1	1	-	1	-	1	-	-	-
Venezuela	*	*	*	-	-	-	-	-	1	-	-	-	-	-	-	1	-	-	1	-	-	-	-	-	-	1	-
Bahamas	*	*	*	*	*	*	-	-	-	-	1	-	-	-	1	-	-	-	-	-	-	-	-	-	-	-	-
Peru	-	-	-	1	-	-	*	*	*	-	-	-	-	-	-	-	-	-	-	-	-	-	-	-	-	-	-
Chile	-	-	-	-	-	-	2	-	-	2	2	-	-	-	-	-	-	-	-	-	-	-	-	-	-	-	-
Korea	*	*	*	-	-	2	-	-	2	-	1	1	-	-	-	-	2	1	-	1	1	*	*	*	*	*	*
Portugal	*	*	*	1	-	1	-	-	2	-	-	-	-	-	-	-	1	2	-	-	-	-	-	1	-	-	-
Trinidad and Tobago	-	1	1	*	*	*	*	*	*	*	*	*	*	*	*	*	*	*	*	*	*	*	*	*	*	*	*
Latvia	-	-	1	-	-	-	-	-	-	-	-	-	-	-	-	1	-	-	-	-	-	-	-	-	-	-	-
Philippines	*	*	*	*	*	*	*	*	*	*	*	*	*	*	*	-	-	-	1	1	3	-	1	-	-	1	-
Mongolia	*	*	*	*	*	*	*	*	*	*	*	*	*	*	*	-	-	-	*	*	*	*	*	*	-	-	-
Haiti	*	*	*	-	-	-	-	1	1	*	*	*	-	-	-	-	-	-	-	-	-	1	-	-	-	-	-
Lebanon	*	*	*	-	-	-	-	1	1	*	*	*	-	-	-	-	-	-	-	-	-	-	-	-	-	-	-
Taiwan	*	*	*	*	*	*	-	-	-	*	*	*	-	1	-	-	-	-	1	-	-	-	-	-	1	-	-
Ghana	-	-	1	-	1	1	-	-	1	-	-	-	-	1	-	-	-	-	-	-	-	-	-	-	-	2	-
Uganda	*	*	*	*	*	*	*	*	*	-	-	-	-	-	-	-	-	-	-	-	1	1	1	1	-	-	-
Ceylon (Sri Lanka)	*	*	*	-	1	-	-	-	-	-	-	-	-	-	-	-	-	-	-	-	-	-	-	-	-	-	-
Iceland	-	-	-	-	-	-	-	-	-	-	1	-	-	-	-	-	-	-	-	-	-	-	-	-	-	-	-
Morocco	*	*	*	*	*	*	*	*	*	*	*	*	-	1	-	-	-	-	-	-	-	-	-	-	-	-	-
Singapore	*	*	*	-	-	-	-	-	-	-	-	-	-	1	-	-	-	-	-	-	-	-	-	-	-	-	-
Cameroon	*	*	*	*	*	*	*	*	*	*	*	*	*	*	*	-	-	-	-	1	-	-	-	-	-	-	-
Panama	*	*	*	-	-	2	-	-	-	*	*	*	-	-	-	-	-	-	-	-	-	-	-	-	-	-	-
Nigeria	*	*	*	*	*	*	-	-	-	-	-	-	-	-	-	-	-	-	1	-	-	-	-	-	1	-	-
Puerto Rico	*	*	*	-	-	1	-	-	-	-	-	-	-	-	-	-	-	-	-	-	-	-	-	-	-	-	1
Iraq	*	*	*	-	-	-	*	*	*	*	*	*	-	1	-	-	-	-	-	-	-	-	-	-	-	-	-
South Korea	*	*	*	*	*	*	*	*	*	*	*	*	*	*	*	*	*	*	*	*	*	-	1	-	1	1	4
North Korea	*	*	*	*	*	*	*	*	*	*	*	*	*	*	*	*	*	*	*	*	*	1	1	3	1	1	-
Netherlands	*	*	*	*	*	*	*	*	*	*	*	*	*	*	*	*	*	*	*	*	*	3	1	1	-	2	3

MATHEMATICS

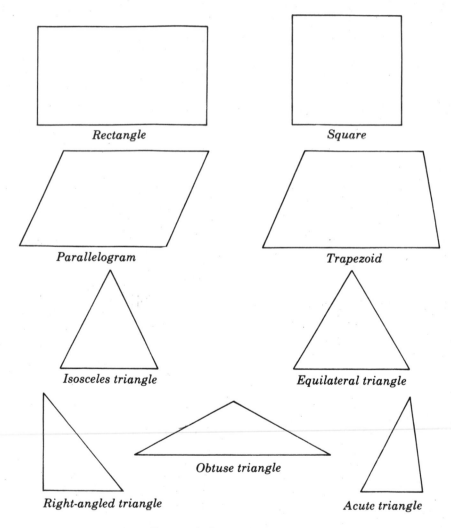

Rectangle

Square

Parallelogram

Trapezoid

Isosceles triangle

Equilateral triangle

Obtuse triangle

Right-angled triangle

Acute triangle

Geometric figures (see page 236)

Mathematics is the science of space and number. Pure mathematics includes arithmetic, algebra, geometry, calculus and trigonometry. Applied mathematics is used in various sciences such as mechanics, physics and astronomy.

Very early peoples learned to count, measure and calculate for practical, everyday purposes. The pyramids of Egypt, built about 4,500 years ago, are miracles of precise measurement. Algebra was developed by astronomers in ancient Egypt, Babylon and India.

One of the earliest theoretical mathematicians was a Greek, Thales of Miletus (624–565 BC). He gave us the first theorems in plane geometry. His pupil, Pythagoras, established geometry as a science among his fellow Greeks. This paved the way for the school of Alexandrian mathematicians which produced Euclid and Archimedes in the 4th and 3rd centuries BC.

Euclid wrote 13 books called the *Elements*, nine of which were devoted to plane and solid geometry and four to arithmetic. Euclid's geometry books remained as standard textbooks until the present century.

The numerals we use today reached Europe about AD 1000. They came from the Arabs whose knowledge of mathematics was sought by European scholars. From the 15th century onwards mathematics began a continuous development in the West. Descartes connected algebra with geometry in 1637. Napier invented logarithms (published 1614) and the modern notation of fractions. Isaac Newton and Gottfried Leibnitz independently invented the differential and integral calculus in the 17th century. The Russian mathematician Lobachevski (1793–1856) rejected Euclid's basic assumptions and developed a non-Euclidian geometry; Einstein followed in the 20th century.

MATHEMATICAL SIGNS

equal to $=$

not equal to $\neq$

approximately equal to $\doteq$ or $\simeq$

identical to $\equiv$

greater than $>$

not greater than $\not>$

less than $<$

not less than $\not<$

plus $+$

minus $-$

plus or minus $\pm$

multiplication (times) $\times$

division $\div$

brackets indicating that the quantities enclosed are to be treated together as forming a single term or expression $(\ ),[\ ],\{\ \}$

varies as $\propto$

infinity ∞

square root $\sqrt{\ }$

per cent $\%$

therefore $\therefore$

because $\because$

the difference between $\sim$

the sum of $\sum$

parallel to $\parallel$

angle $\angle$

triangle $\triangle$

perpendicular to $\perp$

integration sign $\int$

Algebra

Algebra is the branch of mathematics in which quantities are indicated by symbols in the solving of problems. A quantity represented by a symbol is called a *variable*. Any collection of symbols, or numbers and symbols, combined by operations such as addition, subtraction, multiplication or division is an *expression*, e.g. 3a, $\sqrt{x} + y$. An *equation* is a mathematical sentence saying that two expressions are equal, e.g. $a + b^2 = 2(y)$. *Factors* are two or more expressions, the product of which is a given expression. A *term* is part of an expression connected to the rest by $+$ or $-$, e.g. $3ab^2 + x - ay$ has three terms. An *exponent* is a number placed at the upper right of a number or variable indicating how many times it is to be used as a factor, e.g. a^2.

SOME ALGEBRAIC EQUATIONS

$a\,(b + c) = ab + ac$

$a(b - c) = ab - ac$

$(a + b)(c + d) = ac + bc + ad + bd$

$(a - b)(c - d) = ac - bc - ad + bd$

$(a + b)^2 = a^2 + 2ab + b^2$

$(a - b)^2 = a^2 - 2ab + b^2$

$(a + b)(a - b) = a^2 - b^2$

$x^m \times x^n = x^{m+n}$

$x^m \div x^n = x^{m-n}$

$(x^m)^n = x^{mn}$

Trigonometry

Trigonometry is a branch of mathematics whose principles are based on the fixed proportion of angles and sides in a right-angled triangle. The three principal ratios are:

The sine (sin) of an angle $= \dfrac{\text{side opposite angle}}{\text{hypotenuse}}$

The cosine (cos) of an angle $= \dfrac{\text{side adjacent to angle}}{\text{hypotenuse}}$

The tangent (tan) of an angle $= \dfrac{\text{side opposite angle}}{\text{side adjacent to angle}}$

Three further definitions are:

$\dfrac{1}{\text{sine}} = $ cosecant (cosec)

$\dfrac{1}{\text{cosine}} = $ secant (sec)

$\dfrac{1}{\text{tangent}} = $ cotangent (cot)

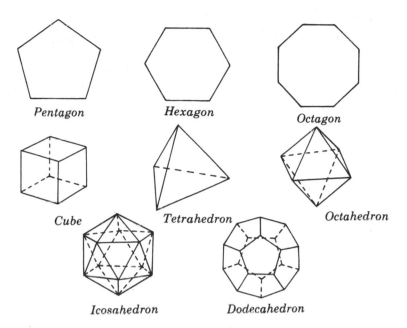

Pentagon   *Hexagon*   *Octagon*

Cube   *Tetrahedron*   *Octahedron*

Icosahedron   *Dodecahedron*

Geometry

Geometry is the branch of mathematics which deals with the properties of space. Kinds of geometry are:

Plane geometry is concerned with points, lines, circles and polygons on a flat surface. One can use it to prove that two triangles have the same shape or are of the same size; that two angles are equal or two lines are equal; and that two lines are parallel.

Solid geometry is the study of points, lines and planes in space. One can use it to find the dimensions of cubes, rectangular boxes, pyramids, spheres, cones, cylinders and prisms. Spherical geometry is particularly useful in navigation because the Earth is almost spherical in shape.

Analytic geometry solves problems by algebraical methods. To understand analytic geometry one needs to be able to understand graphs. Graphs can make an exact picture of an algebraic equation describing many kinds of lines and curves.

Non-Euclidian geometry breaks away from the basic assumptions of the Greek mathematician Euclid. Euclid's geometry describes the world as we see it and is useful for most practical purposes.

POLYGONS

A pentagon is a five-sided figure.
A hexagon is a six-sided figure.
An octagon is an eight-sided figure.

THE PLATONIC SOLIDS

These are any of the following regular polyhedra: **tetrahedron; cube; octahedron; icosahedron and dodecahedron.**

GEOMETRIC FIGURES

Quadrilaterals are closed figures with four straight sides. Squares, rectangles, parallelograms and trapezoids are all quadrilaterals.

A rectangle is a quadrilateral with four right angles and adjacent sides unequal.

A square is a quadrilateral with four right angles and equal sides.

A parallelogram is a quadrilateral whose opposite sides are parallel.

A trapezoid is a quadrilateral with one pair of sides parallel.

Triangles are closed figures with three straight sides.

An isosceles triangle has two sides the same length, also two equal angles.

An equilateral triangle has all sides equal, and all angles equal.

A right-angled triangle has one angle of 90°.

An obtuse triangle has one angle larger than 90°.

An acute triangle has all angles less than 90°.

MEASUREMENTS

TRIANGLE
area $= \frac{1}{2}$ ah

SQUARE
area $= a^2$

CIRCLE
diameter (d) $= 2r$
circumference $= 2\pi r$
area $= \pi r^2$
(N.B. the constant $\pi = 3.1415$)

TRAPEZOID
area $= \frac{1}{2}(m + n)h$

CUBE
surface area $= 6a^2$
volume $= a^3$

SPHERE
surface area $= 4\pi r^2$
volume $= \frac{4}{3}\pi r^3$

CONE
curved surface area $= \pi rl$
volume $= \frac{1}{3}\pi r^2 h$
total surface area $= \pi rl + 2\pi r$
$\qquad\qquad\qquad = \pi r(l + r)$

CYLINDER
curved surface area $= 2\pi rh$
total surface area $= 2\pi rh + 2\pi r^2$
$\qquad\qquad\qquad = 2\pi r(h + r)$

PYRAMID
surface area $= a^2 + 2la$
volume $= \frac{1}{3}a^2 h$

ELLIPSE
area $= \pi ab$

Triangle

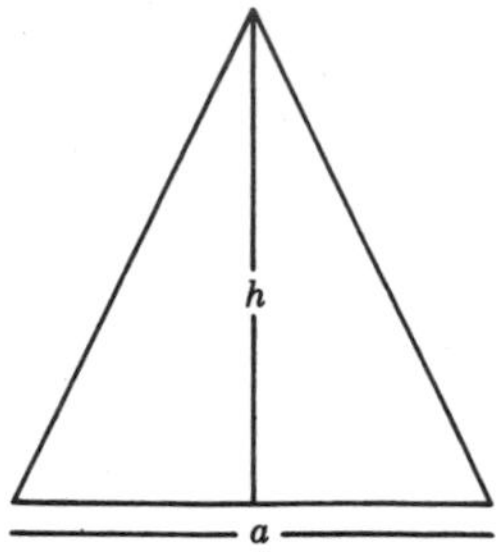

Square

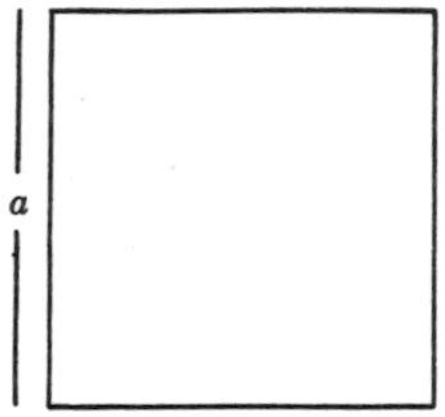

Circle

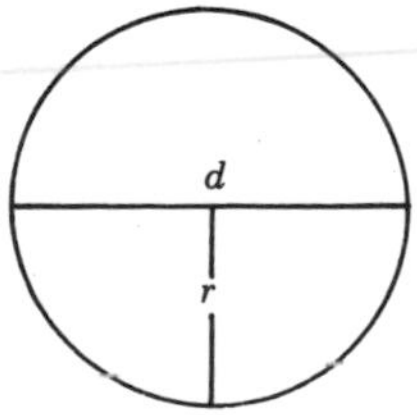

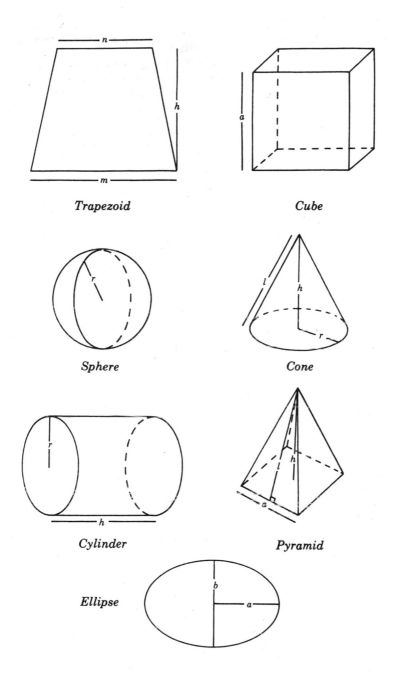

Trapezoid

Cube

Sphere

Cone

Cylinder

Pyramid

Ellipse

GENERAL INFORMATION

Foreign Words and Phrases

Fr = French   L = Latin   Ger = German   It = Italian

à bas (Fr) down with
ab incunabilis (L) from the cradle
ab initio (L) from the beginning
à bon marché (Fr) cheap; a good bargain
ad astra (L) to the stars
ad hoc (L) arranged for this purpose; special
ad infinitum (L) to infinity
ad interim (L) in the meantime
ad nauseam (L) to disgust, satiety
affaire d'amour (Fr) a love affair
affaire de coeur (Fr) an affair of the heart
affaire d'honneur (Fr) an affair of honour; a duel
a fortiori (L) with stronger reason
à la belle étoile (Fr) under the stars
à la mode (Fr) according to the fashion, custom
al fresco (It) in the open air

alter ego (L) one's other self
amour-propre (Fr) vanity; self-love
anno mundi (L) in the year of the world
à pied (Fr) on foot
a priori (L) from the cause to the effect (in reasoning)
à propos (Fr) to the point
au contraire (Fr) on the contrary
au courant (Fr) fully acquainted with
au fait (Fr) well acquainted with
au fond (Fr) at bottom
auf wiedersehen (Ger) goodbye till we meet again
au revoir (Fr) goodbye till we meet again
à votre santé (Fr) to your health
bel esprit (Fr) a wit
ben trovato (It) cleverly invented
bête noire (Fr) a black beast; one's abomination
billet doux (Fr) a love letter
bona fide (L) genuine
bonhomie (Fr) good nature
bon mot (Fr) witty saying
bonne bouche (Fr) a tasty titbit
bon vivant (Fr) one who lives well
carte blanche (Fr) a blank paper; full discretionary powers
casus belli (L) that which causes or justifies a war
causa sine qua non (L) an indispensable cause or condition
cause célèbre (Fr) a law-suit that excites much attention
ceteris paribus (L) other things being equal
chacun son goût (Fr) everyone to his taste
comme il faut (Fr) as it should be; well-bred
compos mentis (L) in right mind
contretemps (Fr) an unlucky accident or hitch
corrigenda (L) things to be corrected
coup de grâce (Fr) a finishing stroke
coup d'état (Fr) a violent or illegal change in the government of a country
de facto (L) in point of fact, actual
dei gratia (L) by God's grace
de jure (L) rightful by law
de profundis (L) out of the depths
de rigueur (Fr) required by etiquette
deux ex machina (L) providential intervention at a critical moment
en bloc (Fr) in a lump; wholesale
en famille (Fr) at home, among one's family
enfant terrible (Fr) a terrible child, who asks awkward questions for example
en masse (Fr) all together
en passant (Fr) in passing; by the way
en rapport (Fr) in harmony, sympathy
entre nous (Fr) between ourselves
erratum, errata (L) error, errors (especially in a list attached to a book)
esprit de corps (Fr) the animating spirit of a group or collective body of people
ex cathedra (L) from the chair (of high authority)
ex officio (L) in virtue of one's office

fait accompli (Fr) a thing already done
faux pas (Fr) a false step; mistake in behaviour
genius loci (L) the guardian spirit of a place
honi soit qui mal y pense (Old Fr) evil to him who evil thinks
hors de combat (Fr) out of the fight; disabled
hors-d'oeuvre (Fr) a dish served at the beginning of a meal
ich dien (Ger) I serve
idée fixe (Fr) a fixed idea
in absentia (L) in (his or her) absence
in extremis (L) at the point of death
in memoriam (L) in memory of
in perpetuum (L) for ever
in situ (L) in its original place
inter alia (L) among other things
in toto (L) completely
ipse dixit (L) he himself said it
ipso facto (L) in the fact itself
je ne sais quoi (Fr) I know not what
laissez-faire (Fr) leave matters alone; policy of non-interference
magnum opus (L) great work
modus operandi (L) manner of working
mutatis mutandis (L) with necessary alterations made
nil desperandum (L) there is no reason to despair
noblesse oblige (Fr) much is expected from those in high position
nolens volens (L) willing or unwilling
nom de plume (Fr) a pen-name
non sequitur (L) it does not follow; an illogical inference
obiter dictum (L) a thing said by the way
omnia vincit amor (L) love conquers all
outré (Fr) eccentric
par excellence (Fr) by virtue of special excellence; above all others
pari passu (L) at an equal pace
passim (L) everywhere
pax vobiscum (L) peace be with you
per annum (L) by the year
per capita (L) by the head; each
per se (L) by itself; considered apart
persona non grata (L) an unacceptable person
pièce de resistance (Fr) the chief dish of a meal; main item
pied-à-terre (Fr) a lodging for occasional visits
poco a poco (It) little by little
post mortem (L) after death
prima facie (L) at first view or consideration
pro forma (L) for the sake of form
pro patria (L) for our country
pro rata (L) proportionally
quid pro quo (L) one thing for another; tit-for-tat
raison d'être (Fr) the reason for a thing's existence
reductio ad adsurdum (L) reduction to a logical absurdity
re vera (L) in truth
sans souci (Fr) without care

sauve qui peut (Fr) let him save himself who can
savoir faire (Fr) tact, quickness to see and do the right thing
sic (L) so (written)
sine die (L) indefinitely
sine qua non (L) without which, not; indispensable
sobriquet (Fr) nickname
sotto voce (It) in an undertone
stet (L) let it stand; do not delete
sub judice (L) under judicial consideration
summum bonum (L) the principal good
tant mieux (Fr) so much the better
tant pis (Fr) so much the worse
vice versa (L) the other way round; the reverse
viva voce (L) orally
voilà (Fr) behold; there is
vox populi (L) the voice of the people; public opinion
zeitgeist (Ger) spirit of the times

The Greek Alphabet

NAME	CAPITAL	LOWER CASE	ENGLISH EQUIVALENT
Alpha	A	α	a
Beta	B	β	b
Gamma	Γ	γ	g
Delta	Δ	δ	d
Epsilon	E	ε	ĕ
Zeta	Z	ζ	z
Eta	H	η	ē
Theta	Θ	θ	th
Iota	I	i	i
Kappa	K	κ	k
Lambda	Λ	λ	l
Mu	M	μ	m
Nu	N	ν	n
Xi	Ξ	ξ	x
Omicron	O	o	ō
Pi	Π	π	p
Rho	P	ρ	r
Sigma	Σ	σ ς	s
Tau	T	τ	t
Upsilon	Y	υ	u *or* y
Phi	Φ	ϕ	ph
Chi	X	χ	ch
Psi	Ψ	ψ	ps
Omega	Ω	ω	o

Roman Numerals

I	1	XVII	17	DC	600	MV̄	4,000
II	2	XVIII	18	DCC	700	V̄	5,000
III	3	XIX	19	-DCCC	800	X̄	10,000
IV	4	XX	20	CM	900	L̄	50,000
V	5	XXX	30	M	1,000	C̄	100,000
VI	6	XL	40	MM	2,000	D̄	500,000
VII	7	L	50	MMM	3,000	M̄	1,000,000
VIII	8	LX	60				
IX	9	LXX	70				
X	10	LXXX	80				
XI	11	XC	90				
XII	12	C	100	**EXAMPLES**			
XIII	13	CC	200				
XIV	14	CCC	300	**1980**	MCMLXXX		
XV	15	CD	400	**1981**	MCMLXXXI		
XVI	16	D	500	**1979**	MCMLXXIX		

Latin Abbreviations

AD = *anno Domini* (in the year of the Lord)

ad lib. = *ad libitum* (at pleasure)

a.m. = *ante meridiem* (before noon)

c. = *circa* (about)

do. = *ditto* (the same)

et al. = *et alii* (and others)

etc. = *et cetera* (and the rest, and so on)

et seq. = *et sequens* (and the following)

ex lib. = *ex libris* (from the books of)

fl. = *floruit* (flourished)

ibid. *ibidem* (in the same place)

id. = *idem* (the same)

i.e. = *id est* (that is)

ign. = *ignotus* (unknown)

incog. = *incognito* (unknown, unrecognized)

in loc. = *in loco* (in its place)

loc. cit. = *loco citato* (in the place cited)

N.B. = *nota bene* (note well)

nem. con. = *nemine contradicente* (nobody contradicting, unanimously)

no. = *numero* (number)

non seq. = *non sequitur* (it does not follow)

ob. = *obiit* (died)

op. = *opus* (work)

op. cit. = *opere citato* (in the work cited)

pinx. = *pinxit* (he painted)

p.m. = *post meridiem* (afternoon)

p.p. = *per procurationem* (by proxy)

pro tem. = *pro tempore* (for the time being)

prox.	= *proximo* (of the next month)	**sqq.**	= *sequentes, sequentia* (the following)
p.s.	= *post scriptum* (postscript)	**ult.**	= *ultimo* (in the last month)
Q.E.D.	= *quod erat demonstrandum* (which was to be demonstrated)	**v.**	= *vide* (see); *versus* (against)
		verb. sap.	= *verbum sapienti sat est* (a word to the wise is enough)
q.v.	= *quod vide* (which see)		
R.I.P.	= *requiescat in pace* (rest in peace)	**viz.**	= *videlicet* (namely, that is to say)

Morse Code

The Morse code is a system of dots and dashes named after its inventor, an American called Samuel F. B. Morse (1791–1872). It is used for conveying messages by wireless, telegraph, etc. The dot is a signal of short duration, the dash is three times this length. A gap equal to one dot is left between each symbol, and twice as much is left between each letter. There is a longer break between words.

Morse code can be sent on a hand key, a skilled operator being able to tap out up to 25 words a minute. Automatic transmitters can exceed this speed many times.

The international Morse code is as follows:

Full stop · − · − · −
Semicolon − · − · − ·
Comma − − · · − −
Colon − − − · · ·
Question mark · · − − · ·
Apostrophe · − − − − ·
Hyphen − · · · · −
Bracket − · − − · −
Inverted commas · − · · − ·
Invitation to transmit − · −
Wait · − · · ·
Break − · · · · −
Understood · · · − ·
Error · · · · · · · ·
Received · − ·
Position report − · − ·
End of message · − · − ·
Finish of transmission · · · − · −

A · −	K − · −	U · · −	1 · − − − −
B − · · ·	L · − · ·	V · · · −	2 · · − − −
C − · − ·	M − −	W · − −	3 · · · − −
D − · ·	N − ·	X − · · −	4 · · · · −
E ·	O − − −	Y − · − −	5 · · · · ·
F · · − ·	P · − − ·	Z − − · ·	6 − · · · ·
G − − ·	Q − − · −		7 − − · · ·
H · · · ·	R · − ·		8 − − − · ·
I · ·	S · · ·		9 − − − − ·
J · − − −	T −		0 − − − − −

Weights and Measures

AVOIRDUPOIS WEIGHT

16 drams (dr)	= 1 ounce (oz)
16 ounces	= 1 pound (lb)
14 pounds	= 1 stone (st)
28 pounds (US : 25 pounds)	= 1 quart (qr)
4 quarters	= 1 hundredweight (cwt)
20 hundredweight	= 1 ton

METRIC WEIGHT

1,000 milligrams (mg)	= 1 gram (g)
1,000 grams	= 1 kilogram (kg)
1,000 kilograms	= 1 tonne

LENGTH

12 inches (in)	= 1 foot (ft)
3 feet	= 1 yard (yd)
5½ yards	= 1 rod, pole or perch
40 poles	= 1 furlong (fur)
8 furlongs	= 1 mile
1,760 yards	= 1 mile
3 miles	= 1 league

METRIC LENGTH

10 millimetres (mm)	= 1 centimetre (cm)
100 centimetres	= 1 metre (m)
1,000 metres	= 1 kilometre

LIQUID MEASURE

4 gills	= 1 pint (pt)
2 pints	= 1 quart (qt)
4 quarts	= 1 gallon (gal)
8 gallons	= 1 bushel

METRIC LIQUID MEASURE

1,000 millilitres (ml)	= 1 litre (l)
1,000 cubic centimetres (cc)	= 1 litre

MEASURES OF AREA

144 square inches	= 1 square foot
9 square feet	= 1 square yard
30¼ square yards	= 1 square rod, pole or perch
40 square poles	= 1 rood
4 roods	= 1 acre
640 acres	= 1 square mile

METRIC MEASURES OF AREA

100 square metres	= 1 are
100 ares	= 1 hectare
100 hectares	= 1 square kilometre

MEASURES OF VOLUME

1,728 cubic inches	= 1 cubic foot
27 cubic feet	= 1 cubic yard

METRIC MEASURES OF VOLUME

1,000 cubic centimetres	= 1 cubic decimetre
1,000 cubic decimetres	= 1 cubic metre

NAUTICAL MEASURE

6 feet	= 1 fathom
100 fathoms	= 1 cable
10 cables	= 1 nautical mile
6,080 feet	= 1 nautical mile
3 nautical miles	= 1 league

CONVERSION TABLE

WEIGHT

1 ounce	= 28.350 grams	**1 kilogram**	= 2.205 pounds
1 pound	= 0.454 kilogram	**1,000 kilograms**	= 0.984 ton
1 ton	= 1.016 tonnes		

LIQUID MEASURE

1 Imperial pint	= 0.568 litre	**1 litre**	= 0.220 Imperial gallon
1 American pint	= 0.473 litre	**1 litre**	= 0.264 American gallon
1 Imperial gallon	= 4.546 litres		
1 American gallon	= 3.785 litres		

SURFACE MEASURE

1 square foot	= 0.093 square metre	**1 square metre**	= 1.196 square yards
1 square yard	= 0.836 square metre	**1 are**	= 119.599 square yards
1 acre	= 4,046.850 square metres	**1 hectare**	= 2.471 acres
1 square mile	= 258.998 hectares	**1 square kilometre**	= 0.386 square mile

LENGTH

1 inch	= 2.540 centimetres	1 centimetre	= 0.394 inch
1 foot	= 30.480 centimetres	1 metre	= 3.281 feet
1 yard	= 0.914 metre	1 metre	= 1.094 yards
1 mile	= 1.609 kilometres	1 kilometre	= 0.621 mile

MEASURE OF VOLUME

1 cubic inch	= 16.387 cubic centimetres	1 cubic centimetre	= 0.061 cubic inch
1 cubic yard	= 0.765 cubic metre	1 cubic metre	= 1.308 cubic yards

TEMPERATURE

To convert degrees Fahrenheit (°F) to degrees Centigrade (°C), use the following formula: $(F - 32) \times \frac{5}{9}$.

To convert Centigrade to Fahrenheit, the formula is: $F = (C \times \frac{9}{5}) + 32$.

To convert Centigrade to degrees Kelvin (°K) or absolute, the formula is: $K = C + 273$.

Knots

The reef knot is used for tying together two ropes of equal size. It tends to slip if the ropes are of unequal diameter. These should be tied with a sheet bend.

The sheet bend is used for tying together two ropes of different diameters. If the end is passed round again the result is a double sheet bend.

The clove hitch is a knot by which a rope is secured around another rope or a rod that it crosses. When fastened it will slip neither up nor down.

A bowline makes a fixed loop at the end of a rope that will never slip. It can be used for making fast to a ring, post, bollard or cleat.

The sheepshank is used for shortening a rope.

The figure of eight is a knot used for stopping a rope running through a block.

The half-hitch is used to tie a rope to a ring or post.

The round turn and two half-hitches holds a rope to a ring or post even more securely than a simple half-hitch.

The timber hitch is used for dragging things along, such as a piece of wood.

The wall knot is used to finish off a rope that is unravelling.

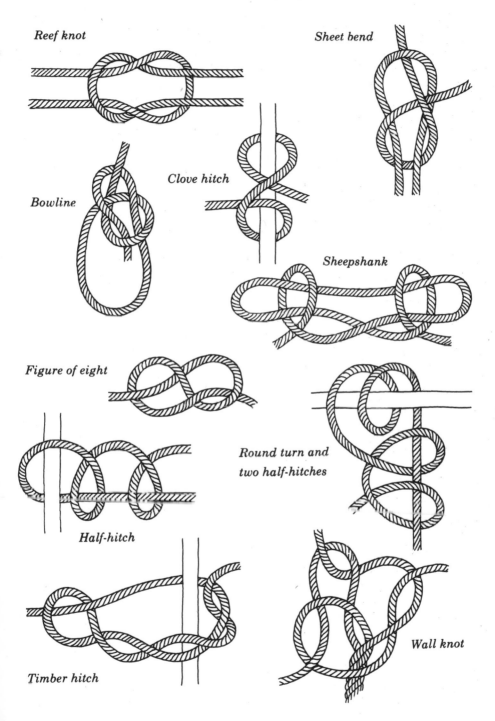

Reef knot

Sheet bend

Bowline

Clove hitch

Sheepshank

Figure of eight

Round turn and
two half-hitches

Half-hitch

Timber hitch

Wall knot

INDEX

Your Own Notes